annie bell's
baking bible

PHOTOGRAPHY BY CON POULOS

KYLE BOOKS

contents

introduction

My fourteen-year-old son has been extremely concerned about the publication of this book. 'But mum, if you've put absolutely everything you know about cakes into one volume, what are you going to do next?' A good point, except that he really needn't worry. As the deadline has approached (or rather been and gone), I feel as though I am back there taking my finals. One last chance to perfect that Swiss Roll, to test the difference between making pastry in a food processor, a traditional mixer or by hand, one last chance to try soaking the dried fruit for a Dundee in rum, and to work the little tweaks into the Angel Smartie Cake my son has insisted on for his birthday every year since he was six. Just one more day. Which is what makes his fear so very misplaced. I could never come to the end. Baking goes hand in hand with existing, it's something I do almost every day, something I do compulsively, that I both want and need to do, that I love. If I look at this collection of recipes, I feel a huge sense of pleasure at putting everything I've enjoyed cooking up until now in writing.

the book may be in print, but it is really no different to the handwritten notebook that I've inherited from my mother, the recipes that carried her through life. It is also a work in progress, because I will always go on adding, go on learning and changing methods, revisiting old favourites, perhaps with a new twist or the revelation of how to improve on some step that came to me at three o'clock on a sleepless night. Baking for me is a rather lovely journey without end; thankfully the world is round and I can just keep on walking. And if this book can infuse you with any of the magic that it has cast on my own life, then I shall be very happy.

After writing my last book on the subject, *Gorgeous Cakes*, I started talking to friends about what they really wanted. And what they asked for was a book that had everything they might need between two covers, quite literally a 'bible'. I hope you will find everything you need here – all the basics, all the favourites, every occasion catered for, but I also like to think there's enough for Volume 2. After all, I don't want to do myself out of the fun of baking 'fat rascals' for the first time, or trying out French 'carrés chocolat'. But this is where I've got to so far, after a lifetime of baking and twenty-five years of doing it pretty much day in and day out.

The choice of recipes has been born of a certain frustration at the direction that cakes have been leading us for some years now, when they have become ever more highly decorated – more icing, more frills, ever prettier. Which is lovely, and cakes do lend themselves to that, but it has left me with a longing to retreat from this, and to get back to real cakes. I want to be able to sink into the comfort of my sofa with a no-nonsense slice of Victoria Sponge filled with fluffy buttercream and jam, or a thick cushion of sticky ginger cake, I also want the recipe for the perfect brownie to take to a friend as

a present, and to be able to reel off a Red Velvet Cake or Coca-Cola Cake for a special tea – or simply to have some fun with a Tomato Soup Traybake. With or without the frills, I suppose that is the point. There is an inherent beauty in these cakes, and who could capture it better than the photographer Con Poulos?

On a practical note, with this in mind, I have separated out the decoration of the cake from the method itself, listing it as 'little extras' or 'tips' below the actual recipe. The idea is that you can go to town if you want to, rather than presenting every cake as though it has to be dressed to the nines for a night on the town. Frills don't make for a tastier cake, they simply make for a prettier one, and even then I feel they are stacked in women's favour. I very much wanted this book to appeal to male cooks as well, most of whom are not interested in Barbie sprinkles, and are probably happy to forego the flurry of icing sugar too.

So with longevity at its heart, this is a collection of unapologetically classic recipes. I have tried to squeeze absolutely every single favourite cake, biscuit, meringue and pancake into one volume, including the less fashionable ones that I still love and feel should be up there with the others. These are the cakes that I return to again and again, tweaking this and changing that, trying out my mum's version or a friend's mum's version, or making it in a different way. The aim of this book is that it should be lovely but real. I am most concerned that you have a recipe for a really good banana bread when there happen to be a couple of over-ripe bananas in your fruit bowl, and that you can lay your hands on a foolproof recipe for pancakes on the tired morning following a sleepover. I don't want you to be fazed because a child happens to be gluten intolerant or it's your turn to send in something for the cake stall tomorrow.

Now two words in particular fill me with dread – rule and technique. I swear by 'if it works, do it'. I have never believed there is a right and a wrong way of cooking a particular dish or recipe. There are good and bad results, but how you get there is frankly immaterial. So even where a method might seem unconventional, trust me. All the recipes have been tested, and if they do deviate from the norm, it's generally because they're designed to make life easier rather than more difficult.

Which leads to my second bête noire, 'technique'. Central to writing this book was a consuming desire to produce a handbook that anyone would be able to use. The greatest compliment for me is hearing from a fellow mum that her eight-year-old daughter likes cooking my recipes. They are intended to be child's play (without ruling out adults), and the younger the readership the better the endorsement. The recipes have been pared down to the barest minimum wherever possible.

And to further ensure the low-tech approach, there are no specialist or tricky methods. No piping bags, even where a recipe might normally call for one – when making éclairs, for example, or macaroons. If I felt you couldn't get halfway decent results shaping an éclair with a teaspoon, I wouldn't have included the recipe in the first place. For this reason, too, there is no yeast in the book. Perhaps in the future, baking with yeast will prove the starting point for a subsequent book. However, it is specialised and there is no doubt that the greater your experience and understanding of how it works, the better the results are likely to be. Which is not the stuff of this book, where I want you to succeed first time round, without practising.

As far as possible the ingredients list will tell you how to prepare an ingredient, whether it is flour to be sifted, lemon to be zested, or fruit to be cut in a particular fashion. But if, for instance, several of the dry ingredients need sifting together, this will be detailed in the method itself. Either way, it is always worth reading through a recipe from start to finish first – and ideally a little way in advance of cooking – just in case, say, the butter needs to be softened, dried fruit soaked, or dough rested.

It was serendipity that I found myself writing this book at a time when it was particularly poignant. When my mum died last year it was the end of a lifelong, ongoing conversation. Like anyone in that situation, I have tried to sort through and organise the emotional chaos in a way that is lasting and meaningful – where she is still with me, rather than as a sum of fragmented possessions that no longer hold any great meaning now they are removed from their original context. Taste and smell are some of the greatest reminders, and one of my most precious memories. When my brother and I were sorting through her books and we came to her battered handwritten notebook of recipes, I was so very relieved when he said 'you have it'. It is probably, for me, the most precious of her belongings.

I had no idea until that time quite how powerful a memento handwriting is. But combined with her wonderfully insouciant take on anything she cooked, 'what's the matter with you, I don't understand why my fruitcake didn't work for you, I've been making it for years and all my friends love it.' Well maybe mum, something to do with the fact there's no method and no temperature, just a list of ingredients. Another entry reads 'Shortbread V. G'. Probably it is if you know how to make it. Now though, she's not here to ask. But she still infuses this book, and I inherited my own love of down-to-earth classic cakes from her. It is that continuity that I hope this book captures.

There are no specialist or tricky methods. No piping bags, even where a recipe might normally call for one.

art of baking

YOUR OVEN

It is fan ovens that I swear by and have used to test everything that follows, as they consistently guarantee great results. With a fan oven, there are no pockets of hot or cool air and everything cooks at the same rate and evenly, so you shouldn't have to move trays up and down, or to turn cakes round to prevent them from cooking more on one side or the other. Occasionally the lower tray might take a couple of minutes longer than the top, but only marginally.

So all of the temperatures that follow have 'fan' as their default; the electric temperature in my own experience is about 10–20 degrees higher, but this can differ depending on the oven. You will probably know from cooking with your own oven what this differential is. Most ovens today come with the option of both. And it may also be useful to know that I test on a Miele fan oven.

FOOD PROCESSOR V MIXER

My very earliest memories of baking are of a lovely flour-ridden fest with my mother's Kenwood mixer, which churned and whirred in a comforting fashion, giving out the odd sea spray of flour or powdery sugar when the paddle hit a large knob of butter. And I still think that traditional mixers are delightful machines, but I jumped ship a long time ago.

The wedding gift of a food processor from one of my best friend's parents revolutionised my life in the kitchen and the way that I bake. Having always had relatively compact kitchens I have never been able to justify the presence of both machines, and over time have come to realise that in many cases you get better results with a food processor. Its sheer power and speed cannot be matched for amalgamating cake ingredients or softening butter, and its efficiency in making pastry is awesome – by rubbing butter into flour in seconds, it remains cold and reduces to tiny crumbs in a way that you could never match by hand or in a mixer. I also find the idea of having endless different attachments for different jobs offputting; a food processor is endlessly adaptable if you never get further than the main blade. It's the most minimal of the various options. And then there are the all-in-one methods, which feature throughout the book. The very first time I baked an all-in-one Victoria Sponge, where basically you place all the ingredients in a food processor and press GO, I was transfixed. If it works for that mixture, maybe it works for others. And it does, not always, but again this method plays to the power and speed of the machine. It would be disingenuous to pretend that there is no difference at all between a lovingly whisked sponge and a whizzed-up version, but in these time-challenged days, many is the occasion when speed and ease of preparation will win out over perfection (see page 157, Victoria Sponge).

The only addendum here is that not all processors are made equal. A good domestic machine is one of the best investments you could make, my own choice being Magimix, who lie at the helm of professional domestic processors. They operate with the speed and efficiency of a professional machine, but are designed for the home kitchen. You don't need the biggest machine – all the cakes that follow have been tested on a 'Compact 3 litre bowl', which I appreciate for not taking up too much kitchen space.

I swear by 'if it works, do it.' I have never believed there is a right and a wrong way of cooking a particular dish or recipe. There are good and bad results, but how you get there is frankly immaterial.

ELECTRIC WHISK

This is your next best friend to a food processor, indispensible for any number of preparations that involve beating air into ingredients. This might be egg whites, or whisking butter for buttercream. In the absence of a traditional mixer, I also use my electric whisk for making sponges in the step-by-step fashion – where first you whisk the butter with the sugar, then you whisk in the eggs, and finally you fold in the flour and so forth. It is always worth going for a reliable household name, but bear in mind that often it is the lower grade ranges that are the lightest and the easiest to wield.

MEASUREMENTS

Teaspoons and tablespoons mean rounded rather than flat; for spoonfuls of syrup or honey, it's however it comes out the jar. This may, in particular, affect bakers in the US who are accustomed to levelling off cups when measuring, which may leave you short.

I recommend electronic scales for accuracy. Most can be set at zero with a bowl in place, which makes for easy measuring compared to the system of old that only allowed for a single bowl or dish on top of the scale.

As liquid measurements are frequently quite small in cakes, I find the feeding tube on my Magimix food processor is ideal for measuring quantities up to 100ml, which can be difficult to measure accurately in a jug. Bear in mind that 15ml is equal to a tablespoon.

SKEWER TEST

A clean skewer inserted into the centre of a cake is frequently the all-important marker that it is done. If the skewer comes out coated in a sticky goo of raw cake mixture, this indicates the cake requires a little longer – the exception being brownies that by design should immerse a skewer in sticky-crumbs-cum-goo if they are to remain true to form.

But there are skewers and there are skewers, and thin round ones will often emerge clean when in fact the cake is still undercooked. The ideal is a flat skewer, or else a very fine knife (as you don't want to visually damage the centre of the cake). Either way, it is necessary to surround an instrument with enough of the cake mixture to be a true marker. I have in the past come across special skewers for the job, but frankly these belong in the same dusty archive as egg squarers and electric spaghetti spoons.

COOLING CAKES

A non-stick wire rack is ideal for cooling any cakes that require unmoulding. But as you will see from many recipes, I frequently suggest cooling in the tin, which I find just as effective. The practice of turning cakes out was largely, I am sure, born at a time of fixed-base tins, when to have left them in the tin would have resulted in them sticking. With the advent of Springform and loose-based tins, this isn't an issue if you run a knife around the collar once it comes out of the oven. And in many cases the base serves as a handy plinth for serving – although bear in mind you'll need to go easy with any metal utensils that might damage or scratch the non-stick surface. Some cakes, especially those that shrink on cooling, benefit from being cooled upside-down in the tin.

STORAGE

The majority of sponges freeze well, but you should ideally leave the icing and decorating until after defrosting. Not only will the results be altogether fresher, it can be tricky to freeze a finished cake without bashing the edges – so it's on the grounds of looks too.

Lock & Lock containers are great for storing cakes that benefit from being in an airtight environment. They will keep a dry meringue or biscuit crisp, and a moist cake succulent. Certain goodies benefit from being allowed to breathe – Cannelés Bordelais, soft-bake cookies and flapjacks and so on – and here I find the best route is a loosely tied plastic food bag, which will keep the cake moist without softening the edges. Pretty cake tins are a good halfway house, especially for fruit and ginger cakes that are long-keepers, as these benefit from a little air. Cheesecakes are best covered with foil to protect them from drying out while allowing them to mature and breathe.

Equally important is the temperature at which they are stored, the ideal being an old-fashioned larder. If possible, choose a well-ventilated and cool storage space, not so cold that butter will harden – an unheated utility room or a garage or shed. Sometimes though, during the summer, a fridge will often end up being the optimum environment.

Cakes made with vegetable and groundnut oil tend to recover better from chilling than butter-rich sponges such as a Victoria. Equally, sponges made with ground nuts and eggs should bounce back to form within half an hour of being removed from the fridge. And occasionally chilling is actually a part of the process – when making brownies, for example, or when you need cream cheese frosting to set. However, if you are simply storing cakes in the fridge in order to preserve them, ensure you allow 30–60 minutes for them to come back to room temperature before serving.

PRESENTATION

I am inclined to take the lazy route at home, and leave a round cake on its base or, in the case of a traybake or brownie, to cut and lift slices out to order. But otherwise lining the base with baking paper can help with moving a cake from base to plate. Today you can buy pre-cut silicone paper for the ultimate convenience, but I tend to take a roll of baking paper, using the base of the tin as a cutting guide.

One of the most useful cake plates I own is a completely flat plate with no rim – I acquired it from my mum in a design that I thought would never see the light of day in my kitchen, and haven't stopped using it ever since. A white china cake stand with a pedestal is a lovely way to present any cake, but they do take up more space.

Cake stalls, however, and those 'bring a little something occasions' present us with an entirely different set of criteria. While you may send something in beautifully presented with the best of intentions, this is a very good opportunity of loaning a favourite plate or tray and never seeing it again. Or – as happened to one of my own cake tins that emerged from my small son's locker a matter of months after the event, unwashed – I would rather not have seen it again. Still more reason for something disposable.

Paper cake cases, which come in pretty much every size from muffin and fairy cake to loaf or round cakes, are a great solution, particularly if you are going to be doing this on a regular basis. I also keep a pile of pretty paper plates and thin ply disposable ones for such occasions. Otherwise, I find small melamine trays or enamelled tin ones are perfect in so far as they are unbreakable. And if you really want to appear like a pro, then those cellophane bags tied with ribbon give an artisan patisserie look.

raw materials

Cakes are a team effort between the ingredients that go to make them up. However simple, the better the component parts, the tastier your confection will be. Each ingredient has something to say.

BUTTER

For the most part the recipes recommend using unsalted butter. A sponge cake made with butter will taste resonantly creamy and delicate, while one that is made with margarine, well, it won't taste of butter at all. The trend for using margarine was largely born of post-war thrift, but it is not a natural ingredient or a quality one. Just occasionally a recipe will call for salted butter, and the only addendum here is that if you are using Breton or Norman butter that is liberally laced with sea salt crystals, and tends to come up saltier than others, then it is a good idea to use half and half in conjunction with unsalted butter. But otherwise a lightly salted butter is what is intended. And I would avoid spreadable butters, useful as they are for crackers and the like – most are cut with vegetable oil, so you can't be sure of their make-up.

SUGAR

I remember my mum once saying that the question she was asked most frequently in relation to my recipes was 'why does it always say "golden" caster sugar? Won't ordinary do?' And yes, it will do, but golden caster sugar is unrefined and carries with it something of the flavour of the cane before it was stripped of all its colour, a very slight caramelisation. Once we get further into the brown sugars – demerara, light and dark muscovado – this flavour is even more apparent. However, if all you have in the cupboard is white caster sugar, it won't risk the success of your cake. I also think there can be some confusion between 'light brown' and 'light muscovado'; effectively they can be used interchangeably, but muscovado is that much fudgier and more aromatic. The Billington's brand make beautiful unrefined sugars, lovely for baking.

The exception to using unrefined sugars is for those cakes where you want a lily-white hue – angel cakes and meringues, in particular – and here I have indicated a refined sugar. Icing sugar should always be refined. Even though you can buy faintly beige unrefined icing sugar, it doesn't have the lightness of texture of white icing sugar and tends to clog, and it's altogether coarser.

Just as important as refined v unrefined, is texture. Caster is not interchangeable with granulated, which bakes in a completely different way – caster dissolves and combines with the other ingredients in a particular fashion. But you can always give granulated a quick whizz in a coffee grinder if it happens to be late in the evening and you have to get that cake ready for the school stall the following morning and that's all there is to hand.

EGGS

Eggs need to be at room temperature for the recipes that follow. If you do happen to store your eggs in the fridge, remember to remove them at least 30 minutes, and ideally an hour, before baking. This is essential if you are whisking the whites, but temperature also affects the way they combine with other ingredients.

The majority of recipes use 'medium' eggs, which weigh 53–63g, and so conform to the traditional ratio of eggs, flour, butter and sugar that in equal quantity go to make up a Victoria Sponge, a quatre-quart or pound cake. As a child, I remember my granny using eggs as the starting point to weigh out the other ingredients on an old-fashioned set of balance scales. Occasionally 'large' eggs are specified, which weigh 63–73g.

Always use free-range or organic eggs. Every country will have its own system of controlling egg production and in the UK the British 'Lion' mark accounts for some 85 per cent of our eggs. This not only guarantees that the poultry have been vaccinated against salmonella, but also all the eggs are stamped with a 'best before date' too. As a rule of thumb, if the eggs are likely to be used in their raw or under-cooked state, I always buy organic.

SALT

Recipes often call for a pinch of sea salt, but what I mean here is the fine variety rather than coarse stuff. Much as we love using it elsewhere, you don't want to be crunching on savoury crystals – the idea is the very faintest challenge to the sugar. At very least, scrunch it between your fingers.

FLOUR

The majority of the cakes rely on refined wheat flour. A reliable cake flour, be it own-brand or one of the bigger names, is likely to cook up one and the same.

But there are, of course, a large range of different types of flour on the market. I would like to be able to say that these are all interchangeable, so if you happen to be gluten intolerant, no problem, just use chestnut or quinoa, and of course you can substitute polenta or ground almonds for the plain flour in the muffins. But you can't!

I learnt the hard way here (actually it was a lot of fun and very interesting). Set the challenge of coming up with a range of recipes using different flours, I felt the only way forward was to go back to the beginning – rockcakes. In fact, I'm not sure I had made them since those very early childhood buns, but I needed something forgiving and speedy, and so I knocked out batch after batch of rockcakes using different flours. While a handful cooked up in a similar fashion (rice, chestnut and rye), the spelt rockcakes spread outwards rather than upwards, the polenta ones were a pile of lumpy sand, and the ground almond ones were perhaps predictably on the oily side, and spread themselves in an unseemly fashion all over the baking tray.

The conclusion is that if you want to play around with different flours then do it, I am afraid, at your own risk – and I would suggest trying rice, chestnut or rye flours before any others. That said, I cannot speak highly enough of ground almonds, which you will see feature in any number of recipes that follow. This is the Continental baker in me. I love the texture and the perfume that results from using ground almonds, it is an ingredient that makes for truly luxurious results. You can, however, fairly safely substitute ground hazelnuts for ground almonds. Again on the Continent you can readily buy these, but elsewhere you may have to grind them yourself in a coffee grinder.

equipment

CAKE TINS

With space in our kitchens at a premium, I have pared down my own range to a minimum. Nearly all the cakes in this book rely on just a handful of sizes.

NON-STICK

Modern cake tins and moulds make the baker's life easier than ever and are recommended for all the recipes that follow. Gone are the days of rusting cake tins with fixed bases, when it was necessary to butter, then line the tin and butter the paper. For the most part what is on offer to the domestic consumer comes lined with a non-stick coating. The best among these are solid and heavy; sometimes described as heavy-gauge or commercial weight, and the more layers of non-stick coating the better. It is really worth investing in the best tins here, in one that will last. The more robust the less likely the cake is to burn, and the better the fit of base and collar, the less chance there is of any mixture leaking out. It is also worth noting that 'insulated' cake tins that have two layers of metal change the cooking times, in my experience by up to 30 per cent.

LOOSE BASE OR SPRINGFORM?

There are two choices here: loose-based or Springform cake tins, which come with a collar that clips onto the base. Both do away with the need for lining the tin (unless the sponge is particularly shallow), always one of the fiddliest bits, and have the added advantage that you can leave the cake on the base to serve it, which means it's less likely to crack. I recommend buttering the tin in the majority of cases. This is generally more successful than brushing with oil, even if the cake itself relies on it.

SANDWICH V DEEP CAKE TINS

If you are going to invest in just one type of round tin, then the deeper the better. A deep tin is essential for fruitcakes and other deep sponges, but is versatile enough for baking shallow sandwich sponges too. Loose-based tins tend to come up deeper than Springform, which generally measure approx. 7cm in height; the very deepest tins are 8–9cm. Sandwich tins are limited in use, and I quite often suggest baking a deeper cake and splitting it in half in any case, which makes for a particularly moist slice – unless it is a delicate sponge that needs to be made as a shallow layer.

SILICONE MOULDS

It was many years before I embraced these, and I still prefer the old-fashioned procedure of baking in a tin. I think you achieve a particular crust, as the metal itself is partly responsible for toasting the outside crumb. But I wouldn't be without racks of silicone moulds for small cakes, which so often stick to the tin even when buttered. With silicone moulds, the cake can be popped out with ease, however intricate the design.

MIXING BOWLS

I have stacks of different-sized Mason Cash pudding bowls, which I use for all my measuring and mixing. I find them especially pleasurable and relaxing to work with. And there is also something enormously satisfying about mixing up a cake in a traditional mixing bowl.

In fact, an interesting tale surrounds my favourite cane weave mixing bowl. The traditional bowls were first manufactured by Mason Cash in the 19th century using a local clay, which accounts for their colour. Then in the 20th century the T.G. Green pottery, who were keen to exploit the success of Mason Cash's bowl, developed the gripstand, using a white clay and spraying it. While almost identical in appearance, the gripstand has one flat panel to stand the bowl on its side while beating a mixture or whisking egg whites. Today both designs of bowl are produced by Mason Cash who now own T.G. Green pottery. www.rayware.co.uk

CAKE TIN SIZES

If you do want to ring the changes with shape, then the importance is volume. Simply measure the volume of the recommended cake tin with water, and choose a different shape that offers the same. You may have to keep an eye on the timing and temperature – if it is deeper it may take longer for instance, or you might need to bake at a lower temperature to avoid overcooking the top.

Loaf tins are more complicated, with some manufacturers specifying the length and others the weight of the finished loaf. If in doubt, the most accurate gauge again is volume, measured by filling it with water.

The following sizes should cover you for the cakes that feature. It is worth bearing in mind that the size of traybake and roasting tins can vary by 1–2cm, depending on whether the manufacturer has included the lip at either end in the final measurement. And where a tart tin has sloping sides, the measurement refers to the top of the tin.

PAPER CASES

For the best results with small cakes, set paper cases inside the moulds of fairy cake or muffin trays. Failing this, put two cases inside each other, and lay these out on a baking tray. When a recipe specifies fairy cake, it means a shallow paper case 2.5cm high with a base measurement of about 4cm. A muffin is approximately 4cm high with a base measurement of 5cm. There are other sizes out there, in which case you may find the recipe makes more or less depending, and you might need to heed the cooking time too.

RECOMMENDED SIZES

2 x 20cm non-stick cake tins with a removable base, at least 7–9cm deep

2 x 23cm non-stick cake tins with a removable base, at least 7–9cm deep

22cm/1.3 litre non-stick loaf tin

30cm x 23cm non-stick traybake or roasting tin, 4cm deep

32cm x 23cm non-stick Swiss roll tin or shallow oven tray

2 non-stick fairy cake trays or shallow bun trays

2 non-stick muffin trays

23cm non-stick square brownie tin, 4cm deep

25cm non-stick bundt tin or fluted cake ring (18cm tube [angel cake] tin)

20cm tart tin with a removable base, 3cm deep

23cm tart tin with a removable base, at least 3cm deep

Gingerbread Family Cookie Cutter Set

Set of fluted cutters

2 non-stick baking trays

SIEVE

The ingredients to sift religiously are those prone to caking, or that by dint of not being used that often are inclined to take on the moisture in the air. Ground spices, bicarbonate of soda, cream of tartar, and baking powder being the forceful little agent that it is, all merit being sifted to ensure there are no small lumps in there. Icing sugar, equally, is hygroscopic and likely to clog.

Flours for the most part are free-flowing in their present day incarnation. And I am the first to cut corners here even where I've specified sifting, but that one is over to you. In my food-processing world, rarely does sifting have much to do with adding air, unless it is clear that the mixture is based on whisked egg whites and sifted flour, and then it does play a part.

Most important is the sieve itself, which should be open-textured as opposed to gossamer fine. You need to be able to see actual holes, which will allow for any dry ingredients to pass through with ease, otherwise you will be there for hours. This is something that I took for granted, until I went out to Mallorca to teach a team of Spanish chefs how to bake British cakes – the equipment that had been ordered in prior to my arrival included drum sieves, with a mesh so tight that water would have been challenged to drip through. It was a shame that what were supposed to be foolproof and simple recipes were rendered almost unachievable by this one fault. Equally though (if you are reading dear husband), a vegetable colander won't do.

BAKING TRAYS

The best heavy-gauge non-stick baking trays such as the Tala range (see e-address book) shouldn't require any buttering, although this can be good insurance with enamel and other steel trays. You want a couple of these for biscuits and cookies, 25cm x 40cm is a good size.

BAKING PAPER

Baking paper and greaseproof are one and the same. They probably get less of an outing these days, given the non-stick nature of most cake tins, but they are still indispensible for when you want to lift a traybake, loaf or some rocky road out of a tin with a fixed base. Baking paper also serves to protect fruitcakes which call for a long slow baking from colouring overly, so it's a good staple to keep to hand.

PERFECT PANCAKE PAN

While special pancake pans do exist, not being able to find it or having to drag it out from the back of the cupboard for occasional use is one more reason for not making pancakes as often as we might. The ideal is an all-purpose frying pan that just happens to make perfect pancakes into the bargain, and you will be well served here by a legendary non-stick 'Scanpan'. The patented ceramic titanium surface is famously durable and will withstand metal utensils (turning pancakes with a metal spatula is by far and away the easiest route), so this is an important consideration. The 24cm is an ideal size. www.scanpan.dk

CLINGFILM

Indispensible for any number of tasks, not just covering the food to keep it fresh. I use it for wrapping doughs to rest, and for spreading out shortbread or pastry dough in a tin using fingers in lieu of rolling.

FOIL

Sometimes this is preferable to baking paper when pre-baking a case, making it easier to secure the pastry sides to the tin. Indispensible for maturing cheesecakes too.

BAKING BEANS

A packet of dried pulses will stand in as baking beans to weight pastry when pre-baking the case, but the revival of ceramic baking beans is a welcome one as pulses inevitably have a certain scent when heated. So if you plan on making lots of tarts, then this is a good investment. www.talacooking.com

the art of decoration

ICING

When making a simple glace icing, the ideal is to cautiously edge your way towards the perfect consistency by adding the liquid to the icing sugar just a little at a time, and working it thoroughly. It should be creamy rather than claggy, and slowly run off a spoon rather than trickle in a stream, in which case it is too thin. And if you do accidentally add too much liquid, it's not the end of the world, just add a little more sugar.

To achieve really pale pastel shades, it is best to dip a skewer into the colouring and then wave this through the icing until you are happy with the colour. A trickle of liquid colour or a small piece of paste can dye it rather dramatically. Of the two, I find paste more effective than liquid.

FLOWERS

Fresh rose petals are one of my favourite ways of dressing up a cake for an occasion; a shower of small inner petals of red or white roses will always look magical. Be sure these are organic or homegrown to avoid any pesticides.

CRYSTALLISED ROSE PETALS One step on from fresh rose petals, and you do need to make them several hours in advance. A fan oven with a defrost setting provides an ideal environment for drying them. Otherwise a warm and draughty spot. Carefully pull the rose petals off the stalks. Lay them out on a worksurface, and very lightly paint the topside with egg white. Sift over an even layer of white caster sugar until they appear frosted. Turn them over and repeat on the other side. Lay them on the rack of a grill pan and leave to dry for several hours, until they are brittle and crisp.

FLOWER WATERS Rose and orange blossom can be used to delicately scent a sponge or frosting in the same way as vanilla. But there is a huge difference in strength between the delicate flower waters sold in Middle Eastern delis, which you can add with relative abandon, and the potent culinary essence that comes in a small bottle and needs to be added by the drop. All the recipes that follow call for traditional flower water, except for Rose Sugar on page 20.

CRYSTALLISED VIOLETS The ultimately pretty cake decoration.

flavourings

VANILLA

The scent of vanilla in a sponge cake is as central as the key ingredients that go to make it up; somehow it brings them all together. So a small bottle of the very finest extract is a must-have, as opposed to vanilla flavouring or essence which implies a concentrated artificial flavouring rather than an extraction of the real thing.

The key name here is Nielsen-Massey, a third generation producer. Made from Madagascan vanilla beans, the ensuing vanilla is known as 'Madagascar Bourbon Vanilla', the highest quality of pure vanilla available; it is deliciously creamy, sweet and mellow. While it might seem on the pricey side, a small bottle goes a long, long way and should see you through many cakes. They also produce a vanilla paste, a mass of tiny, sticky black vanilla seeds, that is equally gorgeous stuff. The key to Nielsen-Massey's production is their 'cold extraction' process that very gently draws the delicate flavour from the vanilla beans, that differs from others as it doesn't involve heat or pressure.

VANILLA CHANTILLY (SERVES 6)

A lovely way of turning a cake into a pud, one step up from a spoonful of crème fraîche.

Whisk together 200ml whipping cream, 40g sifted icing sugar and ¾ teaspoon vanilla extract in a bowl until light and fluffy using an electric whisk. Cover and chill until required. If leaving for longer than an hour or two, it may need a quick stir before serving.

VANILLA-RUM MASCARPONE (SERVES 6)

This is another lovely vanilla cream for dishing up with fruit tarts and pies, as well as cakes. You can also make a thick pouring cream using crème fraîche.

Place 250g mascarpone in a bowl. Open out a slit vanilla pod and run a knife along the inside to remove the tiny black seeds, or you can use half a teaspoon of vanilla extract. Blend the seeds, 40g sifted icing sugar and 2 tablespoons dark rum with the mascarpone, beating well with a wooden spoon until smooth. Transfer to an attractive serving bowl, cover and chill until required. You can make this a day in advance, in which case stir it before serving.

VANILLA SUGAR (MAKES 225G)

In France, potent little sachets of vanilla sugar are the norm for scenting cakes, and they make a great convenience should you chance across them. That much more potent than homemade vanilla sugar, I would mix them one part to three with ordinary caster. But otherwise it is easy to make your own, and a good use for any discarded pods where you've already used the seeds to flavour a dish. Simply whizz a chopped vanilla pod in a food processor with 225g caster sugar. Sieve and keep it in an airtight jar.

CHOCOLATE

Many of the recipes involving chocolate rely on one with 50 per cent cocoa solids, lower than most eating chocs today, which can be too forceful in a cake or icing as well as being tricky to cook with. Whereas cooking chocolate was once a derogatory term, today there is a wide selection of high-quality cooking chocolate on the market. Look for cocoa butter in the small print, which has a profound effect on how the chocolate melts and combines with other ingredients.

LEMON

Zest: Large firm lemons zest better than small soft ones. Remove the zest with a fine grater rather than a zester, as it is the outer yellow layer that contains the essential oils.
Extract: Our favourite source of vanilla extract, Nielsen-Massey, make an equally exquisite lemon extract using natural botanical oils.

CANDIED PEEL

Those sugary sheaves of candied peel in the local deli promise so much more than the commercial pots laden with preservatives, but also cast a thought to how easy it is to make at home. The scent alone while it is cooking makes this worth considering, especially if you are making a once-a-year fruitcake for some celebration.

Quarter and remove the skin from two thick-skinned oranges. Place this in a medium-sized saucepan, cover with water and bring to the boil; drain it and repeat about five times until softened. Return the peel to the pan with 100ml water and 200g golden caster sugar and simmer over a low heat for 20 minutes until glossy and the syrup is thickened. Drain the peel and lay it on a rack to dry for about 36 hours. It will still look glossy at this point. Loosely stack it in a jar with plenty of airspace and use as required. It will dry out further in the coming days.

COFFEE

I am hooked on my Nespresso machine and this is a great route to a really strong aromatic coffee for using as an extract or essence in sponges and icings. Select one of the stronger espressos such as the classic 'Ristretto' – you want max flavour in relation to liquid. www.magimix.com

flavoured sugars

As well as sprinkling flavoured sugars over pancakes, try them as you would vanilla sugar in buttery shortbread biscuits, or dusted over the top of simple sponges or fruitcakes.

LEMON SUGAR

Pour 1 tablespoon lemon juice over 225g caster sugar in a bowl, and stir until it is uniformly moist. Scatter it over a baking tray or roasting dish, and place somewhere warm overnight to dry out. Transfer it to a food processor and whizz to a free-flowing consistency. Peel off the zest from a lemon using a potato peeler, and store the sugar with the zest in an airtight jar.

CINNAMON SUGAR

Whizz a cinnamon stick with 225g caster sugar in a food processor, then pass through a sieve. Store in a jar with a cinnamon stick in the centre until required.

ROSE SUGAR

Make as for lemon sugar, using 1 tablespoon rosewater. Here a pungent extract or essence is ideal. Pull off the petals from an organic red rose, and mix these into the sugar before storing it in a jar.

e-address book

ONE-STOP SHOPS

www.lakeland.co.uk With an eye on up-to-the-minute trends and clever labour-saving devices, as well as lovely presentation kits. A wide range of cake tins and silicone moulds, biscuit cutters, excellent flavourings, paper cases and loaf-tin liners.

www.talacooking.com For all the suggested cake tins plus paraphernalia galore. This traditional kitchenware maker has been going since 1899. I am sure the icing syringe set that I used to play with as a child would have been Tala. Their range, which is based on the decades since the 1950s when we truly fell in love with baking, has a lovely sense of continuity, comfort and familiarity.

www.divertimenti.co.uk A great resource for the serious cook. They have all manner of out-of-the-ordinary cutters and tins, as well as the standard sizes. They also sell tart tins with 4cm sides, the minimum you should look for.

SPECIALISTS

www.magimix-spares.co.uk For Magimix food processors and Nespresso machines, as well as spare parts.

www.kenwood.co.uk For hand-held electric whisks.

www.rayware.co.uk For stockists of Mason Cash pudding bowls and cane weave mixing bowls.

www.george-wilkinson.com For an excellent wide range of durable non-stick bakeware.

www.scanpan.dk The Danish non-stick Scanpan is brilliant for pancakes. Its ceramic titanium surface allows for the use of metal utensils, where other plastic coatings will tear and scratch. The Classic 24cm is a great all-round size.

www.brabantia.com For compact reliable digital electronic scales, and lightweight stainless-steel mixing bowls with non-slip silicone bases.

www.salterhousewares.com For electronic timers that show seconds as well as minutes.

www.johnlewis.com and www.jwpltd.co.uk For airtight Lock & Lock plastic containers.

www.janeasher.com For specialised decorating supplies and equipment, including edible decorations.

www.supercook.co.uk Great for everyday baking ingredients, including chocolate decorations and cooking chocolate, icings and marzipan, flavourings and candles.

www.squires-shop.com This online decorating emporium has everything you need to set up shop, and to decorate and present your cakes – including boxes and boards.

www.sugarshack.co.uk Another online shop with the semi-professional in mind, or someone with a fervent imagination they are keen to let run wild.

cookies and biscuits

CHAPTER ONE

MAKES 10–12

220g unsalted butter, diced

120g icing sugar

finely grated zest of 1 lemon

2 medium egg yolks

300g plain flour

approx. 100g seedless strawberry jam, worked until smooth

KIT

Food processor

Clingfilm

8cm fluted cutter

2–3cm plain or fluted cutter

2 non-stick baking trays

Palette knife

LITTLE EXTRAS

Plain flour for rolling

Icing sugar for dusting

lunettes

The French tradition of 'lunettes' or spectacles loosely mirrors our own jammy dodgers, but as we might expect they come loaded with Gallic charm. For starters there is their size, they are cut as a large oval 7–8cm long, with two 'eyes' or lovely jammy holes, which instantly doubles their allure. Their sides are fluted, and the biscuit itself is made using a short sweet 'sable', not dissimilar to shortbread, containing equal quantities of butter and icing sugar, twice the amount of flour, and also egg.

In my own take on these, the dough is generous with the butter and is made with egg yolks, and in the interests of accessibility the biscuits are cut round rather than oval, but that is not to stop you cutting out two holes. I have come across these sandwiched with all manner of jams – from myrtle or blueberry to raspberry and strawberry – so you can use anything your cupboard offers up.

Cream the butter and icing sugar together in a food processor with the lemon zest, then add the egg yolks and finally the flour. The dough will be soft and sticky at this point, wrap it in clingfilm and pat into a flattened block. Chill for several hours or overnight.

Preheat the oven to 160°C fan oven/180°C electric oven. Roll out half of the dough at a time on a lightly floured worksurface to a thickness of about 5mm and cut out biscuits using an 8cm fluted cutter. Cut out a small circle from the centre of half of the biscuits using a 2–3cm plain or fluted cutter.

Arrange the biscuits separately on a couple of non-stick baking trays, spacing them slightly apart.

Bake the biscuits for 10–12 minutes, with the ones with holes on the lower rack, until they are just starting to colour. Remove and loosen with a palette knife and leave to cool. Dust the biscuits with the holes with icing sugar until they are white. Dollop half a teaspoon of the jam in the centre of each of the other biscuits and thickly spread to within a couple of centimetres of the rim. Sandwich with the dusted biscuits.

TIP

The biscuits can be made up to a week in advance, stored in an airtight container and sandwiched and dusted with icing sugar on the day they are to be served. The dough can also be made a couple of days in advance, and it freezes well.

fab choc chip cookies

MAKES 20–30

110g lightly salted butter, diced

125g light muscovado sugar

1 medium egg

1 teaspoon vanilla extract

175g plain flour

1 teaspoon baking powder

150g dark chocolate (approx. 70 per cent cocoa solids), coarsely chopped

KIT

Food processor

2 non-stick baking trays

Palette knife

Wire rack

LITTLE EXTRAS

Vegetable oil for greasing

I fall for those over-sized chocolate cookies at the railway station café every single time, it can only be hope over experience combined with the numbing boredom of scanning the departure board. Still, that's plenty of time to dream up what they should be like, generously scented with vanilla and set with an indecent amount of really dark craggy nibs of chocolate.

Choc chip cookies fall into two camps depending on their texture. 'Soft-bake', as they are known, are something like a biscuit meets a cake, crispy around the edges and soft and fudgy in the centre. These are seriously divine but they're not keepers – leave them overnight and the cake-like centres will win out over the crispy edges as they relax all over, although they can be rescued (see TIP). Or, if you want something that stays buttery and crumbly for a while, the trick is to make them smaller and bake until uniformly crisp.

Cream the butter and sugar together in a food processor, then incorporate the egg and vanilla. Sift and add the flour and baking powder and process briefly. Transfer the mixture to a large bowl and mix in the chopped chocolate. Cover and chill for a couple of hours or overnight if preferred.

Preheat the oven to 170°C fan oven/190°C electric oven and lightly oil a couple of non-stick baking trays – you will probably need to cook the cookies in batches. Roll the dough into balls the size of a walnut (about 30g) for soft-bake, and slightly smaller than this (about 20g) for crisp cookies. Arrange the balls on the baking trays, spacing them about 5cm apart. For soft cookies, bake for 10–12 minutes until pale gold around the edges; for crisp cookies, bake for 15–17 minutes until golden all over. The lower tray may take a few minutes longer. Loosen the cookies with a palette knife straight away, transfer them to a wire rack and leave to cool. They will keep well in an airtight container for a couple of days.

TIP

The point here is the 'chips', don't stint on the quality of the chocolate, 70 per cent cocoa should have just the right bitter edge. The other secrets to flavour are to use a lightly salted butter and a muscovado sugar.

Soft-bake cookies are at their most decadent slightly warm when the edges are crisp and the chocolate is gooey. They can be rewarmed for 5 minutes at 170°C fan oven/190°C electric oven. Or you can make the dough a day in advance.

mont-saint-michel choc chip cookies

Should you ever have visited Mont-Saint-Michel or the surrounding area of Normandy, then you may well have fallen under the spell of the Mère Poulard's cookies, in particular their chocolate chip ones. Neither overly sweet or rich, they are crisp and golden, studded with chocolate chips and finished with a shiny glaze.

Whizz the egg with the caster sugar and salt in a food processor. Add the flour and demerara sugar and whizz again. Add the butter and whizz until the mixture resembles fine crumbs, then keep whizzing until it starts to cling together into larger crumbs. Transfer the mixture to a bowl and mix in the chocolate chips. Bring the dough together into a ball, wrap in clingfilm and chill for a couple of hours or overnight.

Preheat the oven to 170°C fan oven/190°C electric oven. Knead the dough until it is pliable and then roll it out to a thickness of about 7mm on a lightly floured worksurface. Cut out biscuits using an 8cm fluted cutter, rolling the dough twice, which should give you about 12 biscuits. Arrange these on a couple of non-stick baking trays spaced slightly apart. Lightly brush with egg yolk and bake for 20–22 minutes until evenly golden. Leave to cool and then store in an airtight container. They should be good for several days.

TIP

It is important that your butter is really cold for this recipe, since it is the tiny nibs of butter within the dough that give the biscuits their light, flaky texture. To be on the safe side, it is worth spreading the diced butter out on a plate and popping it into the freezer for 10 minutes before using.

MAKES 12

1 medium egg, plus 1 egg yolk to glaze

75g golden caster sugar

pinch of sea salt

240g plain flour

1 tablespoon demerara sugar

160g salted butter, chilled and cut into 1cm dice (see TIP)

75g dark chocolate chips or chunks (approx. 70 per cent cocoa solids)

KIT

Food processor

Clingfilm

8cm fluted cutter

2 non-stick baking trays

Pastry brush

LITTLE EXTRAS

Plain flour for rolling

soft-bake chocolate and fennel cookies

I love dreaming up slightly outlandish combinations of flavours, and biscuits in particular allow for this. There is something in their character that accommodates a bold hand – dark chocolate, apricot and fennel? It works, I promise you. These blowsy amorphous cookies are crisp around the edges and chewy within. They look something like a treasure island map with their nooks and crannies.

Preheat the oven to 200°C fan oven/220°C electric oven and butter a couple of non-stick baking trays. Cream the butter and sugar together in a food processor, then beat in the egg and vanilla extract. Add the ground almonds, flour and baking powder and process to a soft dough. Transfer the mixture to a large bowl.

Coarsely grind the fennel seeds in a pestle and mortar and stir into the cookie batter with the apricots and chocolate.

Drop generous heaped teaspoons of the mixture onto the baking trays, spacing them well apart – I allow about six per tray – and cook them in two batches. Bake for 8–10 minutes until golden around the edges but pale within. The lower tray may take a little longer than the top. Leave the cookies to cool for 3 minutes, then loosen them with a palette knife and leave to cool completely. They are at their best the day they are made, while the chocolate is gooey and the outside crisp.

MAKES APPROX. 20

125g unsalted butter, diced

200g golden caster sugar

1 medium egg

½ teaspoon vanilla extract

100g ground almonds

75g plain flour, sifted

1 teaspoon baking powder, sifted

1 heaped teaspoon fennel seeds

100g dried apricots, chopped

200g dark chocolate (approx. 70 per cent cocoa solids), coarsely chopped

KIT

2 non-stick baking trays

Food processor

Pestle and mortar

Palette knife

LITTLE EXTRAS

Unsalted butter for greasing

125g unsalted butter, diced

75g demerara sugar

3 tablespoons golden syrup

175g wholemeal flour

½ teaspoon baking powder

½ teaspoon bicarbonate of soda

FOR THE COATING

100g dark (approx. 70 per cent cocoa solids) or milk chocolate, broken into pieces

KIT

Food processor

Clingfilm

2 non-stick baking trays

Palette knife

Wire rack

chocolate digestives

Digestive or sweetmeal biscuits have been around since, I was about to say our grandmother's generation, but probably better make that our great grandmother's, who believed them to have 'digestive' properties on account of the bicarbonate of soda.

I will happily secrete a packet in my suitcase when going away for the familiar comfort they provide in the middle of the night in a strange bedroom, one that is entirely their own, no other biscuit quite does it. I have even been known to hide a packet in my son's luggage too as he's heading off on some trip, 'just in case they don't feed you properly'. As if I need worry.

These are 'soft-bake' by comparison to the classic McVitie's biscuit, but the charm of that rustic biscuit with its sandy wholemeal finish and crunch of demerara is just as comforting. You can choose from dark or milk chocolate to suit your craving. Either way go for a really good eating choc.

Cream the butter and sugar together in a food processor until light and fluffy, then add the golden syrup. Add the flour, and sift and add the baking powder and bicarbonate of soda. Process briefly until the mixture comes together in a ball, then wrap in clingfilm and chill for several hours or overnight.

Preheat the oven to 170°C fan oven/190°C electric oven. Roll the dough into balls the size of a large walnut (about 30g) and place on a couple of non-stick baking trays, spacing them about 5cm apart. Bake for 15–20 minutes until risen and evenly golden. Leave to cool for 5 minutes, then loosen them with a palette knife and transfer to a wire rack to cool.

Gently melt the chocolate in a bowl set over a pan with a little simmering water in it. Drizzle the melted chocolate over the biscuits, first in a zigzag in one direction and then at right angles to this. Either pop into the fridge for 20 minutes for the chocolate to harden or set aside for a couple of hours.

TIP

The biscuits will be too soft to loosen the minute they come out of the oven and will break if you try, but equally they will adhere to the tray if you leave them for too long. So set the timer for 5 minutes as soon as you take them out. Once cold, they can be stored in an airtight container for a couple of days.

polka dot cookies

MAKES APPROX. 10
10CM COOKIES

125g unsalted butter, diced

75g golden caster sugar

3 tablespoons golden syrup

1 teaspoon vanilla extract

180g plain flour

½ teaspoon baking powder

½ teaspoon bicarbonate of soda

2 and a bit tubes of Smarties

KIT

Food processor

Clingfilm

2 non-stick baking trays

Palette knife

LITTLE EXTRAS

Vegetable oil for greasing

An over-sized biscuit with half a packet of Smarties thrown in is going to prove irresistible to any child, *et moi aussi*. Hard to pass by the tray strategically placed on the counter between me and the exit at my health club, one easy way of undoing all those lengths of the pool. But they always make me smile, and hey, another day another swim.

Cream the butter and sugar together in a food processor until pale and fluffy, then add the golden syrup and vanilla. Sift the flour, baking powder and bicarbonate of soda together, add to the butter and sugar mixture and whizz to a dough. Remove from the bowl, wrap in clingfilm and chill for 30 minutes.

Preheat the oven to 180°C fan oven/200°C electric oven and lightly oil two non-stick baking trays. Form the dough into balls the size of a walnut (about 30g) and gently flatten them between your palms into chubby discs about 5cm in diameter. Arrange on the prepared baking trays, spacing them well apart, and bake for 12–14 minutes until evenly golden and slightly risen. Remove from the oven and immediately press the Smarties into the surface of each – one in the centre and six around the outside for max appeal. Leave to cool for 5 minutes before loosening the cookies with a palette knife and setting aside to cool completely. They keep well for several days in an airtight container.

black forest cookies

MAKES APPROX. 25

110g lightly salted butter, diced

75g golden caster sugar

50g light muscovado sugar

1 medium egg

½ teaspoon vanilla extract

150g plain flour

1 teaspoon baking powder

50g dried cherries

150g dark chocolate (approx. 70 per cent cocoa solids), chopped

KIT

3 non-stick baking trays

Food processor

Palette knife

Wire rack

LITTLE EXTRAS

Vegetable oil for greasing

Choc chip cookies with strains of Black Forest Gateau. Eat these warm when they are soft and crumbly in the centre with crispy edges. Serve with some vanilla ice cream for a treat.

Preheat the oven to 170°C fan oven/190°C electric oven and lightly oil three non-stick baking trays. Cream the butter and sugars together in a food processor, then incorporate the egg and vanilla. Sift and add the flour and baking powder and process briefly to a soft dough.

Transfer the mixture to a large bowl and mix in the cherries and chopped chocolate. Drop heaped teaspoons of the mixture in mounds onto the trays, spacing them well apart. Bake for 12–17 minutes until pale gold all over, but slightly darker around the edges. Loosen the cookies with a palette knife straight away, then leave them to cool. You can transfer them to a wire rack after a few minutes if you wish. These are at their best the day they are made, but still in good form the day after.

150g unsalted butter, diced

75g icing sugar, sifted

finely grated zest of 1 lemon

25g cornflour, sifted

150g self-raising flour, sifted

1–2 tablespoons seedless raspberry jam

KIT

Food processor

Fairy cake paper cases

2 fairy cake trays

LITTLE EXTRAS

Icing sugar for dusting

melting moments

Basically these are a kind of shortbread, and as a child they were one of the first cakes or biscuits I tried my hand at. I clearly remember one Sunday afternoon setting out 'en famille' on a treasure hunt with a hopeless set of clues and getting horribly lost, a batch of these were the panacea. Supremely short, they dissolve to nothing in the mouth, and it's useful to know they are egg free.

Preheat the oven to 170°C fan oven/190°C electric oven. Cream the butter, sugar and lemon zest together – you can do this in a food processor – then add the cornflour and flour to give a soft, squidgy dough. Arrange 14–17 paper cases inside a couple of fairy cake trays. Roll the dough into balls the size of a walnut (about 30g), and use your finger to indent a shallow hole into each one. Place these hole-up in the baking cases, gently pressing them onto the base to steady them. Bake for 15–17 minutes until lightly coloured, then remove and leave them to cool. If using two tins, the bottom may take a little longer than the top.

Drop a little jam into the middle of each cake to fill the holes and lightly dust with icing sugar. Set aside for an hour or two for the jam to set a little. If you like you can now peel the paper off. The cakes will keep well for up to a week in a sealed container.

chocolate melting moments

These readily transcribe to Chocolate Melting Moments. Simply omit the lemon zest, and replace 30g of the flour with 30g cocoa powder. To fill them, whisk 30g softened unsalted butter, 30g icing sugar and 2 teaspoons cocoa powder in a small bowl until pale and fluffy using an electric whisk. Fill each hollow with ½ teaspoon of the butter icing.

gingerbread men

Have fun with these – dream up gingerbread men, women, boys and girls with a tube of spidery white icing. For cookie cutters, see page 21.

Place the flour, sugar, butter, salt and spices in the bowl of a food processor and reduce to a crumb-like consistency. Add the egg yolk and bring the dough together into a ball. Wrap it in clingfilm and chill for 1 hour.

Preheat the oven to 180°C fan oven/200°C electric oven and brush two non-stick baking trays with oil. Knead the dough until it is pliable, then thinly roll it out to a thickness of about 3mm on a lightly floured worksurface. Cut out biscuits using a 7cm gingerbread cutter, rolling the dough twice, and lay these 1cm apart on the baking trays. Bake the biscuits for 9–12 minutes until very lightly coloured. The lower tray make take longer than the top. Remove the trays from the oven and leave the biscuits to cool for a couple of minutes, then loosen them with a palette knife and leave to cool completely.

Ice the gingerbread men with spidery white icing and leave this to set. The gingerbread men will keep well in a covered container for several days.

MAKES APPROX. 20

150g plain flour

50g caster sugar

115g unsalted butter, diced

pinch of sea salt

½ teaspoon ground ginger

½ teaspoon ground cinnamon

1 medium egg yolk

KIT

Food processor

Clingflim

2 non-stick baking trays

7cm gingerbread cutter

Palette knife

LITTLE EXTRAS

Vegetable oil for greasing

Plain flour for rolling

White writing icing

stem ginger and chilli biscuits

These peppery soft-bake ginger cookies take this genre to its logical extreme, accentuating the ginger with a touch of chilli. But this isn't essential, and you can leave it out for a more classic ginger biscuit.

Cream the butter and sugar together in a food processor, then add the syrup. Sift the flour, bicarbonate of soda, ginger and cayenne pepper together and add to the syrup mixture. Process to a soft dough, transfer the mixture to a medium-sized bowl and work in the stem ginger. Cover with clingfilm and chill for several hours or overnight.

Preheat the oven to 180°C fan oven/200°C electric oven and lightly oil a couple of non-stick baking trays. Form the dough into balls the size of a walnut (about 30g), rolling them between your palms. Arrange on the baking trays, spacing them about 5cm apart, and bake for 12–14 minutes until golden. Leave to cool on the baking trays for 5 minutes to firm up, before loosening them with a palette knife and transferring them to a wire rack. They should keep well in an airtight container for several days.

MAKES APPROX. 20

125g unsalted butter, diced

75g light muscovado sugar

3 tablespoons golden syrup

180g self-raising flour

½ teaspoon bicarbonate of soda

1 level teaspoon ground ginger

1/8 teaspoon cayenne pepper

50g crystallised stem ginger, finely chopped

KIT

Food processor

Clingflim

2 non-stick baking trays

Palette knife

Wire rack

LITTLE EXTRAS

Vegetable oil for greasing

MAKES APPROX. 20

60g unsalted butter, diced

100g golden caster sugar

½ medium egg, beaten

10–15 saffron filaments, ground and blended with 1 teaspoon boiling water

finely grated zest of 1 lemon

50g ground almonds

70g plain flour, sifted

½ teaspoon baking powder, sifted

¼ teaspoon sea salt

KIT

Food processor

Clingfilm

2 non-stick baking trays

Palette knife

Wire rack

LITTLE EXTRAS

Unsalted butter or vegetable oil for greasing

saffron lemon crisps

Buttery and crisp, with the hidden charm of saffron and lemon.

Cream the butter and sugar together in a food processor, then beat in the egg along with the saffron infusion and lemon zest. Add the ground almonds, flour, baking powder and salt and process briefly to a sticky dough. Spoon the mixture into a bowl, cover with clingfilm and chill overnight.

Preheat the oven to 180°C fan oven/200°C electric oven and grease two non-stick baking trays with oil or butter. Roll the dough into balls the size of a cherry and place well apart on the prepared baking trays. I would bake them in two batches, with 5–6 biscuits per tray. Bake for about 12 minutes, checking them after 10 minutes. The bottom tray may need a little longer than the top. Immediately loosen the biscuits with a palette knife and transfer them to a wire rack to cool. They will keep well in an airtight container for several days.

almond thins

These little almond-crusted biscuits are meltingly tender, leaving a hint of cinnamon in their wake.

Place the flour, sugar, butter, salt and cinnamon in the bowl of a food processor and whizz to a crumb-like consistency. Add the egg yolk and process briefly to bring the dough together into a ball. Wrap in clingfilm and chill for 1 hour.

Preheat the oven to 180°C fan oven/200°C electric oven and brush two non-stick baking trays with oil. Knead the dough until it is pliable and then roll out thinly to a thickness of about 2mm on a lightly floured worksurface. Cut out biscuits using a 5cm round biscuit cutter, rolling the dough twice, and lay them 1cm apart on the baking trays. Brush the surface of the biscuits with the eggwash and scatter over the flaked almonds. Bake in the oven for 9–12 minutes until lightly golden. The lower tray may take a little longer than the top. Remove the trays and leave the biscuits to cool. Transfer them to a plate using a palette knife. They will keep well in a covered container for several days.

MAKES 30–40

FOR THE BISCUITS

150g plain flour

50g golden caster sugar

115g unsalted butter, diced

pinch of sea salt

1/3 teaspoon ground cinnamon

1 medium egg yolk

FOR THE TOPPING

1 egg yolk blended with 1 tablespoon milk to form an eggwash

40g flaked almonds

KIT

Food processor

Clingfilm

2 non-stick baking trays

5cm round cutter

Palette knife

LITTLE EXTRAS

Vegetable oil for greasing

Plain flour for rolling

classic shortbread

MAKES APPROX. 15

110g unsalted butter, chilled and diced

50g golden caster sugar

100g plain flour

60g ground almonds

finely grated zest of 2 oranges or lemons

KIT

Food processor

Clingfilm

2 non-stick baking trays

4cm fluted cutter

Palette knife

LITTLE EXTRAS

Vegetable oil for greasing

Plain flour for rolling

Golden caster sugar for dusting

Shortbread could really do with a chapter to itself, but this is my default recipe, which I use endlessly as a starting point either as a biscuit or as a basis for bars and so forth. You can vary the flavourings – it could be lemon, orange or lime zest, or sometimes I substitute about a tablespoon of the sugar with vanilla sugar. The basic dough can be made into all manner of shapes and thicknesses that in turn dictate its end texture. So over to you. I was given this recipe years and years ago by Clarissa Dickson Wright, whose passion for Scotland makes her the perfect sage. We both agreed that bad shortbread was like a 'bit of old pavement' and took it from there.

Place all the ingredients in the bowl of food processor and whizz to a dough. Wrap in clingfilm and chill overnight.

Preheat the oven to 140°C fan oven/160°C electric oven and grease two non-stick baking trays with vegetable oil. Roll out the dough to a thickness of 1cm on a lightly floured worksurface and cut out 4cm biscuits using a fluted cutter. You should get 15–20 biscuits if you roll the dough twice. Arrange on the baking trays, spacing them slightly apart, and chill for 30 minutes. Bake in the oven for 35–40 minutes until just starting to colour. Dust with caster sugar, loosen with a palette knife and leave to cool.

brown sugar
shortbread

MAKES 10–14

110g lightly salted butter, chilled and diced

50g light brown sugar

160g plain or spelt flour

KIT

Food processor

Clingfilm

2 non-stick baking trays

Palette knife

LITTLE EXTRAS

Demerara sugar for rolling

Unsalted butter for greasing

Cookie rolls, where the dough is formed into a sausage shape, rolled in sugar and sliced after chilling, are one of the simplest and visually effective ways of making shortbread biscuits. Their edge here has the crystalline sheen of demerara sugar, but you could roll them in all manner of other sugars or seeds.

Whizz all the ingredients for the shortbread together in a food processor to form a dough – at first the mixture will reduce to tiny crumbs, which will start to cling together in lumps as you continue to whizz them. Sprinkle some demerara sugar over a worksurface and roll the dough into a sausage 4–5cm in diameter, coating it in the sugar. Wrap in clingfilm, twisting the ends, and give it another little roll to smooth out any imperfections. Chill overnight. (You can also make up the dough several days in advance.)

Preheat the oven to 140°C fan oven/160°C electric oven and grease two non-stick baking trays with butter. Cut the shortbread roll into slices 1cm thick to give 12–14 biscuits and arrange on the baking trays, spacing them slightly apart. Bake for 30–40 minutes until just starting to colour, then loosen with a palette knife and leave to cool. The biscuits should keep well for some days in an airtight container.

lemon spelt sables

MAKES 20–25

115g lightly salted butter, chilled and diced

50g caster sugar

150g refined spelt flour

60g ground almonds

finely grated zest of 2 lemons

KIT

Food processor

Clingfilm

2 non-stick baking trays

Palette knife

LITTLE EXTRAS

Demerara sugar for rolling

Many people who are unable to tolerate wheat gluten find they can eat spelt, but its virtues go way beyond this. These biscuits play on one of spelt's great strengths, its lightness of being – these little sables are supremely short and melt in the mouth. For a slightly gutsier flavour you could use lightly salted goat's butter, which has a defined savour reminiscent of the cheese. It works well.

Place all the ingredients in the bowl of a food processor and whizz to a soft, squidgy dough.

Sprinkle some demerara sugar over a small section of a board or worksurface. Remove one-third of the dough and shape into a rough sausage, 3–4cm in diameter, then roll it in the sugar to coat the outside. Lay it on a sheet of clingfilm, 5–10cm longer than the roll at either end. Roll it up and twist the ends to neaten them. Repeat with the rest of the dough to give you three sausage shapes and chill for several hours or overnight.

Preheat the oven to 140°C fan oven/160°C electric oven. Unwrap the rolls and cut them into slices 1cm thick. Arrange on a couple of non-stick baking trays, spacing them slightly apart, and bake for about 30 minutes until a pale even gold. Loosen the biscuits with a palette knife and leave to cool on the trays. They will keep well for about a week in an airtight container.

MAKES APPROX. 30

2 x shortbread dough (see page 40) made using lemon zest

golden caster or granulated sugar for rolling

crunchy lemon shortcakes

Rolling the biscuits in sugar gives them a lovely crunchy finish. You could also use granulated for this, which makes for a coarser and even crunchier texture.

Preheat the oven to 140°C fan oven/160°C electric oven and grease two non-stick baking trays with vegetable oil. Place some caster or granulated sugar in a shallow bowl ready for coating.

Roll the dough into balls the size of a walnut (about 30g) between your palms, dip them in the sugar and roll lightly to coat. Arrange on the baking trays, spacing them slightly apart, and bake for about 40 minutes until an even pale gold. Leave to cool. These should keep well for a week in an airtight container.

150g lightly salted butter, softened

75g golden caster sugar

15 drops lavender essence (available from www.hopshop.co.uk)

150g plain flour

75g ground rice

finely grated zest of 1 lemon

pinch of dried or fresh lavender flowers

KIT

27 x 18cm baking tray

Baking paper

Electric whisk

LITTLE EXTRAS

Golden caster sugar for dusting

Lavender flowers for decorating (optional)

lavender shortbread

I was given this recipe by Crispin Alexander, whose parents own and run the wonderful Castle Farm in Kent that specialises in culinary lavender. While his method was new to me (see TIP), I had forgotten how good the inclusion of a little ground rice is, it gives the biscuit an alluring sandiness. I grew up with this ingredient, many was the milky pud that was placed on the table at supper, and I have started to use it again myself in this way. But it was always the secret ingredient of shortbreads too, the only caveat being that you are more likely to find it in a gargantuan bag in the Indian section of a supermarket than you are sold as a traditional pudding ingredient.

Preheat the oven to 150°C fan oven/170°C electric oven and line a 27 x 18cm baking tray with baking paper, taking it up the sides. Cream the butter, sugar and lavender essence in a large bowl using an electric whisk, then add the flour, ground rice, lemon zest and lavender flowers and continue to whisk until the mixture is crumb-like in consistency. Press into the lined tin, without totally compressing it, to leave it quite crumbly. Bake for 30–35 minutes until a pale gold, then remove and dust with caster sugar. Leave to cool and then cut into fingers. If you wish, you can scatter over a few more lavender flowers.

TIP

There is method in the apparent eccentricity of using an electric whisk here, as opposed to a food processor, that is all important to the crumbly finish of the biscuit. By only lightly pressing it into the tin, you encourage this further.

Failing ground rice, you can grind white rice in a coffee grinder as finely as possible. You could also use rice flour.

100g milk chocolate, broken into pieces

100g dark chocolate (approx. 70 per cent cocoa solids), broken into pieces

25g unsalted butter, diced

125g Rice Krispies

25g white chocolate chips

KIT

Fairy cake paper cases

2 fairy cake trays

triple choc crispies

One of our best-loved easy treats, a world apart if you give it the red carpet treatment of a high-end chocolate.

Gently melt the milk and dark chocolate with the butter in a large bowl set over a pan with a little simmering water in it. Stir in the Rice Krispies. Arrange about 14 paper cases in a couple of fairy cake trays and fill with heaped tablespoons of the mixture. Scatter a few chocolate chips over the top of each one and chill for 30–60 minutes until set. Store in an airtight container for up to one week.

MAKES APPROX. 12

100g dark chocolate (approx. 70 per cent cocoa solids), broken into pieces

100g milk chocolate, broken into pieces

25g unsalted butter, diced

100g cornflakes

80g milk chocolate chips or chunks

KIT

Fairy cake paper cases

Fairy cake tray

cornflake crispies

An oldie but a goodie, these remain a classic favourite of children, teenagers and a few grown-ups. You can also make them using dark chocolate only, but the mix of milk and dark creates a good balance.

Gently melt the dark and milk chocolate with the butter in a large bowl set over a pan with a little simmering water in it. If necessary, leave to cool to room temperature. Gently mix in the cornflakes using a metal spoon, folding them over until they are evenly coated, without worrying about the odd speck showing through. Fold in two-thirds of the chocolate chips. Arrange 12 paper cases in a fairy cake tray and heap the mixture inside. Scatter the remaining chocolate chips over the top of each. Chill for 30–60 minutes until set. Bring back to room temperature to serve and store in an airtight container. They should keep well for several days.

SERVES 8

225g plain flour, sifted

110g golden caster sugar

110g icing sugar, sifted

225g lightly salted butter, diced (see TIP)

5 medium egg yolks

¾ teaspoon vanilla extract

125g strawberry jam, e.g. Bonne Maman Strawberry and Wild Strawberry Conserve

1 egg yolk blended with 1 teaspoon water to form an eggwash

KIT

Food processor

Clingfilm

20cm non-stick cake tin with a removable base, at least 5cm deep

Pastry brush

LITTLE EXTRAS

Unsalted or lightly salted butter for greasing

Plain flour for rolling

breton gateau

Time spent in Normandy has given me a complete passion for this cake-cum-shortbread. There, I habitually chance across it filled with a purée of dried prunes, with chocolate and all manner of other variations. But it's the salty butter that defines its character and has you hewing off slivers long after you were sated. That and the inclusion of egg yolks, but not the whites, gives it the most gorgeous fudgy consistency.

Place the flour, two sugars and butter in the bowl of a food processor and whizz until the mixture forms a crumb-like consistency. Blend the egg yolks with the vanilla in a bowl, add to the dry ingredients and whizz to a soft, sticky dough. Wrap in clingfilm and chill for at least a couple of hours.

Preheat the oven to 170°C fan oven/190°C electric oven and butter a 20cm non-stick cake tin with a removable base, at least 5cm deep. Press half the dough into the tin, lay a sheet of clingfilm over the top and smooth out the surface carefully with your fingers. Work the jam in a bowl to loosen it and spread over the surface to within 1cm of the rim. Roll out the remaining dough on a well-floured worksurface (it will still be quite sticky) into a circle fractionally larger than the cake tin. Lay this on top of the jam and press it into place, tidying the edges using your fingers. Liberally paint the surface with the eggwash and make a lattice pattern using the tines of a fork. Bake for 45–55 minutes until deeply golden, crusty and risen. Run a knife around the collar and leave to cool in the tin. To serve, remove the collar and cut into wedges. It will keep well for several days in an airtight container.

TIP

If using Breton salted butter, replace with half salted butter and half unsalted.

50g unsalted butter

100g golden caster sugar

100g runny honey

225g plain flour

½ teaspoon baking powder

½ teaspoon bicarbonate of soda

1 teaspoon ground ginger

1 teaspoon ground cinnamon

½ medium egg

KIT

Clingfilm

2 non-stick baking trays

10cm star-shaped or other cutter

Skewer

Palette knife

Wire rack

LITTLE EXTRAS

Vegetable oil for greasing

Plain flour for dusting

White writing icing

Ribbon for hanging

lebkuchen

This is the classic honey-sweetened gingerbread of Germany and Austria, which appears in so many different forms there – from the shell of your gingerbread house to the biscuits that hang on the tree. The spices can be varied, a pinch of ground cardamom, cloves or nutmeg can be included too, but ginger and cinnamon are a must. This is a great recipe for involving children, the more dextrous can make the biscuits, and the more artistic (for which read young) can decorate them. A kit of biscuits, icing and ribbon also makes a good present for any friends' children, nephews or nieces.

Gently heat the butter, sugar and honey together in a small saucepan, stirring until melted and smooth. Working off the heat, add the dry ingredients and stir until crumbly, then add the egg and work to a dough. If the mixture seems very sticky you can add a little more flour. Tip out onto a worksurface, bring it into a ball and then pat it between your palms until you have a pleasingly smooth and shiny dough. Wrap in clingfilm, leave to cool and then chill for several hours or overnight.

Preheat the oven to 160°C fan oven/180°C electric oven and brush a couple of non-stick baking trays with vegetable oil. Thinly roll out the dough on a lightly floured worksurface to a thickness of about 2mm and cut out 10cm stars. A biscuit cutter is the quickest route here, but you could also make a template from thin card and cut around that. Roll the dough twice and arrange the biscuits on the baking trays – they don't spread much, so you can place them quite close together. If you are planning on hanging them, make a hole at the base of one of the points of the star using a skewer.

Bake the biscuits for about 12 minutes until golden. The lower tray may take a little longer than the upper one. The holes will have closed up slightly in the oven, so make them a bit larger using a skewer. Loosen the biscuits straight away with a palette knife before they harden and become brittle, and then transfer them to a wire rack to cool. Ice them as you fancy and leave this to set for an hour or two.

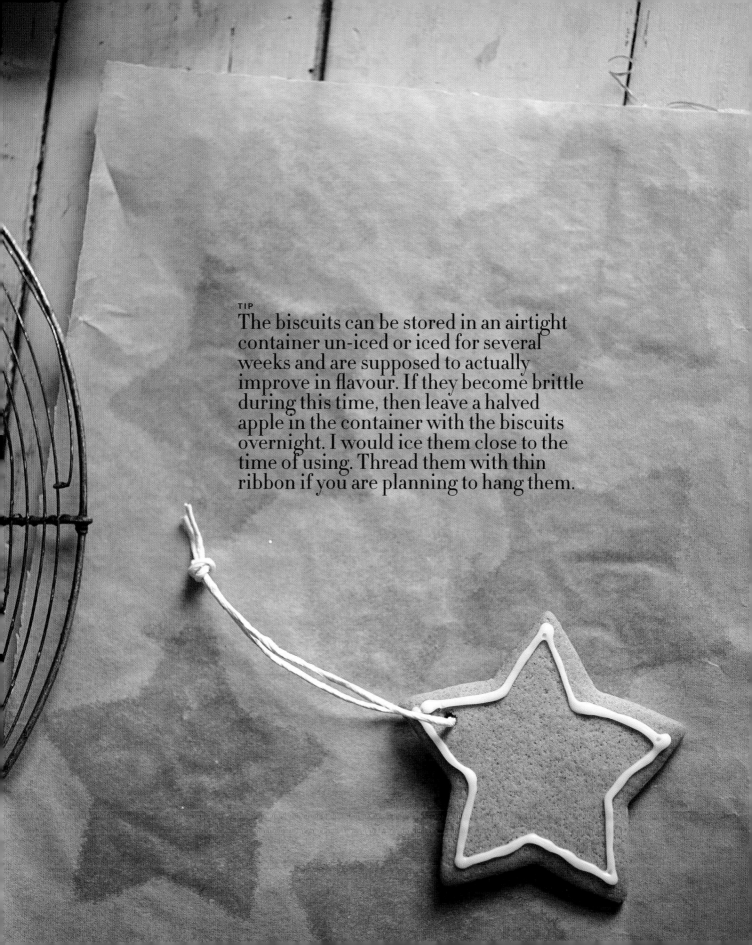

TIP
The biscuits can be stored in an airtight container un-iced or iced for several weeks and are supposed to actually improve in flavour. If they become brittle during this time, then leave a halved apple in the container with the biscuits overnight. I would ice them close to the time of using. Thread them with thin ribbon if you are planning to hang them.

white chocolate florentines

MAKES APPROX. 17

25g unsalted butter

25g caster sugar

1 teaspoon runny honey

25g plain flour

20g flaked almonds

20g diced candied peel

20g undyed glace cherries, sliced

150g white chocolate chips or chopped white chocolate

KIT

2 non-stick baking trays

Large palette knife

Wire rack

Small palette knife

LITTLE EXTRAS

Unsalted butter for greasing

Plain flour for dusting

Florentines aren't the simplest of biscuits, which is why I tend not to go overboard on making them, but this is a pared down recipe that shouldn't tie you in too many knots. This is the cocktail-size version of these dainties, which make a lovely present as well as an after dinner treat.

Preheat the oven to 170°C fan oven/190°C electric oven and butter and flour two non-stick baking trays. Melt the butter, sugar and honey in a small saucepan, then stir in the flour and straight away afterwards the almonds, candied peel and cherries. Using your fingers, shape half teaspoons of the mixture into flattened patties and place them well apart on the baking trays. Bake for 8–10 minutes until golden. You may need to turn the trays around at the end to colour them evenly. Leave to cool for a few minutes before loosening the florentines with a palette knife and transferring them to a wire rack to cool completely.

Gently melt half the chocolate in a bowl set over a pan of simmering water. Using a small palette knife (or unserrated table knife), coat the underside of each biscuit with the melted chocolate. Leave to set, chocolate-side up, on a wire rack in a cool place for an hour or two. Repeat the process with the remaining chocolate to give two layers, but this time use the tines of a fork to draw waves on the surface of the chocolate. Leave to harden in a cool place for several hours. Florentines are at their best freshly made.

TIP

When shaping the mixture into patties, you need to work quite quickly otherwise the mixture will dry out and turn crumbly.

traybakes
and
bars

flapjacks

MAKES 1 X 23CM TIN/
25 SQUARES

240g lightly salted butter, diced

180g demerara sugar

225g golden syrup

350g rolled oats

KIT

23cm non-stick square brownie tin, 4cm deep

It seems right to be kicking off this chapter with what must be the best-loved bar of all. I feel as though I am endlessly knocking out batches of flapjacks, in the time it takes for a cup of tea to brew, for wrapping in foil to take on some journey or occasion as a neat package of pure home comfort, they always disappear. Everyone, it seems, loves a good flapjack, just as they do apple crumble and brownies.

Tempting as it is to experiment, it is hard to improve on the humble basic. I like to make them with lightly salted butter, which offsets their gooey sweetness. Demerara is a must, for that treacly crunch, and golden syrup acts as a go-between for the two.

Preheat the oven to 160°C fan oven/180°C electric oven. Gently melt the butter with the sugar and syrup in a medium-sized saucepan over a medium heat and whisk until smooth and amalgamated. Stir in the oats, tip the mixture into a 23cm non-stick square brownie tin, 4cm deep, pressing it down using the back of a metal spoon. Bake for 20 minutes until very lightly coloured. Leave to cool. Cut into 25 squares or as wished. These will keep in an airtight container or wrapped in foil for several days.

salt caramel flapjacks

MAKES 25 SQUARES

An exception for every rule, here is the first variation on the theme of classic flapjacks, which perhaps I suggested too hastily in the preceding recipe couldn't be bettered.

Make the flapjacks as above, replacing the demerara with light muscovado sugar, and the golden syrup with dulce de leche, e.g. Nestle Caramel. Leave to cool for about 30 minutes, then gently melt 50g dark chocolate (approx. 50 per cent cocoa solids), broken into pieces, in a bowl set over a pan with a little simmering water in it, and drizzle this over the flapjack.

TIP

You want a slightly wimpy oat rather than anything too hearty, but avoid 'value' oats that incline on the powdery side and act as a sop for the butter and syrup. Success here also rests on slightly undercooking the flapjacks. By the time they have turned golden on top, they will also be teeth-challengingly chewy.

apple and oat shortcake bars

MAKES 12–16 SLICES

FOR THE SHORTBREAD

180g unsalted butter, diced

70g golden caster sugar

150g plain flour

100g ground almonds

FOR THE FRUIT

850g Bramley cooking apples, peeled, cored and sliced

100g currants

75g light muscovado sugar

finely grated zest of 1 lemon

FOR THE FLAPJACK

200g unsalted butter

200g golden syrup

1 teaspoon sea salt

225g rolled oats

KIT

Food processor

30 x 23cm non-stick traybake tin, 4cm deep

Clingfilm

LITTLE EXTRAS

Icing sugar for dusting (optional)

I recall that when I first made these (an attempt to roll several of my favourite things into one – flapjacks, apple pie and shortbread), we had a team of Polish builders at home, most of whom didn't speak any English. I soon realised the scent of these brought on pangs of homesickness by the still sadness that seemed to descend when they were baking, instantly alleviated during a tea-break.

It was lovely to have such eager takers lined up at the windowsill, plaster-dusted hands cradling warm slices. On a personal note, I particularly like the way that once cold the buttery syrup soaks through the layers to enrich the biscuit below.

Place all the ingredients for the shortbread in the bowl of a food processor and reduce to crumbs, then keep the motor running until the mixture comes together into a ball. It will be very soft and sticky at this point. Press it into the base of a 30 x 23cm non-stick traybake tin, 4cm deep, cover with a sheet of clingfilm and smooth out the surface with your fingers. Cover the surface of the tin with a fresh piece of clingfilm and chill for 1 hour.

Preheat the oven to 140°C fan oven/160°C electric oven, prick the shortbread all over with a fork and bake for 25–30 minutes until just beginning to colour. Leave to cool. Either turn the oven up to 180°C fan oven/200°C electric oven or preheat if you have turned it off. Toss the apples, currants, muscovado sugar and lemon zest together in a large bowl and then evenly distribute over the shortbread.

Gently melt the butter for the flapjack mixture in a small saucepan with the syrup and the salt, then fold in the oats. Scatter the flapjack mixture over the apples – there should still be some fruit showing through. Bake for 25–30 minutes until the top is golden and crusty. Run a knife around the edge of the cake and leave it to cool. Cut it into two long halves, then across into 2–3cm slices. If you like, dust with icing sugar, then transfer the slices to a plate. They will keep well covered with clingfilm for a day or two.

chocolate truffle macadamia bars

If making these for children, being fussy little things, they may prefer them without the nuts or cocoa.

Butter a 30 x 23cm non-stick traybake tin, 4cm deep. Place all the ingredients for the shortbread in the bowl of a food processor and reduce to crumbs, then keep the motor running until the mixture comes together into a ball. It will be very soft and sticky at this point. Press the mixture into the base of the tin, lay a sheet of clingfilm over the top and smooth out the surface with your fingers. Cover the surface of the tin with clingfilm and chill for 1 hour.

Preheat the oven to 140°C fan oven/160°C electric oven, prick the shortbread all over with a fork and bake for 45 minutes until just beginning to colour. Leave to cool.

To make the truffle cream, gently melt the chocolate in a bowl set over a pan with a little simmering water in it. Gradually whisk in the cream and then the coffee. Pour the chocolate cream over the shortbread, tipping it to coat the surface, and scatter over the macadamia nuts. Cover the tin with clingfilm and chill for a couple of hours until the chocolate truffle has set.

Run a knife around the edge of the shortcake, cut it into two long halves, then across into 3–4cm slices. Dust with cocoa and transfer to a plate. These bars keep well in an airtight container for several days, stored in a cool place. Alternatively keep them in the fridge and remove shortly before eating.

MAKES 14–16 SLICES

FOR THE SHORTBREAD

170g unsalted butter, diced

75g golden caster sugar

150g plain flour

100g ground almonds

FOR THE TRUFFLE CREAM

200g dark chocolate (approx. 50 per cent cocoa solids), broken into pieces

200ml double cream

2 tablespoons strong black coffee

100g macadamia nuts, halved

KIT

30 x 23cm non-stick traybake tin, 4cm deep

Food processor

Clingfilm

LITTLE EXTRAS

Unsalted butter for greasing

FOR THE BISCUIT BASE

100g digestives, broken into pieces

60g walnut pieces

40g cocoa powder, sifted

100g golden caster sugar

80g desiccated coconut

150g unsalted butter, melted

2 medium eggs, beaten

FOR THE BUTTERCREAM

100g unsalted butter, softened

2 tablespoons custard powder

½ teaspoon vanilla extract

250g icing sugar

2 tablespoons milk

FOR THE CHOCOLATE COATING

150g dark chocolate (approx. 70 per cent cocoa solids), broken into pieces

25g unsalted butter

4 tablespoons strong black coffee

KIT

23cm non-stick square brownie tin, 4cm deep

Food processor

Electric whisk

Palette knife

Clingfilm

LITTLE EXTRAS

Unsalted butter for greasing

nanaimo bars

I was a latecomer to these, but I'm busy making up for lost time, they are headily divine. Canadian in origin, they obviously play the role that brownies do across the border in the US. They are deliciously zany, with a biscuity base with coconut and walnuts, a sweet custard buttercream and then a layer of chocolate that I've fused with coffee, a welcome addition to all that sweetness.

Preheat the oven to 160°C fan oven/180°C electric oven and butter a 23cm non-stick square brownie tin, 4cm deep. Whizz the digestives and the walnuts to crumbs in a food processor. Add the cocoa and sugar and whizz again, then transfer the mixture to a large bowl and mix in the coconut. Add the melted butter and blend and then the beaten eggs, stirring until well combined. Transfer the mixture to the tin and level the surface using your fingers or the back of a spoon. Bake for 15 minutes, then leave to cool.

To make the buttercream, whisk the butter in a large bowl for about a minute until pale and fluffy using an electric whisk. Whisk in the custard powder and the vanilla and then the icing sugar. Once the mixture appears crumbly, add the milk and continue to whisk to a pale and mousse-like buttercream. Spread this over the biscuit base using a palette knife and chill for about an hour until set.

To make the chocolate coating, gently melt the chocolate with the butter in a bowl set over a pan with a little simmering water in it, then whisk in the coffee. Should the mixture seem to separate, keep beating until it is completely smooth and glossy – this is important, if it appears oily the butter will harden as a film on the surface. Smooth this over the surface of the buttercream and swirl it using a teaspoon. Loosely cover the tin with clingfilm and chill for several hours until set. To serve, cut into bars about 3cm wide and half the width of the tin, or you could cut them half this size for 'Nanaimo bites'. The Nanaimo bars should keep well for several days and are best served chilled.

TIP

If the glaze still seems oily after beating, simply whisk in 2 teaspoons of cold water.

brownies

Ah, brownies, you can feel the temperature rising at the very mention of the word – yet another type of cake that holds me in its thrall. Recently I was tasked with trying to find the perfect recipe for a client in Mallorca, who owns a group of very chic cafés that extend from Palma to Jeddah. So I baked and baked and baked, and lost count of how many versions I tried, little tweaks here and little changes there. So I am kicking off with the recipe that we eventually settled on. From here, there are all manner of variations and different results that can be achieved, with subtle changes such as the inclusion of nuts, perhaps milk instead of orange juice, more or less ground almonds and so forth.

But perhaps the main consideration is the length of time you cook them for. A true brownie should remain undercooked in the centre. The art to that dense, fudgy texture is to bake them until they appear slightly cracked and risen around the outside while the centre is set but still gooey. If a skewer comes out clean in the usual fashion they will be overcooked and dry.

So underbake, then leave them to cool for a few hours, or for a fudgier texture chill for another few hours or overnight.

If, however, you want something to eat newly cooled, then cook them that little bit longer. A skewer inserted into the centre should come out clean with just a few moist crumbs on it without actually coating the skewer, but nor should it pass the usual clean skewer test.

TIP

If in haste you have pulled your brownies from the oven to prevent them overcooking, but discover actually they seem a little undercooked, simply chill them once cool and order will be restored as they turn suitably fudgy. From there store them in a cool place.

300g dark chocolate (approx.
50 per cent cocoa solids),
broken up

180g lightly salted butter, diced
(see TIP)

180g light muscovado sugar

4 medium eggs, plus 1 egg yolk

115g ground almonds

100g plain flour

15g cocoa powder

1 teaspoon baking powder

2 tablespoons fresh orange juice

1 tablespoon dark rum

70g dark chocolate (approx.
70 per cent cocoa solids),
chopped

KIT

23cm non-stick square brownie
tin, 4cm deep

LITTLE EXTRAS

Cocoa powder for dusting

the ultimate chocolate brownie

The combination of the two different percentage chocolates is all-important here. The 50 per cent cocoa chocolate melts and combines with the other ingredients in a particular fashion (a good cooking chocolate should do it, but check the ingredients for the percentage of cocoa and the all-important presence of cocoa butter), while the 70 per cent cocoa dark chocolate chips provide bite and a slight bitterness.

Preheat the oven to 150°C fan oven/170°C electric oven. You need a 23cm non-stick square brownie tin, 4cm deep. Gently melt 300g dark chocolate with the butter in a bowl set over a pan with a little simmering water in it. Remove from the heat, add the sugar and whisk to get rid of any lumps.

Add the eggs and yolk to the chocolate mixture – one by one and beating after each addition, continuing to beat at the end, having added all of them, until the mixture is very glossy and amalgamated. Gently fold in the ground almonds, then sift over the flour, cocoa and baking powder. Fold in gently without overmixing. Stir in the orange juice and rum, and finally fold in the chopped chocolate.

Pour the chocolate mixture into the tin and bake for 25–30 minutes until the outside of the cake is risen and slightly cracked – a skewer inserted into this section should come out with just a few gooey crumbs, and likewise in the centre. Run a knife around the edge of the tin and leave the cake to cool overnight (see page 63). Slice into squares and dust with cocoa.

date brownies

Dates make for supremely sticky brownies and these are lusciously soft, halfway to being a parfait. Replace the orange juice with 3 tablespoons of strong black coffee or espresso. Include 100g Medjool dates, halved lengthways, pitted and sliced across, with the chocolate chips, separating out the pieces. Scatter 30g of extra chopped chocolate over the top before baking.

pistachio brownies

Pistachios are one of the loveliest nuts to include in a brownie. Omit the chocolate chips and include 75g shelled pistachios instead.

even fudgier brownies

Make the brownies using 50g ground almonds and 75g plain flour.

TIP

A note on the butter: if using Breton salted butter heavily laced with sea salt, substitute with half salted and half unsalted.

MAKES 9–16 LARGE OR 25 MINIATURE

150g unsalted butter

150g golden syrup

150g set honey

1 teaspoon vanilla extract

2 medium eggs

200g plain flour

2 teaspoons baking powder

75g white chocolate, chopped

KIT

23cm non-stick square brownie tin, 4cm deep

LITTLE EXTRAS

Unsalted butter for greasing

blondies

Blondies are of the same sticky genre as chocolate brownies, but draw their character from soft brown sugar. I like to make them using honey and syrup, which makes for an even stickier cake, and to add a little white chocolate in homage to their name.

Preheat the oven to 170ºC fan oven/190ºC electric oven and butter a 23cm non-stick square brownie tin, 4cm deep. Gently heat the butter, syrup, honey and vanilla in a small saucepan until melted. Leave to cool for about 15 minutes and then beat in the eggs one at a time. Sift over and fold in the flour and baking powder, whisking until smooth.

Pour into the prepared tin, scatter over the white chocolate and bake for 25–30 minutes until a skewer inserted in the centre comes out clean. Run a knife around the edge and leave to cool, then cut into squares. They will keep for a couple of days in an airtight container.

flourless chocolate brownies

MAKES 9–16 LARGE OR 25 MINIATURE

250g dark chocolate (approx. 70 per cent cocoa solids), broken into pieces

250g unsalted butter, diced

200g golden caster sugar

4 medium eggs

150g ground almonds

1 heaped teaspoon baking powder, sifted

¾ teaspoon ground cinnamon, sifted (optional)

50g dark chocolate chips

KIT

23cm non-stick square brownie tin, 4cm deep

LITTLE EXTRAS

Unsalted butter for greasing

These are even gooier for being made with ground almonds rather than flour, and literally dissolve in the mouth. A scoop of vanilla ice cream melting on top turns them into one of life's more sought after puds. The cinnamon is optional, if you like a little mystery in your brownies.

Preheat the oven to 150ºC fan oven/170ºC electric oven and butter a 23cm non-stick square brownie tin, 4cm deep. Melt the chocolate with the butter in a bowl set over a pan with a little simmering water in it. Remove from the heat, add the sugar and stir to combine, then leave to cool slightly. Add the eggs to the chocolate mixture, one by one, beating after each addition until the mixture is very glossy.

Gently fold in the ground almonds, baking powder and cinnamon (if using) without overmixing, then add half the chocolate chips.

Spread the chocolate mixture over the base of the prepared tin. Scatter over the remaining chocolate chips and bake for 25–35 minutes. A skewer inserted into the centre should come out clean with just a few moist crumbs on it, and there should be hairline cracks in the sponge to within about 5cm of the centre, which should be just set.

Leave to cool completely in the tin – it will be very crumbly to begin with, but will firm up a little by the following day (see page 63). The brownies will keep well in an airtight container for several days.

FOR THE SHORTBREAD

225g unsalted butter, chilled and diced

100g golden caster sugar

200g plain flour

115g ground almonds

1 teaspoon vanilla extract

FOR THE CARAMEL

100g unsalted butter

70g golden caster sugar

1 tablespoon golden syrup

275g dulce de leche, e.g. Nestlé Caramel

$1/3$ level teaspoon fine sea salt

FOR THE TOPPING

200g dark chocolate (approx. 50 per cent cocoa solids), broken into pieces

25g white chocolate chips

KIT

Food processor

23cm non-stick square brownie tin, 4cm deep

Clingfilm

Cocktail stick or skewer

LITTLE EXTRAS

Unsalted butter for greasing

millionaire's shortbread

Its title precedes it, the lottery winner among bars. There is, however, a lot of mediocre stuff around that is definitely a few bob short of a million, and it is very worthwhile making your own.

Place all the ingredients for the shortbread in a food processor and whizz to a dough. Butter a 23cm non-stick square brownie tin, 4cm deep. Press the shortbread into the base of the tin – you can lay a sheet of clingfilm over the top if you wish and use your fingers to help smooth it. Prick all over with a fork, loosely cover with clingfilm and chill for at least 1 hour.

Preheat the oven to 140ºC fan oven/160ºC electric oven and bake the shortbread for 45 minutes until very lightly coloured, then leave it to cool.

Place all the ingredients for the caramel in a small non-stick saucepan and bring to the boil, stirring until melted and amalgamated. Simmer very gently for 8–9 minutes, stirring frequently and then pour over the shortbread base. Leave to cool for at least an hour until set; overnight is even better.

To make the chocolate topping, melt the dark chocolate in a bowl set over a pan with a little simmering water in it. Pour over the caramel and smooth out in a thin layer. Melt the white chocolate in the same way in a clean bowl. To decorate, drop quarter teaspoons of white chocolate on top of the dark and marble it by swirling with a cocktail stick or skewer. Set aside in a cool place until set but still soft, then cut into squares (a small serrated knife is best for this) and leave to set completely in a cool place. If chilling, remove from the fridge 15–30 minutes before serving. This will keep well in a covered container for several days somewhere cool.

TIP
You want a fine sea salt here rather than the usual coarse one, which may not dissolve effectively.

a luxurious
fridge cake

MAKES 10–15 FINGERS OR
25 SQUARES

180g raisins

120ml Cointreau (or orange juice)

300g dark chocolate (approx. 70 per cent cocoa solids), broken into pieces

180g unsalted butter, diced

1½ tablespoons golden syrup

180g undyed glace cherries, halved

225g digestive biscuits, broken into 1–2cm nibs

KIT

23cm square brownie tin, 4cm deep

Baking paper

Clingfilm

LITTLE EXTRAS

Icing sugar for dusting

A louche take on a fridge cake, where digestive biscuits are bound with a rich truffle cream, with glace cherries and Cointreau-soaked raisins thrown in –although you could use fresh orange juice if you prefer. As well as being cut into fingers or squares for tea, sliced small these make a perfect little after dinner sweetie to serve with coffee in lieu of truffles.

Place the raisins in a small saucepan with the Cointreau (or orange juice) and simmer until they have plumped up and most of the liquid has been absorbed, stirring occasionally. Leave to cool for 15–30 minutes when they will absorb the remainder. Gently melt the chocolate, butter and syrup in a large bowl set over a saucepan with a little simmering water in it, stirring until smooth. Stir in the raisins, cherries and biscuits, tossing until everything is coated in the chocolate mixture.

Line the base of a 23cm square brownie tin, 4cm deep, with baking paper (you can dab a little of the melted chocolate mixture on the four corners to make it stick). Spoon the mixture over the base of the tin. Lay a sheet of clingfilm over the surface and press it level using your hands, although it will still appear slightly craggy. Remove the clingfilm, loosely cover with another sheet and chill for 2–3 hours until hard.

Run a knife around the edge of the tin to remove the slab and lift off the paper. Place the right way up on a board, and liberally dust with icing sugar. Cut into fingers or squares the size of your choice. Store in an airtight container in the fridge.

TIP

This will keep well for a good week, but you may want to give it another flurry of icing sugar close to the time of serving.

You can also make this using 225g stem ginger biscuits in lieu of the digestives and 150g raisins, in which case omit the liqueur.

wafer fridge bars

This is a bar within a bar, and for all its endemic laziness the results are seriously impressive. You need what are sometimes sold as 'Pink Panther' biscuits (although not quite sure what these delicate layered wafer crispies have to do with panthers). Basically they are like a pink Kit Kat or wafer biscuit, less the chocolate, which you will be adding in generous quantities as a surround. It isn't, of course, strictly baking, but as a throw together biscuit that looks as charming as it tastes, it deserves its loophole.

Gently melt the chocolate, butter and syrup together in a large bowl set over a pan with a little simmering water in it, whisking until smooth. Line the base and sides of a 23cm square brownie tin, 4cm deep, with clingfilm. Smooth about 3 tablespoons of the chocolate mixture over the base to coat it. Arrange a layer of wafer biscuits on top so the rows are spaced a couple of millimetres apart – there may be a small gap at the edges

Drizzle over about one-third of the remaining chocolate mixture so that it coats the surface of the biscuits and trickles between the rows. Lay a second layer of biscuits on top at right angles to the first layer. Smooth the rest of the chocolate mixture over the surface and then scatter over the marshmallows. Chill for a couple of hours until set. You may find it easiest to cut the cake if you leave it to soften for 30 minutes at room temperature. Trim the edges of the block and cut into small squares. These will keep well in an airtight container in the fridge for several days. Remove them 30 minutes before eating.

TIP
Imagine you are playing stacking bricks as you assemble this: the idea is to set two rows at right angles to each other, which gives the maximum effect of a grid when you cut into it. Be sure to fill the gaps between the wafers with the chocolate mixture to avoid air bubbles.

MAKES APPROX. 25 SMALL SQUARES

300g dark chocolate (approx. 70 per cent cocoa solids), broken into pieces

150g unsalted butter, diced

4 tablespoons golden syrup

2 x 200g packets of stacked wafer biscuits, e.g. Pink Panther

25g mini marshmallows

KIT

23cm square brownie tin, 4cm deep

Clingfilm

rocky road slab

MAKES 25 SQUARES

100g whole blanched almonds

6 Barratts marshmallow Flumps, or 90g mini pink and white marshmallows (see TIP)

300g dark chocolate (approx. 70 per cent cocoa solids), broken into pieces

400g milk chocolate, e.g. Galaxy, broken into pieces

KIT

Non-stick baking tray

23cm square brownie tin, 4cm deep

Baking paper

Skewer

Rocky Road has come to mean almost anything craggy coated in chocolate, but the real thing of nuts and marshmallow still cuts a dash like no other. The combination of dark and milk chocolate eaten together is one that makes me go weak at the knees, not quite sure why this is, but it remains heart-stoppingly good. This is great at a tea party, or with an espresso at the end of dinner.

Preheat the oven to 180°C fan oven/200°C electric oven. Scatter the almonds over a non-stick baking tray and toast in the oven for about 10 minutes until mid-golden brown. Leave to cool (you can scatter them over a chopping board to speed up the process), and then halve or coarsely chop two-thirds of them. Cut the marshmallow Flumps into 1cm dice using a very sharp knife.

Gently melt the dark chocolate in a bowl set over a pan with a little simmering water in it. Melt the milk chocolate in a separate bowl in the same way. Set both aside to cool to room temperature.

Line the base and sides of a 23cm square brownie tin, 4cm deep, with baking paper, marking the four corners and cutting out a square from each one so that it sits neatly in the tin.

Fold the chopped nuts into the milk chocolate and two-thirds of the marshmallow nibs into the dark. Spoon the milk chocolate mixture into the tin in three rows, one on each side and one in the middle. Now fill the gaps in between with rows of dark chocolate. Using the tip of a skewer, trace a figure-of-eight down each row to marble it. Scatter the reserved whole almonds and marshmallow nibs over the surface and chill for a couple of hours until the slab hardens. Bring back to room temperature for 30–60 minutes, remove the paper and cut into squares the size of your choice using a sharp knife. The slab will be good for a couple of days.

TIP

Be sure to bring the slab back up to room temperature before cutting it, otherwise it will crack as you do so. And what is a 'Flump'? Well, no doubt they will change name before long, but a twisted rope of pink and white marshmallow that looks especially pretty cut into nibs, it's that fairground attraction.

90g rolled oats

225g self-raising wholemeal
flour (see **TIP**)

200g light muscovado sugar

¾ teaspoon bicarbonate
of soda

1 heaped teaspoon ground
ginger

225g unsalted butter, frozen as
a block (see **TIP**)

4 knobs of stem ginger in syrup,
finely chopped, plus
3 tablespoons syrup

KIT

32 x 23cm non-stick Swiss
roll tin

Food processor

LITTLE EXTRAS

Unsalted butter for greasing

Icing sugar for dusting

grasmere gingerbread

If you have ever tasted Sarah Nelson's Grasmere gingerbread, then at a guess you will have been as smitten as I was after my first encounter one Easter holiday. I kept going back into the tiny shop in the Lake District for more, in the hope of being able to glean something of how it is made. Despite the ubiquity of the internet, the recipe for this remains covertly under wraps or, worse even, lock and key. The details are alleged to be secreted in a bank vault, so it is unlikely we will ever discover the true secret. But this is a fine alternative, deliciously chewy and ginger-rich, something of flapjacks and gingernuts combined.

Preheat the oven to 150°C fan oven/170°C electric oven and butter a 32 x 23cm non-stick Swiss roll tin. Whizz the oats in a food processor to finely chop them, add the flour and sugar, and sift over the bicarbonate of soda and ginger. Give the mixture a whizz and transfer it to a large bowl.

Coarsely grate the butter onto a plate a quarter at a time, scattering each batch over the dry ingredients and deftly tossing it in – the butter will return to room temperature in no time so you need to do this with care to avoid it sticking together into lumps. Once all the butter is incorporated, transfer two-thirds of the mixture to another bowl and mix in the chopped stem ginger and syrup. Scatter this mixture over the base of the prepared tin and press down using your hands. Spread the remaining mixture over the top, and pat to semi-compress it, again with your hands. Bake for 25–30 minutes until starting to colour and then remove from the oven and mark into squares. Leave to cool in the tin and dust with icing sugar. It keeps well in an airtight container for several days.

TIP
The easiest route here is to freeze a 250g block of butter and grate what you need. And for once it has to be wholemeal flour, an ingredient I rarely use in sponge cakes but there are certain biscuits such as this one where it defines the texture.

chocolate baklava

Homemade baklava, which by rights contains a heart-stopping quantity of good butter rather than vegetable oil, is awesomely good. That delicate fudgy fusion of syrup, butter and fine pastry is in a league of its own. This is my own take on it – chocolate and hazelnuts have shades of praline, and with rum in there too this belongs in the French Arabic quarter.

Preheat the oven to 140°C fan oven/160°C electric oven. Unroll the stack of filo pastry sheets and lay the pile on a board. Assuming it is rectangle about 45 x 30cm, cut it in half using a sharp knife into two square-ish rectangles.

I find the best dish to assemble this in is a non-stick Swiss roll tin, about 32 x 23cm. Brush the inside of the tin with butter, then layer half the sheets in the tin, brushing each one with butter, and going up the sides if the sheets are slightly larger than the base.

To make the filling, combine the hazelnuts and chocolate in a bowl. Scatter them over the pastry in the tin and layer the remaining stack of filo sheets on top, brushing each sheet with butter as before. Cut the baklava into 4cm diamonds using a sharp knife.

Bake the baklava for 45 minutes, and then turn up the oven to 180°C fan oven/200°C electric oven and bake for a further 10–15 minutes until an even toasted gold.

Meanwhile, place the sugar and lemon juice in a medium-sized saucepan with 150ml water. Bring to the boil, stirring to dissolve the sugar, and then simmer over a low heat for 15 minutes. Remove from the heat and stir in the rum.

Once the baklava is cooked, pour the syrup evenly over the surface and set aside to cool. These should keep well for several days in an airtight container.

TIP
The lemon in the syrup is like salt with potatoes, it brings out the flavour of everything else.

MAKES APPROX. 30 DIAMONDS

1 x 250g packet filo pastry

200g unsalted butter, melted

130g finely chopped roasted hazelnuts

100g dark chocolate (70–80 per cent cocoa solids), finely chopped into chips

270g caster sugar

juice of ½ lemon

1 tablespoon dark rum

KIT

32 x 23cm non-stick Swiss roll tin

Pastry brush

pistachio baklava

MAKES APPROX. 30 DIAMONDS

1 x 250g packet filo pastry

200g unsalted butter, melted

130g shelled pistachios, finely chopped or ground in a food processor

300g caster sugar

juice of ½ lemon

1 tablespoon rosewater (see TIP)

KIT

32 x 23cm non-stick Swiss roll tin

Pastry brush

LITTLE EXTRAS

Finely chopped pistachios (optional)

Scented with rosewater, and made with pistachios instead of walnuts, this is a cut above. It takes a little time to brush the pastry sheets with butter, but in a pleasantly cathartic way, there's no tricky technique involved.

Preheat the oven to 140°C fan oven/160°C electric oven. Unroll the stack of filo pastry sheets and lay the pile on a board. Assuming it is rectangle about 45 x 30cm, cut it in half using a sharp knife into two square-ish rectangles.

I find the best dish to assemble this in is a 32 x 23cm non-stick Swiss roll tin. Brush the inside of the tin with butter, then layer half the sheets in the tin, brushing each one with butter, and going up the sides if the sheets are slightly larger than the base. Scatter over the ground pistachios and layer with the remaining stack of filo sheets, brushing each one with butter as before. Cut the baklava into 4cm diamonds using a sharp knife.

Bake the baklava for 45 minutes, then turn up the oven to 180°C fan oven/200°C electric oven and bake for a further 10–15 minutes until an even toasted gold.

Meanwhile, place the sugar and lemon juice in a medium-sized saucepan with 150ml water. Bring to the boil, stirring to dissolve the sugar, and then simmer over a low heat for 15 minutes. Remove from the heat and stir in the rosewater.

Once the baklava is cooked, pour the syrup evenly over the surface and set aside to cool. These should keep well for several days in an airtight container. Scatter over finely chopped pistachios if wished.

TIP

Rosewater as sold in Middle Eastern delis can be used with some abandon in cakes as it is light and gentle. However, if you are using special culinary essence or extract, only add it by the drop, tasting with each addition, as you might use vanilla.

75g cocoa powder

¾ teaspoon bicarbonate of soda

4 medium eggs

370g light muscovado sugar

180ml groundnut or vegetable oil

200g self-raising flour, sifted

FOR THE ICING

150g dark chocolate (approx. 50 per cent cocoa solids), broken into pieces

2 tablespoons golden syrup

2 tablespoons whipping cream

100g Toblerone, finely sliced

75g glace cherries, halved

KIT

30 x 23cm non-stick traybake tin, 4cm deep

LITTLE EXTRAS

Unsalted butter or vegetable oil for greasing

black forest traybake

The sponge kicks off with the best of intentions, dutifully light and airy, but from there it is all downhill – or uphill depending on your take on the liberal drizzling of chocolate and orgy of Toblerone and glace cherries.

Whisk the cocoa with 200ml boiling water, whisk in the bicarbonate of soda and leave to cool for about 20 minutes. Preheat the oven to 160°C fan oven/180°C electric oven and butter or oil a 30 x 23cm non-stick traybake tin, 4cm deep – there is no need to line it unless you are planning to turn out the cake whole.

Whisk together the eggs, sugar and oil in a large bowl, then fold in the flour, and then the cocoa solution. Pour the mixture into the prepared tin and bake for 30–40 minutes until risen and firm and a skewer inserted into the centre comes out clean. Run a knife around the edge of the cake and leave to cool.

To make the icing, gently melt the chocolate with the syrup and cream in a bowl set over a pan with a little simmering water in it, whisking until glossy and smooth. Drizzle the icing over the cake, scatter over the Toblerone slices and arrange the cherries here and there. Set aside to harden for a couple of hours before cutting into squares. They will keep well in an airtight container for several days.

MAKES 20 SQUARES

FOR THE ICING

150g dark chocolate (approx. 50 per cent cocoa solids), broken into pieces

3 tablespoons milk

Smarties, and hundreds and thousands to decorate

KIT

30 x 23cm non-stick traybake tin, 4cm deep

LITTLE EXTRAS

Unsalted butter or vegetable oil for greasing

smartie traybake

This lovely light chocolate sponge has seen me through more emergency cake stalls than I can count. Par for the course of being a parent is that your offspring only ever let you know it is their turn (i.e. your turn) to contribute around suppertime of the night before.

Like all traybakes, this cuts to the size of your choice, so will stretch. It's also great for children's parties and picnics.

Prepare the sponge as above.

To make the icing, gently melt the chocolate with the milk in a bowl set over a pan with 2cm of simmering water in it, stirring until smooth. Pour over the cake and spread out evenly using the back of a spoon or a palette knife. Scatter over some Smarties and hundreds and thousands and leave for a couple of hours to set. To serve, cut into squares – you should get about 20. They will keep well in an airtight container for several days.

raspberry almond traybake

MAKES 12 SQUARES

225g ground almonds

30g flaked almonds

270g golden caster sugar

2 teaspoons baking powder, sifted

60g fresh white breadcrumbs

6 large eggs

300ml sunflower or groundnut oil

finely grated zest of 2 oranges

125g fresh raspberries

KIT

30 x 23cm non-stick traybake tin, 4cm deep

LITTLE EXTRAS

Vegetable oil for greasing

This delicate almond-rich sponge contains flaked as well as ground nuts, which give it a lovely texture, and also breadcrumbs. The raspberries sink in as it bakes, and the result is a cake that is just as good served for pudding as it is with a cuppa.

Preheat the oven to 190°C fan oven/210°C electric oven and grease a 30 x 23cm non-stick traybake tin, 4cm deep, with vegetable oil. Mix the ground and flaked almonds, 180g caster sugar, baking powder and breadcrumbs together in a large bowl. Beat in the eggs thoroughly using a wooden spoon, and then the oil. Finally stir in the orange zest.

Transfer the mixture to the prepared tin and smooth the surface. Scatter over the raspberries and sprinkle with the remaining 90g sugar. Bake for 25–30 minutes until the cake is golden and a skewer inserted into the centre comes out clean. Run a knife around the edge of the cake and leave to cool in the tin before cutting into squares or slices.

tomato soup traybake

MAKES 12 SQUARES

225g plain flour

2 teaspoons baking powder

¾ teaspoon bicarbonate of soda

½ teaspoon ground cinnamon

½ teaspoon ground ginger

pinch of cloves

225g golden caster sugar

1 x 300g tin of Heinz tomato soup

2 medium eggs

125g unsalted butter, melted and cooled

50g raisins

KIT

30 x 23cm non-stick traybake tin, 4cm deep

LITTLE EXTRAS

Unsalted butter for greasing

No-one will ever guess – you will be there for hours waiting for an answer to what is the secret ingredient in this spiced sponge.

Preheat the oven to 170°C fan oven/190°C electric oven. Sift the flour, baking powder, bicarbonate of soda and spices into a large bowl, then mix in the sugar. Whisk the soup, eggs and melted butter in another large bowl. Combine the two mixtures and whisk until smooth, then stir in the raisins. Grease a 30 x 23cm non-stick traybake tin, 4cm deep – if you wish, you can wipe it over with the melted butter left in the pan using a brush or piece of kitchen paper; there is no need to line it unless you want to turn the cake out. Pour the cake mixture into the tin and bake for 30–35 minutes until risen and firm and a skewer inserted into the centre comes out clean. Run a knife around the edge of the tin and leave the cake to cool. Frost as below (see TIP).

TIP

Traditionally this cake is iced with a cream cheese frosting. Make this up according to the Hummingbird Cake (see page 233) with 120g softened unsalted butter, 100g sifted icing sugar, 300g full-fat cream cheese and $^1/_2$ teaspoon vanilla extract. Decorate it with little jellied red sweets, such as Jelly Tots, in homage to its provenance.

MAKES 16 SLICES

FOR THE SHORTBREAD

175g unsalted butter, diced

75g golden caster sugar

150g plain flour

100g ground almonds

finely grated zest of 1 orange or lemon (optional)

FOR THE SPONGE

120g raspberry jam

110g unsalted butter, diced

150g golden caster sugar

4 medium eggs

150g desiccated coconut

75g ground almonds

1 teaspoon baking powder, sifted

110g sultanas

KIT

Food processor

30 x 23cm non-stick traybake tin, 4cm deep

Clingfilm

Palette knife

LITTLE EXTRAS

Icing sugar for dusting

paradise slice

So aptly named, there is something about the combination of the texture of a biscuit with cake (the secret hit of a Bakewell Tart).

Place all the ingredients for the shortbread in the bowl of a food processor and reduce to crumbs, then keep the motor running until the mixture comes together into a ball. It will be very soft and sticky at this point. Press the mixture into the base of a 30 x 23cm non-stick traybake tin, 4cm deep, lay a sheet of clingfilm over the top and smooth out the surface with your fingers. Cover the tin with clingfilm and chill for 1 hour.

Preheat the oven to 140°C fan oven/160°C electric oven. Prick the shortbread all over with a fork and bake for 25–30 minutes until just beginning to colour. Leave to cool.

Preheat the oven to 170°C fan oven/190°C electric oven. Work the jam with a spoon in a bowl until it is smooth and spread it in a thin layer over the shortbread base using a palette knife.

Now for the sponge. Place the butter and sugar in the bowl of a food processor and cream together, then incorporate the eggs. Pour the mixture into a bowl and fold in the coconut, ground almonds, baking powder and sultanas. Spoon the mixture on top of the jam and spread it out in an even layer. Bake for 25–30 minutes until the sponge has set and the top is golden. Run a knife around the edge of the cake and leave it to cool. Cut it into two long halves, then across into 2cm slices. Dust with icing sugar and transfer to a plate.

lemon drizzle cake

The simplest is so often the best, this relies on a minimum of fuss, just the classic marriage of lemon, butter and the crunch of sugar.

Preheat the oven to 170°C fan oven/190°C electric oven and butter a 30 x 23cm non-stick traybake tin, 4cm deep. Place the butter and caster sugar in the bowl of a food processor and beat together until pale and fluffy. Incorporate the eggs one at a time, scraping down the sides of the bowl if necessary, then add the milk and whizz until creamy. Gradually add the flour and baking powder through the funnel with the motor running, then incorporate the lemon zest.

Transfer the mixture to the prepared tin and smooth the surface. Bake for 30–35 minutes until golden and shrinking slightly from the sides and a skewer comes out clean from the centre. Run a knife around the edge of the tin and prick the cake all over with a skewer at about 2cm intervals. To make the drizzle topping, combine the lemon juice and granulated sugar in a bowl, stirring to distribute it evenly. Spoon over the top of the hot cake and set aside to cool in the tin, allowing the juice to sink into the sponge. The surface should have a lovely crystalline sheen. Cut into whatever size squares you fancy.

MAKES 12 SQUARES

225g unsalted butter, diced

225g golden caster sugar

3 medium eggs

150ml whole milk

225g self-raising flour, sifted

1½ teaspoons baking powder, sifted

finely grated zest and juice of 2 lemons

100g golden granulated sugar

KIT

30 x 23cm non-stick traybake tin, 4cm deep

Food processor

Skewer

LITTLE EXTRAS

Unsalted butter for greasing

MAKES 12 SLICES

FOR THE PASTRY

60g unsalted butter, diced

60g icing sugar

1 medium egg yolk

120g plain flour

FOR THE FILLING

75g unsalted butter, diced

110g golden caster sugar

3 medium eggs

½ teaspoon almond extract

180g ground almonds

1 teaspoon baking powder, sifted

200g raspberry or cherry jam

30g flaked almonds

KIT

Food processor

Clingfilm

23cm non-stick square brownie tin, 4cm deep

Baking paper

Baking beans or dried pulses

LITTLE EXTRAS

Plain flour for rolling

Icing sugar for dusting

bakewell slices

A thick bank of delicate almond sponge with a jam tart below, one of our much-loved classics. But the real thing is altogether more subtle than commercial takes on it that tend to be overpowered with almond extract; there should be just enough to spar with the jam.

To make the pastry, cream the butter and icing sugar together in a food processor. Mix in the egg yolk, then add the flour. As soon as the dough comes together in a ball, wrap it in clingfilm and chill for at least 2 hours; it can be kept in the fridge for several days.

Preheat the oven to 170ºC fan oven/190ºC electric oven. Thinly roll out the pastry on a lightly floured surface and use it to line the base of a 23cm non-stick square brownie tin, 4cm deep, draping the excess up the sides; don't worry if you end up having to patch it as this won't show.

Line the case with baking paper and weight it with baking beans or dried pulses. Cook for 15–20 minutes until lightly coloured, then remove the paper and beans and trim the sides to leave you with a tightly fitting base.

To make the filling, cream the butter and sugar together in a food processor, then add the eggs one at a time, the almond extract, ground almonds and baking powder.

Spread the pastry base with the jam, then spoon the almond sponge mixture on top. Carefully smooth the surface, taking care not to blend it with the jam, and scatter over the almonds. Bake in the oven for 25–30 minutes until golden and risen. Run a knife around the edge and leave to cool in the tin.

To serve, dust with icing sugar, cut in half and slice into 12 bars, or half this size if wished. It will be quite crumbly when very fresh and should keep well for several days in an airtight container.

CHAPTER THREE

the french quarter

The clutch of cakes that follows epitomises the patisseries I have come to know and love over the years in Normandy (and elsewhere in France for that matter), so it is the French quarter of the book if you like, a small self-contained kingdom, which is no lesser for its size.

Among this group, even though macaroons hog the limelight with their zany flavours and bright pastel hues, which look so pretty lined up in a cardboard patisserie box, it is financiers that have stolen my heart. These sponge cakes that are traditionally baked in small oblong moulds are thought to derive their name either from their shape that resembles a bar of gold, or from the fact they were popularised in the financial district of Paris surrounding 'La Bourse du Commerce', as the Parisian stock exchange used to be known. They are heart-stoppingly tender, made with ground almonds as well as flour, egg whites rather than whole eggs, icing sugar and 'beurre noisette' which accounts for their particular scent (see page 90).

In some English-speaking countries, in particular Australia and New Zealand, these are sometimes referred to as 'friands', but in France 'friands' refer to small savoury appetisers. These are often lined up on a counter for sale by the piece during holidays to serve with aperitifs – filled choux puffs, tiny sausage rolls, miniature cheese pastries and the like.

Today financiers are baked in all manner of moulds; they are often made in miniature, chocolate-sized and studded with nibs of fruit or chocolate chips and packaged in cellophane bags. Here silicone moulds come into their own – these are the secret to turning out perfect financiers that have a tendency to stick, which means you can also take advantage of fluted and scallop shapes that might be a no-no for standard metal trays.

When it comes to the now ubiquitous macaroon, the only ones we're really interested in are Parisian – those fragile domes surrounded by a skirt of tiny bubbles with soft fudgy insides. And Ladurée's bright candy-coloured dainties with their intensely flavoured ganache fillings are those by which we judge all others. But they are far from simple, and it would be disingenuous to pretend otherwise. The tricks or techniques employed in professional patisseries are way beyond anything we are likely to want to try at home. Particularly bear in mind that in France, it takes in the region of five years to train as a patissier, and while that takes in several masterclasses in baking baguettes, croissants and the like, there is still considerable skill involved in making most of the other alluring little cakes that are equally traditional.

For this reason, if I am honest, these are the cakes I am least likely to bake at home – easy enough to buy them, and they are by far the hardest to get right. Part of the promise of this book is its low-tech approach, which includes a ban on piping bags, but you can still make perfectly decent macaroons in their absence, albeit slightly rustic ones and you may have to match the pairs up, but that doesn't seem a great hardship for avoiding one of life's fiddlier operations.

And madeleines? These are the little shell-shaped, close-textured sponge cakes immortalised in Proust's *In Search of Lost Time*. Savouring one of these with a cup of tea evokes a world of involuntary memories for Proust, the taste itself for him is synonymous with Sunday morning at Combray as a child, where he would go to visit his aunt Leonie in her bedroom to say good morning before going to Mass, and she would treat him to a morsel of her madeleine, first dipped into her cup of tea or tisane. It is one of the most famous passages in food-related literature, which just so perfectly captures the essence of the relationship or significance of the foods that we grow up with and the memories that are linked to them.

'No sooner had the warm liquid mixed with the crumbs touched my palate than a shudder ran through me and I stopped, intent upon the extraordinary thing that was happening to me. An exquisite pleasure had invaded my senses, something isolated, detached, with no history of its origin.'

MARCEL PROUST

160g icing sugar, sifted

60g ground almonds

150g egg whites (4–5 medium eggs)

1 tablespoon runny honey

90g unsalted butter, melted and cooled

½ teaspoon vanilla extract

70g plain flour, sifted

½ teaspoon baking powder, sifted

TO DECORATE

raspberries, blueberries, 1cm nibs of peeled apple or apricot, or dark chocolate chips

KIT

Clingfilm

2 non-stick fairy cake trays or silicone moulds

Wire rack

LITTLE EXTRAS

Unsalted butter for greasing

classic financiers

These are the real thing, taught to me by Jean-Michel Bellamy whose bakery Au Chant Du Pain in Coutances in Normandy produces quite the best patisserie in the area. He bakes these about twice a week, and they are good for some three to four days.

The real, real thing is made with 'beurre noisette', which imparts a particular nutty savour. This is the subtle but distinctive scent within croissants, la gâche and pain de mie as well as financiers.

However, it takes time – first to gently caramelise the milk solids within the butter by melting and then allowing it to rise and fall over a period of about 30 minutes. So to this end I just use ordinary melted butter. There is no difference in the end texture of the cake, which is what is most important.

Combine the icing sugar and ground almonds in a large bowl, add the egg whites and whisk to blend. Stir in the honey, butter and vanilla, then the flour and baking powder, beating until the mixture is smooth. Cover the bowl with clingfilm and chill for at least half a day, but ideally overnight.

Preheat the oven to 190°C fan oven/210°C electric oven. If using non-stick fairy cake trays, butter them really well; there is no need to grease silicone moulds. Spoon the mixture into the moulds so they are three-quarters full and top with one or two berries, nibs of fruit or chocolate chips. (Place raspberries hole down.) Bake for 14–17 minutes until golden and firm. If using fairy cake trays, run a knife around the moulds as soon as they come out of the oven. Leave to cool in the tin for 5–10 minutes before removing to a wire rack to cool completely. Store in an airtight container for up to 3–4 days.

TIP

It took me a long time to embrace silicone baking moulds, until I realised they were the answer to turning out perfect financiers. If making them in a non-stick fairy cake tray then be sure to butter it well and run a knife around the edge of the cakes as soon as they come out of the oven.

cannelés bordelais

MAKES 18 MINIATURE

250ml whole milk

25g unsalted butter

pinch of sea salt

½ teaspoon vanilla extract

2 teaspoons dark rum

50g plain flour

125g golden caster sugar

1 medium egg, and 1 egg yolk

KIT

Clingfilm

1 x 18-hole tray of silicone mini cannelés moulds

Wire rack

LITTLE EXTRAS

Melted unsalted butter for greasing

Given my adoration of these, I only wish I had known somewhat earlier just how easy they were going to be to produce. I suppose because they are quite ornate in appearance and unlike anything else – caramelised just short of being burnt and chewy on the outside, slightly crisp at the edges but unctuously soft and creamy within – I always assumed the technique would match their apparent sophistication. But in essence they are little batter cakes, and no harder to produce than any other pancake batter or clafoutis.

Bring the milk to the boil in small saucepan with the butter and salt, then remove from the heat and stir in the vanilla and rum. Whisk the flour, sugar, egg and yolk together to a thick paste in a medium-sized bowl, then gradually whisk in the hot milk mixture. Cover the bowl with clingfilm and pop the mixture into the fridge for 1 hour.

Preheat the oven to 250°C fan oven/270°C electric oven and brush an 18-hole tray of silicone mini cannelés moulds with melted butter. Three-quarters fill with the batter – I find it easiest to do this using a jug. Place in the oven for 5 minutes, and then turn it down to 160°C fan oven/180°C electric oven and cook for another hour. Pop out of the moulds onto a wire rack while they are still hot and leave to cool. These are best eaten on the day, when the outside is delicately crisp and caramelised.

TIP

Of all the little French fancies, cannelés have the most distinct outline – tall, fluted domes. The moulds for these come in various sizes, and this recipe is for mini cannelés some 4cm in diameter. Their success lies with the depth of the moulds, not readily transcribed to a shallow bun shape, so if you do want to experiment this needs bearing in mind.

For large canneles (5cm in diameter and 5cm deep), loosely cover the tray with foil after the first hour of baking, and give them another 30 minutes until they are really golden. Makes 8.

These are best eaten on the day, when the outside is delicately crisp and caramelised. Avoid airtight containers, which will instantly soften their edges.

proust's madeleines

MAKES APPROX. 16-17

2 medium eggs

90g golden caster sugar

15g runny honey

½ teaspoon vanilla extract

pinch of fine sea salt

100g plain flour

1 level teaspoon baking powder

80g unsalted butter, melted

KIT

Electric whisk

Clingfilm

2 non-stick fairy cake trays
or trays of silicone moulds
(scallop-shaped are traditional)

LITTLE EXTRAS

Unsalted butter for greasing

Icing sugar for dusting (optional)

It is the 'bosse' or dome here that defines whether it is indeed a madeleine or simply a plain old sponge cake. These meltingly tender little cakes can be flavoured with vanilla, lemon or orange zest, a drop of rum or Calvados, or even studded with chocolate chips. Essentially they are made using a 'Genoise' batter, where melted butter is stirred into a whisked egg, sugar and flour base. The batter needs an hour or two resting in the fridge, but I like to make it the night beforehand.

Whisk the eggs with the sugar, honey, vanilla and salt in a large bowl for 5–8 minutes until very pale and at least doubled in volume, using an electric whisk. Sift over and fold in the flour and baking powder, then the melted butter. Cover the bowl with clingfilm and chill for an hour or two or overnight.

Preheat the oven to 220°C fan oven/240°C electric oven and butter 16–17 holes within two non-stick fairy cake trays or trays of silicone moulds. Give the cake mixture a good stir and fill the moulds by three-quarters with a teaspoon.

Place the trays in the oven, immediately turn it down to 200°C fan oven/220°C electric oven and bake for 4 minutes, during which time a dip will form in the centre of the cake, the beginning of the domed bump. Now turn the oven down to 170°C fan oven/190°C electric oven and bake for a further 3–5 minutes until you have a beautiful dome in the centre of each one, the mixture is set and the edge of the sponge is golden. Run a knife around the edge of each cake as soon as they come out the oven and leave to cool in the tin. Madeleines are probably at their loveliest eaten slightly warm, but they will also be good for dipping in a tisane Proustian fashion for a couple of days thereafter. Store in an airtight container. Dust with icing sugar if you wish.

TIP

The secret to the 'bosse' or dome is partly down to temperature differential – by placing the chilled batter into a very hot oven, you gradually reduce its heat. I suppose in a way it is the opposite to baking a Victoria Sponge: should it unfortunately bolt upwards in the centre this is normally caused by the oven being too hot, whereas here that is a part of the plan.

For Choc Chip Madeleines, fold in 75g dark chocolate chips with the melted butter.

date madeleines

MAKES 15–20

110g pitted dates, chopped

½ teaspoon bicarbonate of soda

2 large eggs

25g vanilla or caster sugar

finely grated zest of 1 lemon

2 tablespoons clear honey

50g self-raising flour

½ teaspoon baking powder

pinch of sea salt

50g ground almonds

110g unsalted butter, melted and cooled

KIT

Electric whisk

Clingfilm

2 non-stick fairy cake trays or silicone madeleine moulds

Wire rack

LITTLE EXTRAS

Unsalted melted butter for greasing

Icing sugar for dusting

These little date cakes are a variation on a theme of a madeleine. Bake them as close to the time of eating as possible, given how good they are fresh from the oven.

Bring 90ml water and the dates to the boil in a small saucepan and simmer for 4 minutes until the dates turn quite mushy, then stir in the bicarbonate of soda. Whisk the eggs and sugar together in a bowl until they are almost white, then add the lemon zest and honey and whisk briefly to combine. Sift the flour and baking powder together and lightly fold into the egg mixture, then carefully fold in the salt and ground almonds, taking care not to overwork. Gently fold in the cooled melted butter, followed by the dates and their water. Cover the bowl with clingfilm and chill the mixture for 30 minutes.

Meanwhile, preheat the oven to 190°C fan oven/210°C electric oven and brush the insides of a couple of non-stick fairy cake trays with a little melted butter. Spoon the mixture into the prepared moulds, filling each one two-thirds full. Bake the madeleines in the oven for 8–10 minutes until golden. Run a knife round the edge of the cakes, turn them out on to a wire rack and dust the tops with icing sugar.

TIP

Traditionally madeleines are baked in a special tray to give small scallop-shaped cakes that are fluted on the underside. Silicone moulds give the best results, but they can be baked in any small cake tins such as fairy cake trays.

rum butter
macaroons

As delicate as they are pretty, don't worry too much about trying to turn out macaroons that look as if you bought them from Ladurée – a certain rusticity is allowed at home. They also make fab meringues and cream, if you sandwich them on the day they are made with a little crème fraîche, or mascarpone blended with just enough milk to achieve a whipped cream consistency.

To make the macaroons, finely grind the almonds and icing sugar together in batches in a coffee grinder. Whisk the egg whites in a large bowl using an electric whisk until they are half risen, then scatter over the caster sugar and continue whisking until the mixture is firm. Keep whisking for a further minute until the mixture is really stiff and then whisk in the vanilla and a little food colouring to dye the mixture a pale pink. Fold the almond and sugar mixture into the meringue in two goes, beating well with a wooden spoon until the mixture forms a thick ribbon on itself.

Preheat the oven to 170°C fan oven/190°C electric oven. Line a couple of baking trays with baking paper, dabbing a little of the mixture on the corners of the trays to help the paper stay in place. Drop half teaspoons of the mixture in neat little mounds onto the paper, spacing them a few centimetres apart. Set aside to stand for 15 minutes, during which time they will spread to about 4cm in diameter.

Bake in the oven for 10 minutes, wedging the door ajar slightly with the handle of a wooden spoon, until they have a shiny domed surface and ideally a small frothy 'foot' at the base – but don't fret too much about this.

The next bit is the trickiest – loosening the macaroons without breaking them, as they are very delicate and gooey within their fragile dome. Loosen the corners of the paper and carefully slide it onto the worksurface, leaving the macaroons in place. Run some cold water over the baking tray to dampen it and then carefully slide the paper back in place. Set aside for 5 minutes, and then carefully loosen each macaroon with a small palette knife, slipping it under the macaroon as close to the paper as possible. Set aside on a worksurface to cool completely.

To make the filling, whisk the butter and icing sugar together in a medium-sized bowl using an electric whisk until light and mousse-like, then whisk in the brandy or rum. Spread a little buttercream onto a macaroon and sandwich with a second one of a similar size. Repeat with the remainder.

These will keep well overnight, loosely covered and stored in a cool place. If chilling them, remove from the fridge 15 minutes before eating.

MAKES APPROX. 20

FOR THE MACAROONS

60g ground almonds

110g icing sugar

2 medium egg whites

15g white caster sugar

½ teaspoon vanilla extract

a little pink food colouring – liquid or paste

FOR THE FILLING

50g unsalted butter, softened

40g icing sugar

2 teaspoons brandy or dark rum

KIT

Coffee grinder

Electric whisk

2 baking trays

Baking paper

Small palette knife

FOR THE CUSTARD

5 medium egg yolks

80g icing sugar, sifted

30g plain flour, sifted

20g cocoa powder, sifted

425ml whole milk

FOR THE ÉCLAIRS

50g unsalted butter

pinch each of sea salt and caster sugar

75g plain flour, sifted

3 medium eggs

FOR THE CHOCOLATE GLAZE

50g dark chocolate (approx. 70 per cent cocoa solids), broken into pieces

2 tablespoons groundnut or vegetable oil

125g icing sugar, sifted

KIT

Clingfilm

1–2 non-stick baking trays

Wire rack

LITTLE EXTRAS

Unsalted butter for greasing

Plain flour for dusting

chocolate éclairs

These are lovely rustic éclairs – no piping bags called for – that drip a sticky chocolate glaze in the most alluring way. Yet another game of French v. English to play here. I favour the Gallic route of éclairs filled with chocolate custard, instead of cream; they are that little bit less rich and that little bit more chocolatey.

To make the custard, whisk the egg yolks and icing sugar together in a medium-sized non-stick saucepan until smooth. Next whisk in the flour and then the cocoa, until you have a thick creamy paste. Bring the milk to the boil in a small saucepan and whisk it into the egg mixture, a little at a time to begin with, until it is all incorporated.

Place over a low heat and cook for a few minutes until the custard thickens, stirring vigorously with a wooden spoon to disperse any lumps that form – if necessary, you can give it a quick whisk. The custard shouldn't actually boil, but the odd bubble will ensure it's hot enough to thicken properly. Cook it for a few minutes longer, again stirring constantly. Pour the custard into a bowl, cover the surface with clingfilm and leave to cool.

Meanwhile, make the éclairs. Preheat the oven to 200°C fan oven/220°C electric oven and butter and flour one or two non-stick baking trays. Place the butter, salt and sugar in a small non-stick saucepan with 200ml water and bring to the boil. Stir in the flour off the heat and beat the dough with a wooden spoon until it is smooth. Return the dough to a medium-high heat and cook it for a couple of minutes, stirring constantly.

Allow it to cool for about 5 minutes, then beat in the eggs one at a time. Spoon heaped tablespoons of the mixture onto the baking trays, shaping them into sausage shapes, 11–12cm long, and spacing them about 5cm apart.

Bake for 10 minutes and then turn the heat down to 160°C fan oven/180°C electric oven and bake for a further 20 minutes until golden. Remove from the oven and immediately slice off the tops of the éclairs to prevent them from becoming soggy.

Scoop out and discard the uncooked insides and leave the éclairs to cool on a wire rack. They are quite delicate so don't be perturbed should a couple of them break.

Fill the éclairs with the custard, mounding it, and replace the lids. Arrange them on a serving plate. To make the glaze, gently melt the dark chocolate with the oil in a medium-sized bowl set over a small pan with a little simmering water in it. Whisk the icing sugar and 2 tablespoons of boiling water into the melted chocolate and spoon a couple of teaspoons along the top of each éclair, letting it trickle down the sides – the little pools that collect at the base are one of the most alluring bits. You may have a little more glaze than you need, as this amount allows for the possibility of all eight éclairs turning out perfectly. Leave to set in a cool place for about an hour. These are best eaten the day they are made.

CHAPTER FOUR

muffins, cupcakes and fairy cakes

blueberry and orange muffins

MAKES APPROX. 12

80ml extra virgin olive oil

180ml smooth orange juice, plus the finely grated zest of 1 orange

2 medium eggs

275g plain flour

2 teaspoons baking powder

200g golden caster sugar, plus extra for dusting

150g fresh blueberries

KIT

Muffin paper cases or wrappers

Muffin tray

Beautifully light and fluffy, and as with all muffins the art lies with the laissez-faire blending of the wet and dry ingredients, not something that comes easily to the conscientious baker who feels there must be more to it than that. Unusually, these are dairy free, and much lower in fat than the norm.

Preheat the oven to 170°C fan oven/190°C electric oven and arrange 12 paper muffin cases or wrappers within a 12-hole muffin tray. Whisk the oil, orange juice, zest and eggs together in a large bowl. Combine the flour, baking powder and sugar in another large bowl. Tip the wet ingredients into the dry ones and stir to loosely blend – there should be no traces of flour, but the mixture should appear wet and lumpy.

Fold in two-thirds of the blueberries and fill the paper cases by two-thirds. Scatter over the remaining blueberries and a little extra sugar and bake for 30 minutes or until risen and crusty. Serve newly cooled, although they keep well overnight if loosely covered.

TIP

It is only one step on in imagination to use extra virgin olive oil in a muffin rather than groundnut or sunflower. It mellows with cooking, and the resulting scent, while distinctive, is very pleasing.

For a crunchier top you could sprinke the muffins with demerara sugar before baking instead of caster sugar.

FOR THE CRUMBLE

70g light muscovado sugar

70g unsalted butter, chilled and diced

80g plain flour

20g cocoa powder

FOR THE CAKE

180g unsalted butter, diced

180g light muscovado sugar

3 medium eggs, and 1 egg yolk

50ml whole milk

160g plain flour, sifted

20g cocoa powder, sifted

¾ teaspoon baking powder, sifted

100g fresh raspberries

KIT

Muffin paper cases

Muffin tray

Food processor

LITTLE EXTRAS

Icing sugar for dusting

chocolate raspberry crumble muffins

This fashionable style of muffin is a personal favourite, but anything that combines crumble with a sponge does it for me. And here a light smattering of buttery chocolate crumble finishes a chocolate sponge studded with raspberries.

Preheat the oven to 170°C fan oven/190°C electric oven and arrange 12 paper muffin cases inside a muffin tray. Place all the ingredients for the crumble in the bowl of a food processor and whizz until the mixture resembles fine crumbs, then transfer it to a bowl.

To make the cake mixture, place the butter and sugar in the bowl of a food processor and cream for several minutes until fluffy. Add the eggs and the yolk, one at a time, scraping down the bowl if necessary, followed by the milk – don't worry if the mixture appears curdled at this point. Incorporate the flour, cocoa and baking powder and transfer the mixture to a large bowl. Gently fold in the raspberries.

Divide the cake mixture between the paper cases, filling them by two-thirds, and then scatter the crumble over the top. Bake the cakes for about 25 minutes until risen and firm when pressed in the centre, then leave to cool. Dust with icing sugar shortly before serving.

TIP

These are at their yummiest the day they are made when the crumble is still crisp, but can also be stored for a day or two. A plastic food bag loosely tied is preferable to an airtight container.

skinny carrot and pineapple muffins

MAKES 8–10

200g wholemeal flour

1 teaspoon baking powder

½ teaspoon ground cinnamon

100g golden caster sugar

1 x 225g tin of pineapple

2 tablespoons tinned prunes, stoned

2 medium egg whites

1 teaspoon vanilla extract

3 tablespoons grated carrots

50g raisins

KIT

Non-stick muffin tray

Muffin paper cases

Pastry brush

Food processor

Wire rack

LITTLE EXTRAS

Vegetable oil for greasing

I was given this recipe many years ago by the founder of the Coffee Republic chain, Sahar Hashemi. It was one of her bestsellers, based on a carrot cake that her mother used to make for her. It is quite unlike any other muffin I have ever encountered, deliciously chewy which is courtesy of the egg whites, and there is no fat. But it is just as moist as any other, so if you are after something sweet but light, these are definitely worth considering.

Preheat the oven to 180°C fan oven/200°C electric oven and brush a tray of non-stick muffin moulds or paper cases set within the moulds with vegetable oil. Place the flour in a large bowl and sift in the baking powder and cinnamon. Add the sugar and stir to combine.

Place the pineapple and its juice in a food processor and whizz until crushed and pulpy. Add this to the dry ingredients, then purée the prunes in the food processor and add these too. Tip in the egg whites and vanilla extract and stir until the dry ingredients are just moistened, then fold in the carrots and raisins.

Spoon the mixture into the moulds, to within 1cm of the top, and bake for 15–20 minutes until risen and lightly golden on the surface. If using a tray of moulds, rather than paper cases, run a knife around the edges to loosen them and turn out onto a wire rack to cool. Eat the muffins warm or at room temperature. They are very moist and keep better than most other muffins.

TIP

Even though we tend to think of fresh fruits being superior to tinned, I find these muffins are very much better for adhering to tinned prunes and pineapple rather than trying to upgrade to the real thing.

courgette and cinnamon muffins

These are a curiosity, but a charming one. Carrot may get the main billing as a vegetable grated for use in cakes, it sweetens and it moistens, but so does courgette, even though it may not seem so obvious.

Preheat the oven to 180°C fan oven/200°C electric oven and arrange 8–10 paper muffin cases inside a muffin tray. Combine the flour, baking powder, 100g sugar and cinnamon in a large bowl and stir to mix them. Whisk the milk, egg and butter with the lemon zest in a medium-sized bowl, and then stir in the courgette and raisins. Tip the wet ingredients over the dry ingredients and loosely combine – the mixture should look wet but lumpy.

Spoon it into the paper cases, filling them by two-thirds, sprinkle over a little more sugar and cinnamon and bake for 25–30 minutes until golden and crusty. Serve warm on their own or with butter and bramble jelly.

MAKES 8–10

225g plain flour

2 teaspoons baking powder

100g golden caster sugar, plus extra for dusting

$1/3$ teaspoon ground cinnamon, plus extra for dusting

200ml whole milk

1 medium egg

75g unsalted butter, melted

finely grated zest of 1 lemon

125g coarsely grated courgette

75g raisins

KIT

Muffin paper cases

Muffin tray

LITTLE EXTRAS

Unsalted butter and bramble jelly, to serve (optional)

milk chocolate cupcakes

These cakes have a soft, fudgy icing, and the sprinkles have max child appeal, but any milk chocolate decoration will do.

Preheat the oven to 180°C fan oven/200°C electric oven and arrange 14 fairy cake paper cases inside a couple of fairy cake trays. Blend the drinking chocolate with 2 tablespoons of boiling water in a small bowl and leave to cool to room temperature.

Place all the ingredients for the cake, including the chocolate paste, in the bowl of a food processor and cream together. Spoon the mixture into the paper cases so they are half to two-thirds full, smoothing the surface. Bake for 17–20 minutes until risen and springy to the touch, then remove and leave them to cool. They may have little mounds in the centre.

To make the icing, melt the chocolate and butter together in a bowl set over a pan with a little simmering water in it. Don't worry if it appears grainy at this stage. Add the milk and whisk until smooth and glossy. Smooth a teaspoon of this over the top of each cake, taking it up to the sides. If you wish, you can press a few mini marshmallows into the glaze and scatter over some chocolate strands. Set aside in a cool place for an hour or two until set. The cakes will keep well in an airtight container for several days.

MAKES APPROX. 14

1 heaped tablespoon drinking chocolate powder

110g plain flour

110g golden caster sugar

100g unsalted butter, diced

2 medium eggs

½ teaspoon baking powder

125g milk chocolate, broken into pieces

30g unsalted butter

1 tablespoon milk

KIT

Fairy cake paper cases

2 fairy cake trays

Food processor

LITTLE EXTRAS

Mini marshmallows and chocolate strands for decorating (optional)

FOR THE CAKES

2 medium eggs, separated

90g golden caster sugar

150g ground almonds

1 level teaspoon baking powder, sifted

1 teaspoon finely grated lemon zest

1 teaspoon lemon extract

3 tablespoons whole milk

FOR THE ICING

200g unsalted butter, softened and diced

300g icing sugar, sifted

4 tablespoons lemon juice, sieved

KIT

Fairy cake paper cases

2 fairy cake trays

Electric whisk

Wire rack

Small palette knife or straight-sided table knife

retro deep-filled lemon cupcakes

Long, long ago, before *Sex and the City* graced our television screens, a cupcake was a deep-iced fancy that came in a box of six, a mixture of primrose yellow lemon and orange, consisting of about two-thirds cake to one-third icing. There was a protocol to eating it; you peeled back the very top silvery edge of the paper casing in order to nibble the icing, and having worked your way around the edge you then tackled the middle island of it before reluctantly eating the sponge.

While it would be disingenuous to pretend that these were superior to the homemade cakes of today (you can in fact still buy them from supermarkets, but they are not as good as they used to be), these are a tribute to the cupcakes of old – homemade and rather better for it, genuinely tasty and rich with lemon. But some silver paper cases play the part nicely.

Preheat the oven to 170°C fan oven/190°C electric oven and arrange about 20 fairy cake paper cases inside a couple of fairy cake trays. Whisk the egg whites in a large bowl until stiff, using an electric whisk. In a separate large bowl, whisk the egg yolks and sugar together – the mixture should not be too pale and thick. Gently fold the egg whites into the egg yolk mixture in two goes. Fold in the ground almonds in two goes, then the baking powder, lemon zest and extract. Finally mix in the milk.

Spoon a generous teaspoon of the mixture into each paper case using up all of it, it should level out of its own accord, and bake for 15 minutes until risen and firm. Don't worry if the surface seems a little craggy, the icing will conceal any sins. Transfer the cakes to a wire rack or worksurface to cool.

To make the icing, whisk the butter in a large bowl until very pale using an electric whisk. In a separate bowl, blend the icing sugar with the lemon juice. Add the icing to the butter and continue to whisk for a couple of minutes until very light and mousse-like. Using a small palette or straight-sided table knife, slather the icing over the top of the cakes so it lies level with the top of the paper cases. Cover and chill for at least an hour, removing them 15 minutes before serving. These keep well for several days.

TIP
For extra lemon factor, try scattering these with a little extra finely grated zest. Scatter the finely grated zest of 2 lemons over a baking tray lined with baking paper and warm for 15 minutes in an oven heated to 100˚C fan oven/120˚C electric oven, giving it a scrunch at the end.

FOR THE CAKES

25g cocoa powder

50g unsalted butter, diced

100g golden caster sugar

1 medium egg

85g plain flour

½ teaspoon bicarbonate of soda

¼ teaspoon baking powder

FOR THE ICING

100ml double cream

100g dark chocolate (approx. 70 per cent cocoa solids), broken into pieces

KIT

Fairy cake paper cases

2 fairy cake trays

Food processor

Small palette knife or straight-sided table knife

LITTLE EXTRAS

Mini dark or milk chocolate curls (optional)

Icing sugar for dusting (optional)

dark chocolate cupcakes

A decidedly chocolatey cake, a tad more bitter and moister than usual, with a dark chocolate truffle icing.

Preheat the oven to 180°C fan oven/200°C electric oven and arrange 18 fairy cake paper cases inside a couple of fairy cake trays. Pour 100ml boiling water over the cocoa in a small bowl and whisk until smooth, then leave to cool to room temperature. Place the butter and sugar in the bowl of a food processor and cream together until pale. Incorporate the egg, the dry ingredients and finally the cocoa solution. Spoon the mixture into the paper cases so they are about half full, and bake in the oven for 17–20 minutes until risen and springy to the touch. Remove and leave to cool.

To make the icing, bring the cream to the boil in a small saucepan. Place the dark chocolate in a small bowl and pour over the hot cream. Set aside for a few minutes, and then stir to melt the chocolate. Leave it a few minutes longer and stir again – you should have a thick glossy cream. If for any reason the chocolate doesn't melt completely, set the bowl over a pan of simmering water and heat gently, stirring until smooth.

Drop a teaspoon of the icing onto each cake and spread it towards the edge using a small palette knife or straight-sided table knife. You can decorate them further if you wish by scattering over some chocolate curls and dusting with icing sugar. Set aside for about 1 hour to set.

TIP

For cartoon fancy, crown with a Malteser instead of the curls.

FOR THE CAKES

110g plain flour

110g golden caster sugar

110g unsalted butter, diced

2 medium eggs

1 teaspoon baking powder

½ teaspoon vanilla extract

FOR THE ICING

125g unsalted butter, softened

125g icing sugar, sifted

½ teaspoon vanilla extract

KIT

Fairy cake paper cases

2 fairy cake trays

Food processor

Electric whisk

Small palette knife or straight-sided table knife

LITTLE EXTRAS

1–2 drops of blue food colouring (optional)

Retro sprinkles

vanilla cupcakes

This is the classic vintage-inspired cupcake – a vanilla pound cake with fluffy buttercream that can be dyed any pretty enamel shade, and there are endless sprinkles out there to choose from. Or why not buck the trend and lose both the colour and the sprinkles – they'll taste just as good.

Preheat the oven to 180°C fan oven/200°C electric oven and arrange 15 fairy cake paper cases inside a couple of fairy cake trays. Place all the ingredients for the cakes in the bowl of a food processor and cream together. Spoon the mixture into the paper cases so they are two-thirds full. Bake for 17–20 minutes until risen and springy to the touch. Remove and leave to cool.

To make the butter icing, whisk the butter in a large bowl for a minute using an electric whisk until very pale and fluffy, then add the icing sugar, vanilla extract and 1–2 drops of blue food colouring if you wish. Continue whisking for another couple of minutes until really mousse-like. Using a small palette knife or straight-sided table knife, trowel the icing over the surface of the cakes and decorate with sprinkles.

TIP

Any bright pastel will keep these in retro mood – pale green is particularly lovely, also dusky orange, yellow and pink.

FOR THE CAKES

175g unsalted butter, softened

175g golden caster sugar

finely grated zest of 1 orange

3 medium eggs, plus 1 yolk

50ml whole milk

175g plain flour

1 teaspoon baking powder

FOR THE DECORATION

250g mascarpone

1 teaspoon vanilla extract

25g golden syrup

10g icing sugar, sifted

KIT

Food processor

Fairy cake paper cases

2 fairy cake trays

Electric whisk

LITTLE EXTRAS

50g white chocolate, broken into pieces

Hundreds and thousands

butterfly cakes

Inspiration for these butterfly cakes comes from those white chocolate buttons smothered in hundreds and thousands, sometimes called Snowies or Jazzies.

Preheat the oven to 170°C fan oven/190°C electric oven. Cream the butter and sugar in a food processor until almost white. Incorporate the orange zest, eggs and yolk, then the milk and continue beating until homogenised. Transfer the mixture to a large bowl. Sift the dry ingredients twice and then fold them, one-third at a time, into the butter mixture. Fill 20 fairy cake paper cases set inside two fairy cake trays about half full with the cake mixture, using up all of it, and bake for 20 minutes. The lower tray may take a few minutes longer. Remove and leave them to cool in the trays.

To make the icing, spoon the mascarpone into a bowl and beat in the vanilla extract, then the syrup and finally the icing sugar. Place the chocolate in a bowl set over a pan of simmering water and gently melt it.

Using a small, sharp knife, cut out a shallow cone from the centre of each cake and halve it to form two butterfly wings. Fill the cavity of each cake with the vanilla cream. Shake some hundreds and thousands into a small bowl. Dip the curved tips of the butterfly wings into the melted chocolate and then into the hundreds and thousands. Set them into the vanilla cream at an angle, tips uppermost. Set aside in a cool place. If keeping longer than a few hours, store in an airtight container.

TIP

You could simply fill the cakes, and dust the wings with icing sugar for a classic simple butterfly bun. You can use the same buttercream as the Vanilla Cupcakes on page 112 if preferred to the mascarpone cream.

200g plain flour

2 teaspoons baking powder

½ teaspoon mixed spice

75g demerara sugar, plus extra for dusting

150g unsalted butter, diced

1 medium egg

100ml whole milk

100g currants

50g mixed peel

KIT

2 non-stick baking trays

Food processor

Palette knife

LITTLE EXTRAS

Unsalted butter for greasing

rockcakes

I think we neglect these cakes, which are half scone and half sponge. They were a staple of my childhood and I still feel a surge of warmth whenever I come across them in bakeries. They are the antithesis of cupcakes, and who knows, maybe the sign of a village that hasn't succumbed to global coffee culture and is a promise of somewhere sleepy and undiscovered.

Preheat the oven to 170°C fan oven/190°C electric oven and butter a couple of non-stick baking trays. Whizz the flour, baking powder, mixed spice, sugar and butter to fine crumbs in a food processor, then add the egg and the milk and process to a very thick, sticky dough. Transfer to a large bowl and work in the currants and peel.

Drop heaped tablespoons of the mixture onto the baking trays, spacing them slightly apart, and sprinkle each one with a pinch of demerara sugar. Bake for 20–23 minutes until golden. The lower tray may take longer than the top. Immediately loosen the cakes with a palette knife and leave to cool. I like these best on the day they are baked, but if you pop them inside a food bag they will be good for a day or two thereafter.

TIP

Rockcakes are quite forgiving little buns, which will accommodate a number of different flours, all with very different results. You can use a wholemeal rye for a hearty, slightly grainy finish; chestnut flour is richer in both texture and flavour; while rice flour gives a lovely delicate and loose-textured bun.

french iced fancies page 120

FOR THE SPONGE

3 large eggs

75g golden caster sugar

50g plain flour, sifted

pinch of sea salt

FOR THE BUTTERCREAM

3 medium eggs

150g icing sugar, sifted

50g plain flour, sifted

325ml whole milk

finely grated zest of ½ lemon

½ teaspoon vanilla extract

180g unsalted butter, softened

FOR THE ICING

225g icing sugar, sifted

2–3 tablespoons lemon juice, sieved

KIT

32 x 23cm Swiss roll tin

Baking paper

Electric whisk

Palette knife

Clingfilm

LITTLE EXTRAS

Unsalted butter for greasing

Mini white marshmallows for decorating (optional)

french iced fancies

These cakes are all about the buttercream filling. French rather than American, it is lighter and less sweet than our own, consisting of about two-thirds custard. And it's great for all sorts of cakes, not just here for these pretty little squares.

Preheat the oven to 180°C fan oven/200°C electric oven. Butter a 32 x 23cm Swiss roll tin, line it with baking paper and butter this also.

Place the eggs and sugar in a bowl and whisk for 8–10 minutes using an electric whisk until the mixture is almost white and mousse-like. You can also do this in a food processor using the whisking attachment, in which case reduce the time to about 5 minutes. Lightly fold in the flour in two goes, then the salt. Pour the mixture into the prepared tin and smooth it using a palette knife. Give the tin a couple of sharp taps on the worksurface to eliminate any large bubbles and bake the sponge for 8–10 minutes until it is lightly golden and springy to the touch. Run a knife around the edge of the cake and leave it to cool.

To make the buttercream, first make a thick custard. Whisk the eggs and icing sugar together in a medium-sized, non-stick saucepan until smooth, and then whisk in the flour. Bring the milk to the boil in a separate small saucepan and whisk it into the egg mixture. Place the pan of custard over a low heat and cook for a few minutes until the custard thickens, stirring vigorously with a wooden spoon to disperse any lumps that form. The custard shouldn't actually boil, but the odd bubble will ensure it's hot enough to thicken properly. Cook it for a few minutes longer, again stirring constantly.

Pass the custard through a sieve into a bowl, stir in the lemon zest and vanilla, cover the surface with clingfilm and leave to cool completely.

To finish the buttercream, beat the softened butter in a bowl until light and creamy. If it's on the hard side, you can cream it in a food processor and then transfer it to a bowl. Using an electric whisk, gradually whisk in the cooled custard. Continue whisking for another few minutes, on a low speed to begin with and then on a higher speed, until the buttercream is very pale and fluffy.

Turn the cake out onto a board and peel off the paper. Cut it in half widthways. Line a large plate or dish with clingfilm and place one of the cake halves on top.

Spread with the buttercream, taking it up to the edge, and then sandwich with the other half. Use a palette knife to smooth the edges of the buttercream level with the cake. Loosely cover the whole thing with clingfilm and chill for a couple of hours.

Remove the cake from the fridge and slice into twelve 4cm cubes – you may find it easiest to lift the whole cake first onto the worksurface using the ends of the clingfilm.

To make the icing, blend the icing sugar and lemon juice in a bowl – it needs to be thick enough to coat the cake and trickle down the sides. Ice the surface of the cubes with the icing, taking it up to the edge of the cake. Leave it to trickle down the sides for a few minutes, and then decorate the top with a few mini marshmallows if you wish.

Set aside in a cool place to set for an hour. Cover and chill if not serving in the near future.

a simple lemon bun

I will always associate these with shopping trips. Despite the ubiquity of espresso-makers at home, stopping off at a pavement café to sip a double espresso with a really good small lemon sponge is a precious ritual. That little bit of sugar and hit of caffeine is a mid-morning tonic like no other, and provides that extra hit of energy needed to keep on shopping.

Preheat the oven to 170°C fan oven/190°C electric oven and arrange about 8 paper muffin cases inside a muffin tray. To make the cakes, blend all the ingredients together in a food processor. Spoon the mixture into the paper cases so they are two-thirds full – the mixture will be quite runny – and bake for 20–25 minutes until risen and set, and lightly coloured.

Meanwhile, gently warm the marmalade in a small saucepan, working it with a spoon until smooth, then press through a sieve into a bowl. Remove the cakes from the oven and brush the sieved marmalade over the surface of each. Place the icing sugar and lemon juice in another small saucepan and bring to the boil, whisking until smooth and translucent. Drizzle one and a half teaspoons of the glaze over the surface of each bun to lightly coat it (a little may collect around the rim) and return to the oven for 1 minute. Remove from the oven, scatter over some chopped pistachios (if using) and leave the buns to cool completely. These are best eaten on the day they are baked, but are still good the day after.

TIP

What you don't get in that pavement cafe is 'raspberries in Champagne'. So divide 350g chilled raspberries between six glasses and pour over half a bottle of chilled pink Champagne. First eat the raspberries with a teaspoon and then drink the Champagne, then eat the bun, down the espresso in one and go shopping.

If using a zester, finely chop the strands before adding them to the mixture.

MAKES APPROX. 8

FOR THE CAKES

2 medium eggs

180g golden caster sugar

150g self-raising flour

finely grated zest of 2 large lemons (see TIP)

60g unsalted butter, softened

75ml whole milk

1 teaspoon lemon extract

FOR THE GLAZE

75g lemon and lime marmalade

100g icing sugar

2 tablespoons lemon juice, sieved

KIT

Muffin paper cases

Muffin tray

Food processor

Pastry brush

LITTLE EXTRAS

Finely chopped pistachios (optional)

pistachio and white chocolate buns

MAKES 12–14

115g unsalted butter, diced

115g golden caster sugar

finely grated zest of 1 orange

2 medium eggs, separated

75ml whole milk

140g plain flour

1 teaspoon baking powder

¼ teaspoon sea salt

25g shelled raw pistachio nuts, coarsely chopped, plus 1 tablespoon

25g white chocolate chips

75g apricot jam

KIT

Fairy cake paper cases

2 fairy cake trays

Food processor

Electric whisk

Coffee grinder

Pastry brush

Golden sticky buns set with pistachio nuts and white chocolate chips.

Preheat the oven to 170°C fan oven/190°C electric oven and arrange 14 fairy cake paper cases inside a couple of fairy cake trays. Cream the butter and sugar in a food processor until almost white. Incorporate the orange zest and egg yolks, then the milk and continue beating until homogenised. Transfer the mixture to a large bowl. Sift the flour and baking powder twice, and then fold them half at a time into the butter mixture. Add the salt, 25g coarsely chopped pistachios and the chocolate chips and fold in carefully. Whisk the egg whites in a separate bowl until stiff peaks form using an electric whisk. Fold them into the cake mixture in two goes, working as lightly as possible. Spoon the mixture into the paper cases so they are two-thirds full and bake for 15–20 minutes. The lower tray may take a few minutes longer. Remove and leave them to cool in the trays.

Place the remaining tablespoon of pistachios in a coffee grinder and finely chop, almost to a powder. Gently heat the jam in a small saucepan until it liquefies, then press it through a sieve. Paint the surface of the cakes with the jam and sprinkle a few ground pistachios in the centre.

coconut macaroons

MAKES 6

150g desiccated coconut

2 medium egg whites

80g icing sugar

40g raspberry jam

KIT

2 non-stick baking trays

Coffee grinder

Electric whisk

Palette knife

LITTLE EXTRAS

Unsalted butter for greasing

These coconut cakes are the English take on macaroons, which shine out from bakery windows alongside doughnuts and sugary iced buns. They are as rough and ready as French ones are demure, the good news being they require zero skill by comparison.

Preheat the oven to 180°C fan oven/200°C electric oven and butter two non-stick baking trays. Grind the desiccated coconut as finely as possible in a coffee grinder in batches.

Whisk the egg whites in a large bowl until stiff peaks form using an electric whisk. Sprinkle over the icing sugar a tablespoon at a time, whisking well with each addition, until you end up with a glossy meringue. Fold the ground coconut into the meringue in several goes. Drop generous heaped tablespoons of the mixture in mounds onto the prepared baking trays, spacing them slightly apart. Using the end of a teaspoon handle, make a little cavity in each one about 2.25cm in diameter – they will spread slightly as you do so. Drop half a teaspoon of jam in the centre of each one.

Bake for 10–12 minutes until lightly golden. Leave to cool and then loosen them with a palette knife. They are at their most delicate the day they are baked, but can also be stored loosely covered on a plate overnight.

meringues

Meringues are very innocent creations and favouring a simple life I have long adopted French meringues as my staple, which require nothing more complex than a whisk and a bowl. In essence all types are a variation on a theme of a spume of sugar and egg whites – from there it is down to how you bake them, depending on whether you want them crisp and melting, or gooey inside.

POINTERS TO SUCCESS

Meringues, for all their simplicity, do demand that we respect certain house rules.

THE EGG WHITES

Egg whites should be at room temperature, so if you normally keep your eggs in the fridge remember to take them out an hour beforehand. In addition be sure they are either organic or free-range. Poor-quality, battery-produced eggs will have watery whites that fail to rise.

THE SUGAR

Meringues conform to a basic ratio of one egg white to 50g of sugar. This is the same whether you are making crunchy individual meringues, layers, nests or a pavlova. What differs and creates the various types is how you bake them. The exception here are meringue crusts for pies, where you can reduce the sugar if the filling is particularly sweet, but the result will be altogether softer and less robust.

A refined white caster sugar will encourage that snowy white hue. I either use caster sugar, or half caster and half icing sugar. Though soft brown sugar can also create a delicious meringue in its own right.

THE BADDIES

Meringues have two arch enemies. The first is water, even a drop in the bowl or on the whisk will prevent the whites from rising. The other enemy is grease, it is oh-so-important that your bowl and whisk are scrupulously clean.

THE UTENSILS

The bowl should be nice and big, but not with such a large base area that the white is too shallow to whip effectively. Pyrex bowls and old-fashioned ceramic mixing bowls are ideal. An electric whisk will make light work of whipping the necessary air into the egg whites.

And now take your time. Add the sugar gradually and whisk well with each addition.

MAKES 6 MEDIUM-SIZED
MERINGUES

3 large egg whites

175g white caster sugar

KIT

1–2 baking trays

Baking paper

Electric whisk

old-fashioned.
meringues

My perfect meringue is one with a thin crisp shell and a soft mousse-like centre that collapses into a messy heap when you bite into it.

Preheat the oven to 120°C fan oven/140°C electric oven and line one or two baking trays with baking paper. Place the egg whites in a large bowl and whisk until they rise into a froth the consistency of shaving foam. From here sprinkle over a heaped tablespoon of sugar at a time, whisking well with each addition until you have a smooth, glossy meringue. You can increase the sugar to 2 tablespoons towards the end. In theory, the meringue should be stiff enough for you to hold the bowl upside down above your head. This is hearsay only.

Drop heaped tablespoons of the mixture onto the paper, leaving plenty of space between each meringue. If you like you can make them bigger than this to give just a handful of large blowsy meringues. Alternatively, if they are destined to be sandwiched together for tea, you can make them smaller – in which case reduce the cooking time accordingly.

Place the meringues in the oven and turn it down to 100°C fan oven/120°C electric oven. Cook for 2 hours; if you are using two trays, switch them around halfway through. The meringues by the end should be crisp on the outside and if you tap the bases they should sound hollow within. Remove and leave them to cool. They can be stored in an airtight container for 2 weeks.

Pam's gooey meringues

An old friend of my husband's family produces meringues of legendary fame that are crisp on the outside and toffeeish within, good enough to eat with coffee or tea without accompanying cream. Prepare your meringue mixture as above. Dollop heaped tablespoons onto trays lined with baking paper and bake for 2 – 2½ hours at 120°C fan oven/140°C electric oven.

chocolate Fold 1 heaped tablespoon of sifted cocoa powder into the finished meringue mixture. Dust over some more cocoa when serving them. Delicious served with butterscotch ice cream, chocolate sauce and toasted flaked almonds.

almond Scatter some flaked almonds over the meringues before baking them. Dust with icing sugar when you come to serve them. Good with vanilla custard and poached fruits such as rhubarb and plums.

hazelnut Scatter a few chopped hazelnuts over the meringues before baking them. Good served with caramelised apples and pears and with whipped cream.

pistachio A few chopped pistachios sprinkled over before baking creates an unusual meringue that is surprisingly adaptable. You can serve these with raspberries and blackberries, as well as with pears in red wine, chocolate and coffee creams, or with lemon and orange sorbet.

brown sugar Replace the white sugar with a light muscovado sugar and bake the meringues for 2 hours at 120°C fan oven/140°C electric oven.

chocolate meringues

MAKES 4 BIG MERINGUES

4 medium egg whites

200g icing sugar, sifted

1 teaspoon cocoa powder

KIT

Electric whisk

Baking tray

Baking paper

Large serving spoon

LITTLE EXTRAS

Vegetable oil for greasing

Preheat the oven to 120°C fan oven/140°C electric oven. Place the egg whites in a large bowl and whisk them until they rise into a froth the consistency of shaving foam using an electric whisk. Sprinkle over a heaped tablespoon of sugar at a time, whisking well with each addition until you have a stiff, glossy meringue. Sift the cocoa powder over the meringue and fold the mixture over about four times, rotating the bowl, until the meringue is streaked with the cocoa, without it actually being mixed in.

Dab a little of the mixture onto the corners of a baking tray and line it with baking paper. Lightly brush this with vegetable oil. Using a large serving spoon drop four large meringues onto the paper, leaving plenty of space between each one.

Place the meringues in the oven and turn it down to 100°C fan oven/120°C electric oven. Cook for 2 hours, by the end the meringues should be crisp on the outside and if you tap the bases they should sound hollow within. Remove and leave them to cool. They can be stored in an airtight container for several days.

raspberry meringues

MAKES 4 BIG MERINGUES

75g raspberry jam

4 medium egg whites

200g icing sugar, sifted

Gently warm the jam in a small saucepan to loosen it, then press it through a sieve. Make the meringue as above, then drizzle the jam over, and fold the meringue over about three times, turning the bowl to streak it. Cook as above. These meringues are quite delicate and should be stored in an airtight container and eaten within a day.

almond meringues

MAKES 4 BIG MERINGUES

4 medium egg whites

200g icing sugar, sifted

30g flaked almonds

Make and shape the meringues as above, then scatter over the almonds and bake.

boutique meringues

With the rise of the boutique patisserie meringues have done a quantum leap from something small and white, a way of using up the unwanted egg whites from an egg custard perhaps, to show-stopping creations streaked with chocolate or swirls of raspberries, scattered with pale green pistachios and flaked almonds. A big picture window with these overblown beauties piled high is promise of greater treats within.

FOR THE PAVLOVA

6 large egg whites, at room temperature

350g white caster sugar

1 tablespoon cornflour

1 teaspoon white wine vinegar

FOR THE TOPPING

800g red berries, hulled

40g icing sugar

2 tablespoons raspberry eau-de-vie or kirsch (optional)

a squeeze of lemon juice

300ml double cream

KIT

Electric whisk

Baking paper

Baking tray

Liquidiser

red berry pavlova

Snowy white meringue and blood-red strawberries look deliciously dramatic. This is something like a composed version of an Eton Mess, but somehow in pavlova form it does for decadent tea times as well as after dinner. Within your choice of red fruits, lean heavily towards raspberries, and, if you can get them, some loganberries and wild strawberries for a real treat.

Preheat the oven to 200°C fan oven/220°C electric oven. Using an electric whisk, whip the egg whites in a bowl until they form stiff peaks, then scatter over the caster sugar a few tablespoons at a time, whisking well with each addition. Gradually whisk in the cornflour and then the vinegar, by which time you should have a very stiff, glossy meringue.

Cut out a circle of baking paper about 23cm in diameter and place this on a baking tray. Spoon the mixture onto the circle, taking it almost to the edge of the paper, and swirl the top with the spoon. Place the pavlova in the oven, reduce the temperature to 110°C fan oven/130°C electric oven and bake for 1½ hours. Remove the pavlova from the oven and leave it to cool.

For the top, place one-third of the berries, the icing sugar, eau-de-vie (if using) and lemon juice in a liquidiser and blend to a purée. Pass through a sieve into a bowl, taste and add more sugar or lemon juice as necessary. Halve or quarter any large strawberries and mix the remaining fruit into the sauce.

Shortly before serving, carefully tip the pavlova onto its side, gently pull off the paper and place the meringue on a large serving plate or cake stand. Pour the cream into a bowl and whisk to fluffy peaks, taking care to stop before it turns buttery. Spoon the cream into the centre of the pavlova and then spoon the berries and sauce on top – don't worry if it trickles down the sides. Serve straight away.

chocolate pavlova

Sift over 25g of cocoa powder with the cornflour. For the top gently melt 100g milk chocolate, broken into pieces, in a bowl set over a pan with a little simmering water in it, then leave to cool to room temperature. Drizzle the chocolate over 300ml whipped cream and fold over a couple of times until it appears marbled. Spoon the cream into the centre of the pavlova and scatter over some chocolate curls or shavings. You can prepare it to this point up to an hour in advance, in which case chill it.

classic lemon meringue pie

MAKES 1 X 23CM PIE

FOR THE PASTRY

150g plain flour

50g golden caster sugar

90g unsalted butter, chilled and diced

1 medium egg, separated

a little whole milk

FOR THE FILLING

25g cornflour

finely grated zest and juice of 3 lemons

300g white caster sugar

40g unsalted butter, diced

2 medium egg yolks, and 3 egg whites

KIT

Food processor

Clingfilm

23cm tart tin with a removable base, 5cm deep

Foil

Baking beans or dried pulses

Electric whisk

LITTLE EXTRAS

Plain flour for rolling

This classic lemon meringue pie is a little bit more work than the retro one on page 138, with a real pastry base, but it does carry with it an air of sophistication, and the sharp jammy layer of lemon curd and mounds of cloudy marshmallow-like meringue are still present and correct.

Place the flour, sugar and butter in the bowl of a food processor and give it a quick burst at high speed to reduce it to a crumb-like consistency. Add the egg yolk and then, with the motor running, trickle in just enough milk for the dough to cling together into lumps. Transfer the pastry to a large bowl and bring it together into a ball using your hands. Wrap the pastry in clingfilm and chill for at least 1 hour or overnight.

Preheat the oven to 170°C fan oven/190°C electric oven. Lightly flour a worksurface and thinly roll out the pastry – it's quite delicate and you may find you have more success rolling it a second time. Use it to line a 23cm tart tin with a removable base, 5cm deep – I usually slide the base underneath the rolled pastry and then lift the whole thing into the case. Don't worry if you end up partly pressing it into the tin. Line the case with foil and baking beans (any dried pulses will do) and cook for 15 minutes. Remove the foil and beans and return to the oven for a further 10 minutes until the case is evenly gold. Leave it to cool.

Meanwhile, make the filling. Blend the cornflour with about one-third of 200ml water in a bowl. Bring the remaining water to the boil in a small saucepan with the lemon zest and 100g of the sugar, stirring until it dissolves. Pour in the cornflour solution and cook, stirring constantly, until the mixture is thick, transparent and silky. Remove from the heat and stir in the butter, then the lemon juice and finally the egg yolks. Smooth the lemon curd over the pastry base and chill for an hour until it firms up. This is to prevent the meringue from sinking in.

Reheat the oven to 170°C fan oven/190°C electric oven if you've turned it off. Whisk the four egg whites (i.e. including the white left over from the pastry) in a large bowl until stiff peaks form using an electric whisk. Whisk in the remaining 200g sugar, 2 tablespoons at a time, whisking well with each addition. Spoon the meringue evenly over the surface of the curd, taking it up to the crust, and bringing it up into peaks. Bake the pie for 30 minutes or until the surface of the meringue is lightly golden and crusty. Leave to cool and then remove the collar. Chill if not eating it straight away. The pie will keep well for a couple of days.

retro lemon meringue pie

MAKES 1 X 20CM PIE

225g digestive biscuits

125g unsalted butter, melted

zest and juice of 3 lemons

1 x 400g tin of condensed milk

4 large eggs, separated

125g white caster sugar

KIT

Plastic bag and rolling pin for biscuit crumbs

20cm non-stick cake tin with a removable base, 7cm deep

Electric whisk

LITTLE EXTRAS

Whipped cream, to serve

This is the easy one of the two, and the recipe I grew up with. This was one of my mum's great hits, all my friends and many relations loved it. It still takes me back every time I taste it.

Now this recipe does sometimes give out a thick sticky syrup, which I have never tried to resolve as I actually quite like it, and the crust does get increasingly louche as the hours pass. But it seems in character with the whole pie really, so don't fret if yours does the same.

Preheat the oven to 170°C fan oven/190°C electric oven. To make the pie crust, reduce the digestive biscuits to a crumb-like consistency either by placing them in a plastic bag and crushing them with a rolling pin, or in a food processor. Tip into a bowl, add the melted butter and toss until it is evenly distributed. Now press the mixture onto the sides and base of a 20cm non-stick cake tin with a removable base, at least 7cm deep.

Before juicing the lemons give them a good roll on the worksurface to release as much juice as possible. Combine the zest and juice with the condensed milk in a bowl, whisking until you have a smooth cream. Now whisk in the egg yolks and pour on top of the biscuit crust.

Whisk the egg whites in a large clean bowl until they form stiff peaks using an electric whisk. Gradually sprinkle over the sugar, whisking well with each addition until you have a glossy, stiff meringue. (NB: This mixture contains less sugar than you would normally use for a meringue, to account for the sweetness of the base.) Mound the meringue mixture on top of the lemon base, fluffing the surface with a spoon. Bake for 30–35 minutes by which time the surface of the meringue should be lightly golden, and the custard below it set. Remove from the oven, run a knife around the collar to loosen the sides and leave to cool. You can cover and chill the pie until required, bringing it back up to room temperature before serving. Serve with cream.

pineapple meringue pie

A thin chocolate pastry and pineapple custard, this is sister to a lemon meringue pie. In keeping it is suitably sticky, and may ooze a sweet syrup as you cut into it.

To make the pastry, place the flour, cocoa, sugar and butter in the bowl of a food processor and give it a quick burst at high speed to reduce it to a crumb-like consistency. Add the egg yolk and then, with the motor running, trickle in just enough milk for the dough to cling together into lumps. Transfer the pastry to a large bowl and bring it together into a ball using your hands. Wrap the pastry in clingfilm and chill for at least 1 hour or overnight.

Preheat the oven to 170°C fan oven/190°C electric oven. Lightly flour a worksurface and thinly roll out the pastry – it's quite delicate and you may find you have more success rolling it a second time. Use it to line a 23cm tart tin with a removable base, 5cm deep – I usually slide the base underneath the rolled pastry and then lift the whole thing into the case. Don't worry if you end up partly pressing it into the tin. Line the case with foil and baking beans (any dried pulses will do), securing the sides to the tin. Bake for 15 minutes, then remove the foil and beans and return to the oven for a further 10 minutes. Leave to cool.

Meanwhile, make the filling. Purée the pineapple in a liquidiser and press through a sieve. This should leave you with about 300ml of frothy juice; discard any more than this or make it up with water if it falls short. Blend the cornflour with about one-third of the juice in a bowl. Bring the remaining juice to the boil in a small saucepan with 50g of the sugar, stirring until it dissolves. Add the cornflour solution and cook, stirring constantly, until the mixture is thick, transparent and silky. Remove from the heat and stir in the butter, then the egg yolks and finally a squeeze of lemon juice. Smooth this on top of the pastry base and chill for an hour until it firms up.

Reheat the oven to 170°C fan oven/190°C electric oven if you've turned it off. Whisk the 4 egg whites (including the white left over from the pastry) in a large bowl until stiff peaks form using an electric whisk. Whisk in the remaining 200g sugar, 2 tablespoons at a time, whisking well with each addition. Sift two-thirds of the cocoa over the meringue and fold it over a couple of times to streak it. Spoon the meringue evenly over the surface of the curd, taking it up to the crust and swirling the surface.

Dust with a little more cocoa. Bake the pie for 30 minutes or until the surface of the meringue is lightly golden and crusty. Leave to cool and then remove the collar. Chill if not eating it straight away. The pie will keep well for a couple of days.

TIP
Chilling the pineapple custard before smoothing the meringue on top prevents it from sinking in.

MAKES 1 X 20CM PIE

FOR THE PASTRY

125g plain flour

25g cocoa powder, sifted

50g golden caster sugar

90g unsalted butter, chilled and diced

1 medium egg, separated

a little whole milk

FOR THE FILLING

½ large pineapple (skin and core removed), diced

25g cornflour

250g white caster sugar

40g unsalted butter, diced

2 medium egg yolks, and 3 egg whites

a squeeze of lemon juice

½ teaspoon cocoa powder

KIT

Food processor

Clingfilm

23cm tart tin with a removable base, 5cm deep

Foil

Baking beans or dried pulses

Liquidiser

Electric whisk

LITTLE EXTRAS

Plain flour for dusting

mont blanc meringue cake

SERVES 6–8

FOR THE MERINGUE

3 large egg whites

175g white caster sugar

2 tablespoons flaked almonds

FOR THE CHESTNUT PURÉE

1 x 435g tin of unsweetened chestnut purée

1 tablespoon dark rum or brandy

60g icing sugar

FOR THE COFFEE CHANTILLY

425ml whipping cream

2 tablespoons strong black coffee, cold

50g icing sugar, sifted

KIT

Baking paper

1–2 baking trays

Food processor

Electric whisk

LITTLE EXTRAS

Cocoa for dusting

This is quite the most decadent meringue cake I know, crisp layers of meringue sandwiched with coffee chantilly and chestnut purée.

Try to find an unsweetened purée – a number of French ones come loaded with sugar. You can make the meringues and the chestnut purée in advance, but whip the cream and assemble the cake as close to serving it as possible, no more than 30 minutes beforehand.

Preheat the oven to 125°C fan oven/145°C electric oven. Make the meringue mixture according to the master recipe on page 130. Cut out three 23cm circles of baking paper – you can do this by laying three pieces of paper on top of each other having traced a circle on the top sheet. Lay these out on one or two baking trays. Spread the meringue mixture over the circles using a metal spoon. Scatter the flaked almonds over one of the circles and bake them for 1½ hours until crisp right the way through.

To make the chestnut purée, place all the ingredients together with 2 tablespoons water in the bowl of a food processor and purée until silky smooth. To make the coffee chantilly, whip all the ingredients together in a bowl until the cream forms soft peaks.

To assemble the cake, peel off the paper from the bottom of each meringue layer. Reserving the almond layer for the top, place one of the remaining layers on a serving plate. Spread with half the chestnut purée and then half the cream. Place another meringue on top and spread with the remaining chestnut purée and cream.

Finish with the almond meringue on top, dust with cocoa and serve in thin slices.

ginger, almond and fig meringue cake

SERVES 6

110g whole blanched almonds, coarsely chopped

4 large egg whites

225g white caster sugar

150g dried figs, coarsely chopped

75g preserved ginger, coarsely chopped

KIT

Non-stick baking tray

Electric whisk

20cm non-stick cake tin with a removable base, 7cm deep

This deep mousse-like meringue cake with its crisp top is an old favourite of mine. It is endlessly adaptable and you can use almost any combination of dried fruits and nuts that takes your fancy.

Preheat the oven to 170°C fan oven/190°C electric oven. Lay the almonds on a non-stick baking tray and toast them for 10 minutes.

Whisk the egg whites in a bowl until they form stiff peaks using an electric whisk. Gradually whisk in the sugar, a tablespoon or two at a time, whisking well with each addition until you have a stiff, glossy meringue. Fold in the almonds, figs and ginger.

Spoon the mixture into a 20cm non-stick cake tin with a removable base, 7cm deep. Bake for 35 minutes until a skewer inserted into the centre comes out clean. Run a knife around the collar and leave the cake to cool. Ideally it should be eaten on the day it is made.

TIP

Like most meringues, this one comes to life with a cooling dollop of whipped cream, or vanilla or chocolate ice cream.

saratoga torte

MAKES 1 X 20CM TORTE

150g digestive biscuits

3 medium egg whites

150g white caster sugar

1 teaspoon vanilla extract

100g pecans or walnuts,
finely chopped

300ml whipping or double cream

KIT

Baking paper

2 plastic bags and a rolling pin
for biscuit crumbs

Electric whisk

Baking tray

LITTLE EXTRAS

Icing sugar for dusting (optional)

When I came across this in my mother's handwritten recipe book (a list of ingredients only, no method) I was overcome with curiosity and had to try it. Delving further I came across a small Australian forum on the subject, having first assumed it was from the US. As a pleasant diversion I found myself engrossed in cruising real estate on both sides of the world, which was somewhat detracting from the main point – which cracker? The Australian forum say 'Yatz' crackers, which are something like a 'Ritz', a lightly salted cocktail biscuit with a hint of sugar. While other takes suggested 'Graham' crackers, which are like our digestive biscuit, and the one that I found the most successful.

Preheat the oven to 160°C fan oven/180°C electric oven and cut out a circle of baking paper 20cm in diameter. Place the digestives inside two plastic bags, one inside the other, and crush them to fine nibs using a rolling pin. Whisk the egg whites in a large bowl until stiff using an electric whisk, then sprinkle over the sugar, a tablespoon at a time, whisking well with each addition until you have a stiff glossy meringue. Stir in the vanilla and fold in the crushed biscuits and three-quarters of the nuts.

Dab a little of the meringue onto the base of the paper to secure it in place on a baking tray and mound the meringue on top to within about 1cm of the rim – it will spread slightly as it cooks. Bake for 25 minutes until lightly golden and crisp on the outside and then leave to cool.

Assemble the torte within an hour or two of serving. Carefully peel off the baking paper and place the meringue on a serving plate. Whip the cream until it forms fluffy peaks using an electric whisk and pile on top of the torte to within a few centimetres of the rim. Scatter the reserved chopped nuts in the centre and, if you like, dust with icing sugar. Chill until required.

TIP
This has the lovely chewy texture of that rather sophisticated praline meringue favoured in France, so often used as a base for patisserie – but with the ease and charm of a retro pud.

sponge
cakes

FOR THE CAKE

225g self-raising flour

225g light muscovado sugar

½ teaspoon sea salt

225ml groundnut oil

4 medium eggs, separated

50ml strong black coffee, cold

50ml whole milk

75g nibbed or chopped walnuts

FOR THE COFFEE CREAM

125g mascarpone

2 teaspoons strong black coffee, cold

1 teaspoon golden syrup

1 teaspoon icing sugar, sifted

FOR THE ICING

100g icing sugar, sifted

1–2 tablespoons strong black coffee, cold

KIT

22cm/1.3 litre non-stick loaf tin

Electric whisk

Wire rack

Palette knife

LITTLE EXTRAS

Unsalted butter for greasing

6–8 walnut halves for decorating

Icing sugar for dusting

coffee walnut loaf

Sister of date and walnut, coffee is the other flavour that harmonises this aromatic but slightly bitter nut. You could also fill this with a buttercream rather than the mascarpone suggested, or simply ice the top if you are after something plainer.

Preheat the oven to 170°C fan oven/190°C electric oven and butter a 22cm/1.3 litre non-stick loaf tin. Sift the flour, sugar and salt into a large bowl. Add the oil, the egg yolks, coffee and milk and beat with a wooden spoon until smooth. Whisk the egg whites until stiff in a large bowl using an electric whisk and fold into the mixture in two goes.

Stir in the walnuts and transfer the mixture to the cake tin, smoothing the surface. Give the tin several sharp taps on the worksurface to bring up any large air bubbles. Bake for 50–55 minutes until a skewer inserted into the centre comes out clean. Leave the cake to cool in the tin for a few minutes, and then run a knife around the edge and turn out onto a wire rack. Place it the right way up and leave to cool. If not icing it straight away, wrap it in clingfilm.

To make the coffee cream, spoon the mascarpone into a bowl and beat in the coffee, then the syrup and icing sugar. Slit the cake in half, about two-thirds of the way up the sides to account for the risen dome. Spread the cream over the lower half and sandwich with the top.

To make the icing, blend the icing sugar and coffee together in a bowl and drizzle down the centre of the cake, smoothing it towards the sides using a palette knife. Don't worry about completely covering the surface or about it trickling down the sides. Decorate the surface with the walnut halves and then dust over a little icing sugar. Leave to set for 1 hour.

TIP

Growing up as a child, coffee cakes were reliant either on Camp Coffee or a slug of strong instant. Now that so many of us can make espressos at home, more so than ever since the advent of Nespresso machines (see page 20) and pods, we also have the potential for a really high quality coffee flavouring.

TIP

Invest in a heavy-duty mould for this, with a non-stick lining (see page 21).

marble
bundt cake

Bundt rings give this traditional cake a new lease of life, bigger and more spectacular than the ring cakes we used to make.

Preheat the oven to 170°C fan oven/190°C electric oven and butter and flour a 25cm non-stick bundt ring mould with a hole in the middle. Cream the butter and sugar together in a food processor. Beat in the eggs one at a time, then the milk – don't worry if the mixture appears curdled at this point, it will cream again in the next stage. Divide the mixture between two large bowls – you can weigh it to be accurate. Sift the flour and baking powder together. Add 150g flour to one bowl and fold in carefully with the vanilla, then fold in the chocolate chips. Fold the remaining 125g flour and the cocoa into the other bowl along with the rum.

Spoon the chocolate mixture into the base of the tin, creating a slight trough, and then smooth the vanilla on top. This arrangement of the two mixtures with the chocolate on the base should minimise the possibility of the cake sticking. Bake for about 50 minutes until risen and set and a skewer inserted into the centre comes out clean. Run a knife around the inner and outer edges and leave to cool in the tin for about 30 minutes. Place a cake stand or plate on top of the tin and invert it. Leave to cool completely.

To make the chocolate drizzle, gently melt the milk chocolate and butter in a bowl set over a pan with a little simmering water in it, stirring until smooth. Add the milk and whisk using a small whisk until amalgamated and glossy. Spoon the glaze over the crown of the cake, letting it trickle down the sides. If you like you can scatter some chocolate chips over the top and dust them with icing sugar. Leave to set for a couple of hours. The cake will be good for several days – it will be very crumbly to begin with, but will firm up on the second day.

MAKES 1 X 25CM BUNDT RING

FOR THE CAKE

300g unsalted butter, diced

300g golden caster sugar

6 medium eggs

150ml whole milk

275g self-raising flour

1 teaspoon baking powder

1 teaspoon vanilla extract

100g dark chocolate (approx. 70 per cent cocoa solids), coarsely chopped into chips, or chocolate chunks

25g cocoa powder, sifted

1 tablespoon dark rum

FOR THE DRIZZLE

100g milk chocolate, e.g. Lindt, broken into pieces

25g unsalted butter, diced

2 tablespoons milk

KIT

25cm non-stick bundt tin

Food processor

Small whisk

LITTLE EXTRAS

Unsalted butter for greasing

Plain flour for dusting

Dark or milk chocolate chips or chunks for decorating (optional)

Icing sugar for dusting (optional)

FOR THE SPONGE

3 medium eggs, separated

125g golden caster sugar

1 teaspoon vanilla extract

100g plain flour, sifted

50g unsalted butter, melted and cooled

FOR THE SYRUP

2 tablespoons golden syrup

2 teaspoons rosewater

FOR THE FILLING

200ml double cream

50g icing sugar

100g raspberries

100g strawberries, hulled and sliced

KIT

20cm non-stick cake tin with a removable base, 8cm deep

Electric whisk

Bread knife

LITTLE EXTRAS

Unsalted butter for greasing

Icing sugar for dusting

Raspberries and small whole strawberries, to serve (optional)

A handful of small edible red rose petals for decorating (optional)

summer berry genoise

A Genoise is a light whisked sponge cake with the addition of melted butter. It is one of the most elegant simple sponges and lends itself to layering, especially with fruit and cream. But if you leave out the butter, you will still have a lovely cake more in keeping with an English whisked sponge, which is supremely light, a great excuse to smother it with whipped cream, but buttercreams are equally lovely.

Preheat the oven to 150°C fan oven/170°C electric oven. Butter a 20cm non-stick cake tin with a removable base, 8cm deep.

Whisk the egg whites in a large bowl until stiff using an electric whisk. Sprinkle over half the sugar, a tablespoon at a time, whisking well with each addition until you have a smooth glossy meringue. In a separate bowl, whisk the egg yolks with the remaining sugar for several minutes using an electric whisk until really pale and mousse-like, then stir in the vanilla. Fold the egg yolk and sugar mixture into the egg whites in two goes, then fold in the flour in two batches and finally the cooled melted butter.

Pour the mixture into the tin, smooth the surface and give it several sharp taps on the worksurface to bring up any large air bubbles. Bake for 40 minutes until lightly golden and firm to the touch. Gently invert the tin onto a worksurface, without running a knife around the edge, and leave to cool.

To make the syrup, blend the golden syrup with the rosewater in a small bowl. The sponge should have levelled on cooling. Run a knife around the edge, remove the collar and split the cake in half using a bread knife. Place both halves on the worksurface, cut-side up, and brush the surface of each with all the syrup.

To make the filling, whip the cream with the icing sugar in a large bowl using an electric whisk until it forms soft, fluffy peaks. Scatter over the raspberries and fold through the cream using a fork to half crush them so that they streak it with crimson juices. Now fold in the sliced strawberries.

If you want to remove the cake from its base, then it is best to assemble it on the serving plate. Smooth the cream over the cake base, sandwich with the top half and liberally dust with icing sugar. Cover and chill until required. Scatter over some more berries and rose petals to serve, if you wish.

TIP
Both a Genoise and a whisked sponge can be flavoured
as wished, rosewater is optional, vanilla is ever apt,
but citrus zests too, or a soupspoon of dark rum.

original victoria sponge cake
page 156

FOR THE CAKE

225g unsalted butter, diced

225g golden caster sugar

4 medium eggs

225g self-raising flour

1 teaspoon baking powder

100ml whole milk

FOR THE FILLING

100g unsalted butter, softened

100g icing sugar, sifted

½ teaspoon vanilla extract

100g strawberry or raspberry jam

KIT

20cm non-stick cake tin with a removable base, 8cm deep

Electric whisk

Bread knife

LITTLE EXTRAS

Unsalted butter for greasing

Icing sugar for dusting

original victoria sponge cake

My own Proustian moment is of eating tea sprawled on the lawn at home, intermittently making daisy chains and helping my mother to shell peas. I remember how the top of the Victoria was always latticed with the bars of the wire cooling rack she upturned it on to cool, and how it would be filled with one of her homemade jams, which somehow always turned out on the runny side, making them just right for slathering in the centre.

Preheat the oven to 170°C fan oven/190°C electric oven and butter a 20cm non-stick cake tin with a removable base, 8cm deep. Using an electric whisk on high speed, first whisk the butter in a large bowl for 1–2 minutes until very pale and fluffy, then add the sugar and continue to whisk for another 1–2 minutes. Whisk in the eggs, one at a time, whisking well with each addition until the mixture is amalgamated, and then sift and whisk in the flour and baking powder in two goes, just lightly, then whisk in the milk. Transfer the mixture to the cake tin, smoothing the surface, and bake for 50–55 minutes or until a skewer inserted into the centre comes out clean. Run a knife around the collar of the cake and leave it to cool.

To make the buttercream filling, whisk the butter in a medium-sized bowl using an electric whisk for about 1 minute until very pale and fluffy, then gradually whisk in the icing sugar and whisk for 1 minute longer. Whisk in the vanilla extract. You can leave the cake on the base or remove it as you prefer. Split with a bread knife. Spread the lower half of the cake first with the buttercream and then with the jam. Sandwich with the top half and dust with icing sugar. Set aside in a cool place for a couple of hours for the buttercream to set.

TIP

There are various routes to filling the Victoria:

Jam – At its simplest, spread with 150g of really good jam – strawberry, raspberry, apricot or plum, some lovely jar you have made yourself or been given.

Jam and Cream –As for jam, but spread 180ml whipped double cream on top of the jam before sandwiching it. Take care not to overwhisk the cream, stopping just as it starts to form soft peaks.

Layers – I am inclined to bake a Victoria as one deep sponge and slit it, as I favour the delicate crumb over the crust. But you can just as easily bake it in two cake tins, at least 4cm deep, for 30–35 minutes, dividing the mixture between them and weighing them for accuracy.

victoria sponge cake
all-in-one method

Which road?

The difference between making a Victoria Sponge the old-fashioned way, where you laboriously whisk it at every stage, and the speedy modern all-in-one creaming method (i.e. place all the cake ingredients in the bowl of a food processor and cream together) might appear small, but it is one that I have agonised over, especially as this book sets out to simplify methods where possible, and this is such an iconic cake. I realised, at the end of writing, that I had been baking Victoria Sponges using the all-in-one method for so long I needed for my own curiosity to return and look at them side by side. So we had a Sunday afternoon bake-off. Was there any difference?

In appearance, there was no difference in height or in the crumb once they were filled and cut. In short, the finished cakes looked identical. But, when you split them to fill, the all-in-one had some larger holes towards the centre, while the whisked sponge appeared more evenly and closely textured. Perhaps not a surprise, as the two were quite different to look at before going into the tin. The whisked sponge was creamy, thick and amalgamated, the all-in-one was thinner.

And to eat? Well, no difference in flavour, but the whisked sponge was slightly the more tender of the two, albeit I felt imperceptibly so. But leaving nothing to chance, I sent the cakes into my son's Greek class the next day, for a 'spot the difference', without telling the boys anything about what this could be. They unanimously came back that the whisked sponge was much lighter, or 'more light and spongy' as they put it; the all-in-one was denser and chewier. Eight 14-year-old boys can't be wrong, so there you have it.

I still think there is a case for the all-in-one method, for those who have never baked before and might be phased by the idea of making a sponge the old-fashioned way; it is a liberating experience to turn out a cake that looks the part and is pretty good, unless you start comparing it. And in our time-challenged days, it is a method that will continue to find fans. Whether or not I will ever be able to get away with it again in my own house is a moot point.

madeira cake

MAKES 1 X 22CM LOAF

175g unsalted butter, diced

175g golden caster sugar

finely grated zest of 1 lemon

3 medium eggs

1 teaspoon vanilla extract

250g plain flour (see TIP)

2 heaped teaspoons baking powder

50ml whole milk

KIT

22cm/1.3 litre non-stick loaf tin

Food processor

Wire rack

LITTLE EXTRAS

Unsalted butter for greasing

Icing sugar for dusting (optional)

So often when I am craving a slice of cake, it is not the icing and the frills or the razzamatazz that is calling, but the inimitable comfort that comes with the magical savour of butter, flour, sugar and eggs when they are baked together. And it is hard to beat a plain Madeira when this is the mood.

A Madeira differs from a Victoria Sponge in that there is slightly less egg to butter and sugar, and more flour. It is usually flavoured with lemon zest and you can also include orange zest and vanilla, or all three. It has a very particular crust that derives from cooking it quite gently for a relatively long time. It is named after the wine, with which it was often served in the 19th century, and has yet to be bettered other than with a fine cup of tea.

Preheat the oven to 150°C fan oven/170°C electric oven and butter a 22cm/1.3 litre non-stick loaf tin. Cream the butter, sugar and lemon zest together in a food processor, then add the eggs one at a time and the vanilla. Don't worry if the mixture appears curdled at this point. Sift together the flour and baking powder, and process briefly, then incorporate the milk. Transfer the mixture to the prepared tin, smooth the surface and bake for 1¼ hours until risen and golden and a skewer inserted into the centre comes out clean. Run a knife around the edge of the cake and either leave it to cool in the tin, or leave it to cool for 10 minutes, then turn it out onto a wire rack to cool, standing it the right way up. Transfer to a plate to serve. A flourish of icing sugar finishes it off nicely if you are serving it plain.

TIP

For a slightly moister cake, you can substitute 50g ground almonds for the same quantity of flour.

For those jam-makers who always have more jam in the cupboard than they know what to do with, this also makes a good basic for slicing and lathering with jam between the layers, and also buttercream.

On day one it is very delicate and crumbly, but if you wrap it in clingfilm and leave it overnight it firms up nicely and the crust softens just slightly to that consistency we associate with a Madeira.

my favourite almond sponge with deep raspberry filling

MAKES 1 X 20CM CAKE

6 medium eggs, separated

250g golden caster sugar

350g ground almonds

1½ teaspoons baking powder, sifted

200g raspberry jam

200g fresh raspberries

KIT

2 x 20cm non-stick cake tins with removable bases, at least 4cm deep

Electric whisk

LITTLE EXTRAS

Unsalted butter for greasing

Icing sugar for dusting

Next to a Victoria Sponge, this is the cake I turn to most often. This version is filled with a thick bank of raspberry jam in the centre to mirror the Victoria on page 156, but it also makes a fab cake for layering or other treatments. It is beautifully moist despite its lack of butter or oil, and relies solely on almonds, with eggs and sugar – no flour.

Preheat the oven to 180°C fan oven/200°C electric oven and butter two 20cm non-stick cake tins with removable bases, at least 4cm deep. Whisk the egg whites in a large bowl until they are stiff using an electric whisk. In a separate large bowl, whisk the egg yolks and sugar together – the mixture should not be too pale and thick. Gently fold the whisked whites into the egg yolk and sugar mixture in three goes. Finally, fold in the ground almonds and baking powder, mixing until they are thoroughly and evenly incorporated.

Divide the cake mixture between the tins (you can weigh it for accuracy) and give them a couple of taps on the worksurface to bring up any large air bubbles. Bake for 30–35 minutes until the top feels springy to the touch and the sides are shrinking away from the tin. A skewer inserted into the centre should come out clean. Run a knife around the collar of each cake, remove and leave them to cool.

Work the jam in a bowl until it is smooth, then stir in the raspberries. Spread the surface of one of the sponges with the raspberry filling, then use it to sandwich with the other one. Dust with icing sugar.

TIP

The layer of raspberry jam in the centre of the cake is vastly improved by the addition of some fresh berries, creating a really deep filling with a hint of tartness to offset the sweetness. It does, however, need to be filled within a couple of hours of eating. So if you want a cake to pop into an airtight container that will be good for several days, store the two cakes unfilled and sandwich with the jam and fruit nearer the time.

cherry pound cake

This is the American equivalent of a French 'quatre-quarts', that contains equal quantities of butter, sugar, flour and eggs, and is as elegant as it is simple. This is set with little dried red cherries in homage to the love of this fruit across the Atlantic.

Preheat the oven to 170°C fan oven/190°C electric oven and butter a 22cm/1.3 litre non-stick loaf tin. Place the butter, sugar, flour, baking powder, eggs and vanilla in a food processor and cream together. Toss the dried cherries with a little flour to coat them and stir them into the cake mixture by hand.

Transfer the mixture to the prepared tin, smoothing the surface, and bake for 50 minutes or until risen and golden and a skewer inserted into the centre comes out clean. Run a knife around the edge of the cake, leave it to cool in the tin for 10 minutes and then turn it out the right way up onto a wire rack to cool completely.

Gently heat the two jellies together in a small saucepan to soften them and whisk until completely smooth. Pour over the top of the cake, covering the top and leaving it to run down the sides. Leave to set for at least an hour. You can decorate the cake further with some fresh cherries if you wish.

MAKES 1 X 22CM LOAF

200g unsalted butter, at room temperature, diced

200g golden caster sugar

200g plain flour, plus a little extra for coating the cherries

2 teaspoons baking powder

4 medium eggs

1 teaspoon vanilla extract

50g dried cherries

75g redcurrant jelly

75g bramble jelly

KIT

22cm/1.3 litre non-stick loaf tin

Food processor

Wire rack

LITTLE EXTRAS

Unsalted butter for greasing

Fresh cherries with stalks for decorating (optional)

lemon loaf

A good lemon cake is a teatime staple for which we need a really good reliable recipe up our sleeves. The inclusion here of some cream gives the texture a little added something.

Preheat the oven to 170°C fan oven/190°C electric oven. Brush the inside of a 22cm/1.3 litre non-stick loaf tin with melted butter and line the base with baking paper. Whisk the eggs, sugar and lemon zest together in a large bowl, then add the cream. Sift the flour and baking powder together and gradually fold in. Finally, stir in the melted butter and 2 tablespoons of the lemon juice. Pour the mixture into the cake tin and bake for 40–45 minutes until golden and risen and a skewer inserted into the centre comes out clean. Run a knife around the edge of the tin to loosen the cake, turn it onto a wire rack, remove the paper and then stand it the right way up. Sprinkle over the remaining tablespoon of lemon juice and leave it to cool.

Place the cake on an upturned plate. Whisk the ingredients for the icing together in a bowl. Coat the top of the cake using a spoon, allowing the icing to run down the sides. Transfer it to a small board or a plate. Leave the icing to set for an hour or two. This cake keeps well for a couple of days.

MAKES 1 X 22CM LOAF

FOR THE CAKE

3 medium eggs

150g golden caster sugar

finely grated zest of 1 lemon

75ml double cream

150g plain white flour

1 teaspoon baking powder

50g unsalted butter, melted and cooled

3 tablespoons lemon juice

FOR THE ICING

150g icing sugar

1–2 tablespoons lemon juice, sieved

KIT

22cm/1.3 litre non-stick loaf tin

Baking paper

Electric whisk

Wire rack

LITTLE EXTRAS

Melted butter for greasing

FOR THE CAKE

200ml Coca-Cola

125g unsalted butter, diced

¾ teaspoon bicarbonate of soda

250g self-raising flour, sifted

1 tablespoon cocoa powder, sifted

300g golden caster sugar

2 medium eggs

125ml buttermilk

1 teaspoon vanilla extract

FOR THE ICING

3 tablespoons Coca-Cola

50g unsalted butter, diced

1 tablespoon cocoa powder, sifted

225g icing sugar, sifted

KIT

25cm non-stick bundt tin

LITTLE EXTRAS

Unsalted butter for greasing

Plain flour for dusting

Chocolate sprinkles for decorating (optional)

coca-cola cake

This Southern cake is slightly chocolatey, and it is almost impossible to guess the Coca-Cola – although if you can lay your hands on some jellied Coca-Cola bottles to adorn it, they might just provide a clue.

Bring the coke to the boil with the butter. Once the butter has melted, stir in the bicarbonate of soda, which will fizz, and set aside for 20 minutes. Preheat the oven to 170°C fan oven/190°C electric oven and butter and flour a 25cm non-stick bundt tin.

Combine the flour, cocoa and sugar in a large bowl, add the cola mixture and whisk until smooth. In a separate bowl, whisk the eggs with the buttermilk and vanilla. Pour over the cake mixture and whisk everything to combine. Transfer the mixture to the prepared tin and give it a couple of taps on the worksurface to bring up any air bubbles. Bake for about 40 minutes until risen and set and a skewer inserted into the centre comes out clean. Run a knife around the inner and outer edges of the tin and set aside to cool for about 30 minutes. Place a cake stand or plate on top of the tin and invert it, and leave to cool completely.

To make the icing, place the cola, butter and cocoa in a small saucepan and bring to the boil, whisking until smooth. Stir in the icing sugar, which will set very quickly, and without delay trickle it over the crown of the ring, letting it drip down the sides – these don't need to be completely covered. Decorate with chocolate sprinkles if you wish. Set aside for about an hour for the icing to set.

TIP
Contrary to so much baking where we take every precaution to ensure the sponge doesn't stick, here the case is the opposite. By not buttering the tin, cooling the sponge upside down and not running a knife around the edge first, you will preserve its lightness and shape.

angel cake page 166

FOR THE CAKE

8 medium egg whites

¼ teaspoon sea salt

1 teaspoon cream of tartar

250g icing sugar, sifted

140g white plain flour, sifted

1 teaspoon vanilla extract

finely grated zest of 1 lemon

FOR THE TOPPING

3–4 tablespoons lemon juice, sieved

300g icing sugar, sifted

200g blueberries

KIT

Electric whisk

18cm angel cake tin (or 20cm cake tin with a removable base, 9cm deep)

Palette knife

LITTLE EXTRAS

Icing sugar for dusting

angel cake

Angel cake pans give satisfyingly deep slices of cake, and show an angel sponge at its best; eating it is something like sinking into a soft white cloud. This one has a heady hit of lemon, but this isn't essential, the vanilla on its own is fine. It's a great keeper, and one of the very few cakes that can claim zero fat, and hence cholesterol. It can be showered with strawberries or raspberries as well as blueberries, or simply served plain or decorated with sugar flowers.

Preheat the oven to 150°C fan oven/170°C electric oven. Whisk the egg whites in a large bowl with the salt and cream of tartar until stiff peaks form using an electric whisk. Whisk in the sugar, a couple of tablespoons at a time, sprinkling it over the egg whites and whisking for about 20 seconds with each addition. Fold the sifted flour into the meringue in three goes, and then the vanilla extract and lemon zest. Spoon the mixture into an 18cm unbuttered angel cake tin and bake for 40 minutes until golden and springy to the touch. Invert the pan and leave the cake to cool.

To make the icing, add just enough lemon juice to the icing sugar in a bowl to achieve a thick coating icing. Run a knife around the edge of the cake and lift it out on its base, then remove this. Place the sponge, base-side up, on a plate and smooth the icing over the top and sides using a palette knife. Leave to set for about 1 hour before transferring the cake to a stand or serving plate. To serve, scatter the blueberries over and around the cake – you can fill the hole if you wish – then dust with icing sugar.

TIP

Remove the lemon zest with a fine or spiked grater rather than a zester, as it is the essential oil that you are after.

For a Chocolate Angel Cake, omit the lemon zest and replace 30g of the flour with sifted cocoa powder.

FOR THE CAKE

150g golden caster sugar

80g plain flour, sifted

½ teaspoon baking powder, sifted

large pinch of sea salt

4 medium eggs, separated

3 tablespoons groundnut or vegetable oil

5 tablespoons smooth fresh orange juice, plus finely grated zest of 1 orange

½ teaspoon vanilla extract

¼ teaspoon cream of tartar

FOR THE AMERICAN FROSTING

2 medium eggs

100g golden caster sugar

225g unsalted butter, softened and diced

1 teaspoon vanilla extract

KIT

Electric whisk

20cm non-stick cake tin with a removable base, 6cm deep

LITTLE EXTRAS

Snowies, white chocolate buttons or jellied orange slices for decorating (optional)

orange chiffon cake

A really light fluffy sponge and altogether different from anything we have to offer in this country or in France. The frosting is mousse-like and silky, and hence the cake should be served lightly chilled – although like most oil-based sponges the texture doesn't change on cooling. You could also eat it plain dusted with icing sugar.

Preheat the oven to 150°C fan oven/170°C electric oven. Setting aside a tablespoon of the sugar, combine the remainder with the flour, baking powder and salt in a large bowl. In another bowl, whisk the egg yolks with the oil, orange juice and vanilla, then stir in the zest. In a separate large bowl, whisk the egg whites with the cream of tartar until stiff using an electric whisk, then sprinkle over the reserved sugar and whisk for about 20 seconds. Add the egg yolk mixture to the dry ingredients and loosely mix, then fold in the whites in two batches.

Transfer the mixture to an unbuttered 20cm non-stick cake tin with a removable base, at least 6cm deep, give it a couple of taps on the worksurface to bring up any bubbles and bake for 45–50 minutes until golden and firm when pressed. Invert the cake and leave it to cool for about an hour, during which time the surface will shrink slightly. This will prevent it from sinking, were it cooled the right way up.

To make the frosting, place the eggs and sugar in a bowl set over a pan with a little simmering water in it. Whisk for several minutes using an electric whisk, until you have a thick frothy mousse-like foam that leaves a trail on itself – a bit like zabaglione.

Remove from the heat and stand the bowl within a larger bowl with a little cold water in it. Continue to whisk for a couple of minutes until the foam and the sides of the bowl are at room temperature. Now whisk in the butter a few pieces at a time and continue whisking for several minutes to a light fluffy buttercream, adding the vanilla halfway through.

Run a knife around the collar of the tin and remove it. Shave a little off the rim of the cake to level it and then invert it onto a cake stand or serving plate – it will be very soft so it is best to decorate it in place. Remove the base, smooth the buttercream over the top and sides of the cake and swirl with a teaspoon – you may have a little leftover. If you like you can decorate the rim and centre with Snowies, white chocolate buttons or jellied orange slices. Chill for an hour and then cover with clingfilm. Remove from the fridge 15 minutes before serving.

TIP

For crispy caramelised orange slices to decorate the cake, line a large roasting dish with baking paper and scatter over a thin layer of white caster sugar. Halve and thinly slice 1–2 oranges into half moons, and lay these on top of the sugar discarding the ends. Scatter over another thin layer of sugar, then pour over a small cup of water to wet the sugar. Bake for 30 minutes at 150°C fan oven/170°C electric oven, then turn and bake for another 15–25 minutes until they start to caramelise and the water has nearly evaporated. Transfer to a wire rack to cool.

lemon polenta cake

MAKES 1 X 20CM CAKE

180g unsalted butter, softened and diced

200g golden caster sugar

3 large eggs

finely grated zest and juice of 2 lemons (see TIP)

130g ground almonds

2 teaspoons baking powder, sifted

100g fine polenta

KIT

20cm non-stick cake tin with a removable base, 5cm deep

Food processor

LITTLE EXTRAS

Unsalted butter for greasing

Icing sugar for dusting

Crème fraîche, to serve (optional)

Here polenta and ground almonds work together to create a lusciously moist cake. This makes a great pudding served with a compote of strawberries for instance.

Preheat the oven to 170°C fan oven/190°C electric oven and butter a 20cm non-stick cake tin with a removable base, at least 5cm deep. Place all the ingredients for the cake in the bowl of a food processor and cream together – the mixture should be smooth and creamy, but grainy. Transfer it to the prepared tin, smoothing the surface with a spoon, and bake for 35–40 minutes until golden, risen and firm, and shrinking from the sides. A skewer inserted into the centre should come out clean. Run a knife around the sides of the cake, remove the collar and leave to cool. Shortly before serving, dust the cake with icing sugar. You can either serve it on the base or remove it as you prefer. It will keep for several days in an airtight container. Delicious served with a spoonful of crème fraîche.

with strawberry compote

To make a strawberry compote, place 450g hulled and quartered strawberries in a bowl and drizzle over 4 tablespoons kirsch. Cover the bowl with clingfilm and chill for several hours or overnight, stirring at least once. Remove the strawberries from the fridge 30–60 minutes before serving. Gently warm 125g strawberry jam in a small saucepan until it begins to liquefy, then press it through a sieve into a bowl. Strain the strawberry marinating liquid into the bowl and stir to blend it with the jam. Pour the warm jammy liquid over the strawberries, stirring to coat. Serve with the cake.

TIP
You can also make this using 2 small oranges in place of the lemons.

raspberry hazelnut gateau

MAKES 1 X 20CM CAKE

FOR THE RICOTTA CREAM

3 tablespoons seedless raspberry jam

2 x 250g tubs of ricotta, drained of any liquid

200g raspberries

FOR THE SPONGE

225g shelled blanched hazelnuts

4 medium eggs, separated

150g golden caster sugar

1 teaspoon baking powder, sifted

KIT

Food processor

Clingflim

2 x 20cm non-stick cake tins with removable bases, 4cm deep

Coffee grinder

Electric whisk

LITTLE EXTRAS

Unsalted butter for greasing

Icing sugar for dusting

As lavish as the finest cream gateau, and virtually fat-free in comparison to other cakes. This keeps well for several days in the fridge; the ricotta seeps down into the sponge keeping it moist.

Whizz the jam in the bowl of a food processor until smooth, then add the ricotta and whizz again (if you do this by hand the ricotta will remain grainy). Transfer to a bowl, cover with clingfilm and chill for several hours, during which time it will firm up slightly.

Preheat the oven to 180°C fan oven/200°C electric oven and butter two 20cm non-stick cake tins with removable bases, 4cm deep. Grind the hazelnuts to a powder in a coffee grinder; you will need to do this in batches. Whisk the egg whites in a medium-sized bowl until stiff using an electric whisk. In a separate large bowl, whisk together the egg yolks and sugar until pale and creamy. Fold the egg whites into the egg and sugar mixture in three goes, then fold in the ground hazelnuts and baking powder.

Divide the cake mixture between the two prepared tins, smooth the surface and bake them for 20 minutes until the sponge has begun to shrink from the sides. Run a knife around the edge of the cakes and leave them to cool in the tin.

Remove the collars from the cakes – you can leave one on the base for ease of serving. Spread half the ricotta cream over the base layer to within 2cm of the edge and sandwich with the other half, gently pressing it down until the cream approaches the edge. Spread the remaining cream over the surface, this time taking it up to the edge, and arrange the raspberries on top. Dust them with icing sugar and set aside in a cool place. If you are keeping the cake longer than a few hours, cover, chill and bring it back up to room temperature for 30–60 minutes before serving.

75g plain flour (see TIP)

pinch of sea salt

5 medium eggs

120g golden caster sugar

200g raspberry jam

KIT

32 x 23cm non-stick Swiss roll tin

Baking paper

Electric whisk

Palette knife

Clean tea towel

LITTLE EXTRAS

Unsalted butter for greasing

Icing sugar for dusting

swiss roll

The allure of a snail-shell spiral of sponge filled with jam is age-old. You can either take advantage of its low-fat profile, or dish it up with some vanilla ice cream for a deconstructed Arctic Roll.

Preheat the oven to 180°C fan oven/200°C electric oven. Butter a 32 x 23cm non-stick Swiss roll tin, line the base with baking paper and butter this also. Sift the flour into a bowl and add the salt. Place the eggs and sugar in a large bowl and whisk for 8–10 minutes using an electric whisk, until the mixture is pale, very thick and several times the volume. You can also do this in a food processor using the whisking attachment, in which case reduce the time to about 5 minutes. Lightly fold in the flour in two goes.

Pour the mixture into the prepared tin and smooth it using a palette knife. Give the tin a couple of sharp taps on the worksurface to eliminate any large bubbles and bake the sponge for 10–12 minutes until set and springy to the touch. It will level a little a few minutes out of the oven.

Lay out a clean tea towel on your worksurface and liberally sift over a fine layer of icing sugar. Run a knife around the edge of the sponge and turn it out on top. Carefully roll it up with the tea towel, leaving the paper in place – start at the short end so you end up with a short fat roll and take care not to squash the cake. Leave to cool for 40–60 minutes, wrapped in the tea towel.

Carefully unroll the sponge with the short side facing you and peel off the baking paper. Work the jam in a bowl until it loosens and thinly spread it over the surface using a palette knife. Roll up the Swiss roll again, using the tea towel to help, and lift or tip onto a serving plate, seam downwards. Loosely cover and set aside. It will be good for a couple of days, although the sponge may darken with the jam juices after a day. Dust with icing sugar close to the time of eating.

TIP

You can also make this using rice flour if you are avoiding gluten.

The Swiss roll can also be filled with vanilla buttercream (see Vanilla Cupcakes on page 112) in place of the jam if preferred.

chocolate cakes

FOR THE CAKE

50g self-raising flour

50g light muscovado sugar

50ml groundnut or vegetable oil

1 medium egg, separated

1 tablespoon strong black coffee, cooled

1 tablespoon milk

FOR THE FILLING

300g dark chocolate (approx. 50 per cent cocoa solids), broken into pieces

4 medium eggs, separated

30g golden caster sugar

250g mascarpone

2 tablespoons kahlúa or strong black coffee

KIT

20cm non-stick cake tin with a removable base, at least 4cm deep

Electric whisk

LITTLE EXTRAS

Unsalted butter for greasing

Edible gold or silver decorations for decorating (optional)

tiramisu torte

The River Café's Chocolate Nemesis has over the years earned itself the accolade of being the ultimate chocolate cake, as well as hard to get right. And I confess I have never actually tried to make it, but enjoyed it on many occasions at the restaurant. So this is a tribute to its greatness, and was very much what I had in mind when I came up with this torte.

Preheat the oven to 170°C fan oven/190°C electric oven and butter a 20cm non-stick cake tin with a removable base, at least 4cm deep. Sift the flour and sugar into a medium-sized bowl. Add the oil, egg yolk, coffee and milk and beat with a wooden spoon until smooth. In a separate bowl, whisk the egg white until stiff using an electric whisk and fold into the cake mixture in two goes. Spoon into the prepared tin, covering the base evenly, and give the tin a couple of sharp taps on the worksurface to allow any bubbles to rise. Bake for 12–15 minutes until lightly golden, firm when pressed and shrinking from the sides. Leave to cool.

To make the filling, place the chocolate in a bowl set over a pan with a little simmering water in it and gently melt. Remove the bowl from the heat and leave the chocolate to cool to room temperature if necessary. Meanwhile, whisk the egg whites in a separate bowl until stiff using an electric whisk. In another bowl, whisk the egg yolks and sugar until very pale and mousse-like. Add the mascarpone to the melted chocolate and blend, then fold in the egg yolk mixture. Finally fold in the egg whites in two goes, followed by the kahlúa or coffee.

To assemble the torte, smooth the chocolate cream over the cake base and decorate with gold or silver decorations if you wish. Cover and chill for several hours or overnight. To serve, run a knife around the collar of the tin to remove it and cut into slices.

chocolate orange macaroon torte

Here a lovely chewy macaroon forms a base for the chocolate cream above. A drop of liqueur underlines the orange, but if you're planning to dish this up to children you could forego this.

Preheat the oven to 150°C fan oven/170°C electric oven and butter the base of a 20cm non-stick cake tin with a removable base, 5–6cm deep. Place the egg whites and light muscovado sugar in a medium-sized bowl and whisk for a couple of minutes using an electric whisk, until very pale and doubled in volume. Combine the ground almonds and icing sugar in a separate bowl and fold into the egg white mixture in two goes. Spoon into the prepared tin, levelling out the surface, and bake for 20 minutes until firm and lightly coloured. Leave to cool.

To make the mousse, gently melt the chocolate in a large-ish bowl set over a pan with a little simmering water in it. Set aside to cool to room temperature – you can transfer it to a cool bowl to speed up the process if you wish.

Place the eggs, sugar and orange zest in a separate bowl and whisk for a couple of minutes using an electric whisk until pale and doubled in volume. In another bowl, whisk the cream until it forms soft, fluffy peaks using clean beaters. Carefully fold the egg and sugar mixture into the cooled chocolate, followed by the cream in two goes. Stir in the liqueur. Smooth over the macaroon base and decorate the edge with chocolate shavings if you wish. Cover and chill for half a day or overnight until set. To serve, run a knife around the collar of the tin to remove it and cut into slices.

MAKES 1 X 20CM CAKE

FOR THE BASE

2 medium egg whites

50g light muscovado sugar

100g ground almonds

100g icing sugar, sifted

FOR THE CHOCOLATE MOUSSE

200g dark chocolate (approx. 50 per cent cocoa solids), broken into pieces

2 medium organic eggs

25g golden caster sugar

finely grated zest of 1 orange

250ml whipping cream

2 tablespoons Cointreau or Grand Marnier

KIT

20cm non-stick cake tin with a removable base, 5–6cm deep

Electric whisk

LITTLE EXTRAS

Unsalted butter for greasing

Chocolate shavings for decorating (optional)

FOR THE SPONGE

4 medium eggs, separated

150g golden caster sugar

30g cocoa powder, sifted

FOR THE MOUSSE

130g dark chocolate (approx. 70 per cent cocoa solids), broken into pieces

5 mediurm egg whites, plus 1 medium egg yolk

20g cocoa powder, sifted

20g golden caster sugar

FOR THE GLAZE

50g dark chocolate (approx. 70 per cent cocoa solids), broken into pieces

2 tablespoons groundnut or vegetable oil

125g icing sugar

KIT

2 x 20cm non-stick cake tins with removable bases, 5cm deep

Baking paper

Electric whisk

Magic whisk

LITTLE EXTRAS

Unsalted butter for greasing

free-from chocolate mousse cake

This lavish layered gateau makes a lovely special occasion cake or pud, with the advantage of being nut, flour and dairy free.

Preheat the oven to 170°C fan oven/190°C electric oven and butter and line the base of two 20cm non-stick cake tins with removable bases, 5cm deep, with baking paper. Whisk the egg whites for the sponge with the sugar in a large bowl for several minutes, using an electric whisk, until several times the original volume and almost white, and the mixture forms a trail on itself. Fold in the egg yolks and the cocoa powder. Divide the mixture between the tins, you can weigh it for accuracy, and smooth evenly over the base. Bake for 12 minutes until risen like a soufflé, immediately run a sharp knife around the skin on top (but not the sponge below it), and leave to cool when they will sink. The sides will remain a little higher than the centre, which won't show once the cake is assembled.

To make the mousse, gently melt the chocolate in a bowl set over a pan with a little simmering water in it. Whisk the egg yolk, cocoa powder and 3 tablespoons of boiling water together in a medium-sized bowl until smooth, a small magic whisk is best for this. In a large bowl, whisk the egg whites until stiff, then scatter over the sugar and continue whisking for about 20 seconds until very glossy. Fold the egg yolk mixture and a quarter of the egg whites into the melted chocolate at the same time, then gently fold in the remaining egg white in two goes.

Run a knife around the edge of each sponge and remove the collars. Peel the base paper off one of the sponges, replace it on the cake tin base, and clip the collar back into place. Pour the mousse into the tin, smoothing the surface. Invert the second sponge on top and peel off the paper. To make the glaze, gently melt the dark chocolate with the oil in a medium-sized bowl set over a small pan with a little simmering water in it. Whisk the icing sugar and 2 tablespoons of boiling water into the dark chocolate and smooth this over the top of the cake. Cover and chill for several hours or overnight until set.

TIP

To dress this up, you can marble it with white chocolate. Gently melt 25g white chocolate chips or chopped white chocolate at the same time as melting the dark for the glaze. Having spread this over, immediately dot with quarter teaspoons of the white chocolate, and swirl using the tip of a fine skewer.

dreamy rice-krispie cake

MAKES 1 X 20CM CAKE

FOR THE CAKE

150g dark chocolate (approx. 50 per cent cocoa solids), broken into pieces

120g unsalted butter, diced

3 medium eggs

30g refined spelt flour

80g golden caster sugar

FOR THE TOPPING

150g dark chocolate (approx. 50 per cent cocoa solids), broken into pieces

40g unsalted butter, diced

1 tablespoon golden syrup

50g Rice Krispies

KIT

20cm non-stick cake tin with a removable base, 4cm deep

LITTLE EXTRAS

Unsalted butter for greasing

100g raspberry jam

Icing sugar for dusting (optional)

I very literally dreamt this up, and am not sure whether this should serve as one of the lovelier parts of my job or as a cautionary tale of someone who never switches off. But frequently I will go to bed feeling troubled by some recipe that hasn't turned out quite as I wanted it to, and after a lot of tossing and turning, I wake up with the answer the next morning.

In this instance, the solution to the slightly troubled chocolate cake recipe I took to bed with me was a trifle outlandish in keeping with the best of dreams – the chocolate crispies of our childhood spread over a brownie base, with a drizzle of raspberry glaze.

Preheat the oven to 160°C fan oven/180°C electric oven and butter a 20cm non-stick cake tin with a removable base, at least 4cm deep. Melt the chocolate and butter for the cake in a large bowl set over a pan with a little simmering water in it. Beat in the eggs, one at a time, and continue beating until the mixture is very smooth and glossy. Finally fold in the flour and sugar. Pour the mixture into the cake tin and bake for 15 minutes until it feels firm in the centre when pressed and the edges have started to rise. Run a knife around the edge and leave to cool in the tin for at least 30 minutes.

To make the topping, gently melt the chocolate, butter and syrup in a large bowl set over a pan with a little simmering water in it, stirring until smooth. Stir in the Rice Krispies and spread over the surface of the cake, pressing down well especially at the edges.

For a little extra glam, gently heat the jam in a small saucepan until it loosens, press it through a sieve and drizzle over the top of the cake. Dust with icing sugar if wished and set aside in a cool place for several hours until set. The top of the cake will be at its crispiest the day it is made.

clarissa's chocolate mousse cake

MAKES 1 X 20CM CAKE

FOR THE CAKE

2 medium eggs, and 2 egg yolks

150g golden caster sugar

450ml whipping cream

1½ tablespoons strong black coffee

300g dark chocolate (approx. 70 per cent cocoa solids), broken into pieces

KIT

20cm non-stick cake tin with a removable base, 4cm deep

Food processor

LITTLE EXTRAS

Unsalted butter for greasing

40g toasted flaked almonds (optional)

Icing sugar or cocoa for dusting (optional)

Many years ago when I was running the little café at the back of Books for Cooks, Clarissa Dickson Wright who was living nearby used to come in every day and order this fabulously rich chocolate mousse cake that stood on the counter. While most of us would have been beaten halfway through the first slice, she used to manage a second. The best possible endorsement. The recipe has evolved over the years.

Preheat the oven to 120°C fan oven/140°C electric oven and butter a 20cm non-stick cake tin with a removable base, 4cm deep. Place the eggs, yolks and sugar in a food processor and whizz for 8 minutes until very pale, almost white, and at least doubled in volume. At the same time, bring the cream and coffee to the boil in a small non-stick saucepan. Place the chocolate in a bowl, pour over the hot cream and leave for a minute or two, then give it a stir and repeat until completely melted. Add the chocolate cream to the whisked egg and sugar mixture and whizz to blend.

Pour the mixture into the prepared tin and give it a couple of sharp taps on the worksurface to bring up any air bubbles. Bake for 30 minutes until the top is glossy and the mixture seems set if gently pressed. The cake should have shrunk away from the sides, but if it hasn't simply run a knife around the rim to release it. Set aside in the tin to cool. The cake is at its best eaten at room temperature on the day it is made while it is really creamy. Cover and chill if keeping any longer than this and remove from the fridge an hour before eating.

Shortly before serving, remove the collar and transfer the cake to a serving plate, leaving it on the base. Scatter over the almonds and dust with icing sugar or cocoa if you wish.

TIP

To toast flaked almonds, scatter them over the base of a baking dish and bake for 8–9 minutes at 180°C fan oven/200°C electric oven.

For a slightly racier take on this you can turn it into a Chocolate Chilli Mousse Cake. The idea here is that the chilli is a silent partner and comes through as an aftertaste. Leave out the coffee and add just a quarter of a teaspoon of chilli powder or cayenne pepper to the mixture to begin with, taste it several times, and then if you feel you want a more pronounced presence, add a little more.

FOR THE FILLING

75g cornflour

600ml whole milk

300g golden caster sugar

1 tablespoon golden syrup

100g cocoa powder, sifted

1 teaspoon vanilla extract

100g unsalted butter, diced

FOR THE CAKE

180g unsalted butter, diced

300g golden caster sugar

3 medium eggs

1 teaspoon vanilla extract

50g cocoa powder

1 teaspoon baking powder

1 teaspoon bicarbonate of soda

280g plain flour

200ml whole milk

KIT

Clingfilm

2 x 20cm non-stick cake
tins with removable bases,
5cm deep

Food processor

Bread knife

LITTLE EXTRAS

Unsalted butter for greasing

brooklyn
blackout cake

This is a wow of a chocolate cake and, quite unlike any other. You sandwich and smother it with lashings of thick chocolate custard, into which you then press a curtain of cake crumbs – the blackout. While the custard is traditionally made with water across the Atlantic, the molly-coddled Brit in me prefers milk.

First make the filling as this requires several hours cooling. Blend the cornflour with about one-third of the milk until smooth. Bring the remaining milk to the boil in a small non-stick saucepan with the sugar, syrup and cocoa, whisking until smooth. Add the cornflour solution and bring to the boil, stirring constantly until you have a rich, thick custard. Remove from the heat and add the vanilla and butter, stirring until it melts. In a perfect world it should be silky smooth; if it seems lumpy, simply give it a whizz in a food processor. Pour into a large bowl, cover the surface with clingfilm and set aside to cool. Give it a stir before using.

Preheat the oven to 170°C fan oven/190°C electric oven and butter two 20cm non-stick cake tins with removable bases, at least 5cm deep. Cream the butter and sugar together in a food processor, then incorporate the eggs one at a time. Add the vanilla, scraping down the sides of the bowl as necessary. Sift together the dry ingredients, and add them half at a time to the creamed mixture. Finally add the milk with the motor running. Divide the mixture between the cake tins, weighing them for accuracy, and smooth the surface of each. Bake for 30–40 minutes until a skewer inserted into the centre comes out clean. Run a knife around the collar of each cake and leave to cool.

When the cakes are cold, remove the collars and slit each one in half using a bread knife. To make the blackout, whizz one of the top halves to crumbs in a food processor – if possible, choose the one that has risen unevenly. To assemble the cake, spread one of the bases on the tin base with one quarter of the custard, taking it almost to the rim. Sandwich with the remaining cake base and spread another quarter of the remaining custard over the surface. Top with the remaining layer of cake and use the remaining custard to coat the top and sides. To finish, liberally coat the whole thing with the cake crumbs. Chill the cake for a couple of hours and then cover with clingfilm. Remove from the fridge 15–30 minutes before eating.

TIP

When coating the sides, imagine you are making a sandcastle. Take handfuls of the crumbs and gently press them against the side, leaving any loose ones to fall down. Discard the excess.

FOR THE CAKE
180g dark chocolate (approx. 70 per cent cocoa solids), broken into pieces

150g unsalted butter, softened

125g icing sugar, sifted

6 large eggs, separated

125g golden caster sugar

140g plain flour

FOR THE GLAZE
350g apricot jam

FOR THE ICING
300g icing sugar

225g dark chocolate (approx. 70 per cent cocoa solids), broken into pieces

KIT
23cm non-stick cake tin with a removable base, 7cm deep

Baking paper

Food processor

Electric whisk

Wire rack

Pastry brush

Jam thermometer

LITTLE EXTRAS
Unsalted butter for greasing

Plain flour for dusting

Lightly whipped cream, to serve (optional)

sachertorte

This is the little black dress and pearls among chocolate cakes, the original classy take that defined luxury at the time it was created in the early 19th century by Franz Sacher, chef to Metternich. This is about as close to the Hotel Sacher's original as you will get, a recipe printed in a favourite cookery book, *Festive Baking in Austria, Germany and Switzerland*, by Sarah Kelly.

Preheat the oven to 160°C fan oven/180°C electric oven and butter a 23cm non-stick cake tin with a removable base, 7cm deep. Line the bottom with baking paper, butter this as well and dust with flour.

Gently melt the chocolate in a bowl set over a pan with about 2cm of simmering water in it, stirring occasionally. Remove the bowl and allow the chocolate to cool.

Cream the butter and icing sugar together in a food processor until pale. Beat in the egg yolks one at a time, then add the chocolate. In a large bowl, whisk the egg whites with an electric whisk until soft peaks form. Beat in the caster sugar, one tablespoon at a time, beating for about 20 seconds with each addition. Keep beating for a couple of minutes until you have a glossy meringue. Transfer the chocolatey mixture to a bowl and carefully fold in the meringue. Sift the flour twice and fold it into the mixture.

Spoon the cake mixture into the prepared tin, smooth the surface and give it a sharp tap on the worksurface to bring up any air bubbles. Bake for about 50 minutes until the top is firm and it has begun to shrink from the sides of the tin, and a skewer inserted into the centre comes out clean. Turn the cake out onto a wire rack, remove the paper and leave it to cool the right way up.

Gently heat the jam in a small saucepan and press it through a sieve. If however it is quite loose, there is no need to heat it. Brush all over the top and sides of the cake. Set aside for a couple of hours for the jam to set.

To make the icing, bring the icing sugar, chocolate and 125ml water to the boil in a small saucepan, and heat to 105°C on a jam thermometer. Remove from the heat and stir continuously for one minute off the heat. To test the consistency, drop a small amount onto a cold plate – it should set on the surface quite quickly. If the icing doesn't set, keep stirring it for another minute.

Place the cake on a rack (I put a sheet of clingfilm underneath to help the clearing up). Pour the icing over the top of the cake to coat it, and around the edges so it runs down and coats the sides. Avoid spreading it with a knife to preserve its glossy surface. Store the cake in a cool place overnight before serving. It will keep well for up to five days in an airtight container. Serve with whipped cream if wished.

warm chocolate dip-in cake

MAKES 1 X 30CM OVAL CAKE

150g dark chocolate (approx. 70 per cent cocoa solids), broken into pieces

180g unsalted butter, softened

325g icing sugar

1 tablespoon golden syrup

1 teaspoon vanilla extract

8 medium egg whites

80g ground almonds

50g plain flour, sifted

KIT

30cm oval gratin or equivalent baking dish

Food processor

Electric whisk

LITTLE EXTRAS

Unsalted butter for greasing

Half rich chocolate cake and half old-fashioned pud. You can have your first pop at it about an hour out of the oven while it is still warm, in which case I would just hand everyone a spoon and let them dip in. And then when it is cold it takes on more the character of a brownie. I searched for many years for a recipe for a chocolate cake from my childhood, similar to one that my neighbour who was a great cook used to make. It had a shiny surface, paler than the soft fudgy cake within, rather like a delicate shell – and this is as close as I have ever found. I reckon the secret is to use just the egg whites, and not the yolks, so it ends up more like a macaroon.

Preheat the oven to 170°C fan oven/190°C electric oven and butter a shallow 30cm oval gratin or equivalent baking dish. Gently melt the chocolate in a bowl set over a pan with a little simmering water in it, and then if necessary leave it to cool to room temperature. Cream the butter and icing sugar together in a food processor, then add the chocolate, golden syrup and vanilla and process briefly to blend.

Transfer the mixture to a large bowl. Whisk the egg whites in another large bowl until nicely frothy, without being stiff, using an electric whisk. Fold these in two batches into the chocolate mixture, which will loosen up, and then fold in the almonds and the flour.

Transfer the mixture to the prepared dish and bake for about 45 minutes, by which time the top should have formed a glossy crust something like a macaroon and a skewer inserted into the centre should come out clean or with just a few moist crumbs clinging. Serve about an hour out of the oven while it's still just warm – the top will sink in the centre, and it will be risen and crusty around the outside.

FOR THE CAKE

75g cocoa powder

¾ teaspoon bicarbonate of soda

4 medium eggs

370g light muscovado sugar

180ml groundnut oil

200g self-raising flour, sifted

FOR THE ICING

250g milk chocolate, broken into pieces

40g unsalted butter, diced

60g cocoa powder, sifted

120ml whole milk

2 tablespoons runny honey

KIT

2 x 20cm non-stick cake tins with removable bases, 5cm deep

Baking paper

Electric whisk

LITTLE EXTRAS

Unsalted butter or oil for greasing

White writing icing for decorating (optional)

devil's food cake

The devil here is the glaze of icing, which remains gooey and sauce-like between the layers but sets to a delicate truffle on top of the cake.

Whisk the cocoa with 200ml boiling water, whisk in the bicarbonate of soda and leave to cool for about 20 minutes. Preheat the oven to 160°C fan oven/180°C electric oven. Butter or oil two 20cm non-stick cake tins with removable bases, at least 5cm deep, and line with baking paper.

Whisk together the eggs, sugar and oil in a large bowl until smooth, if necessary use an electric whisk, then stir in the flour, and then the cocoa solution. Pour two-thirds of the mixture into one tin and a third into the other tin, making sure the mixture is evenly spread – you can weigh them for accuracy. Give each tin a sharp tap on the worksurface to bring up any air bubbles and bake for 40–50 minutes respectively, or until risen and firm and a skewer inserted into the centre comes out clean. Run a knife around the edge of the cakes and leave to cool.

To make the icing, gently melt the chocolate and butter in a bowl set over a pan with a little simmering water in it, stirring until smooth. At the same time, combine the cocoa, milk and honey in a small saucepan and heat almost to boiling point, whisking until smooth. Pass the cocoa and milk mixture through a sieve into the bowl with the melted chocolate and whisk to a thick, glossy icing.

Remove the deeper cake from the base, peel off the paper and slit into two equal layers using a bread knife. Place the lower half on a cake stand or plate and spread with a quarter of the icing. Remove the paper from the smaller cake, lay this on top of the base and spread with another quarter of the icing. Lay the top layer in place and smooth the remaining icing over the top of the cake, taking it up to the sides and leaving it to drip down. Decorate with squiggles of white writing icing if you wish. Set aside for a couple of hours for the icing to set. The cake will keep well in a covered container for several days.

TIP

This fudgy icing sets quickly, so you need to use it straightaway, but if for any reason it starts to appear oily, simply rewhisk over the heat with a teaspoon or two of water.

FOR THE SPONGE

50g cocoa powder

pinch of fine sea salt

3 large eggs

75g light muscovado sugar

FOR THE FILLING

100g dark chocolate (approx. 50 per cent cocoa solids), broken into pieces

1 tablespoon dark muscovado sugar

1 teaspoon vanilla extract

200ml whipping cream

KIT

32 x 23cm non-stick Swiss roll tin

Baking paper

Electric whisk

Palette knife

Tea towel

LITTLE EXTRAS

Unsalted butter for greasing

Icing sugar for dusting

Chocolate curls for decorating (optional)

chocolate.
swiss roll

This is the fresh cream version of this retro classic. It is a great cake, which can also be wheeled out as a 'buche de Noel' come that time of year, with whatever stash of Christmas cake decorations and frills you choose.

Preheat the oven to 180°C fan oven/200°C electric oven. Butter a 32 x 23cm non-stick Swiss roll tin, line the base with baking paper and butter this also. Sift the cocoa into a bowl and add the salt. Place the eggs and muscovado sugar in a bowl and whisk for 8–10 minutes using an electric whisk, until the mixture is pale and mousse-like. You can also do this in a food processor using the whisking attachment, in which case reduce the time to about 5 minutes. Lightly fold in the cocoa in two goes. Pour the mixture into the prepared tin, smooth the surface using a palette knife and give the tin a couple of sharp taps on the worksurface to disperse any large air bubbles. Bake the sponge for 8–10 minutes until set and springy to the touch.

Lay out a clean tea towel on your worksurface and sift over a fine layer of icing sugar. Turn the cake out onto it and carefully roll it up with the tea towel, leaving the paper in place – start at the short end so you end up with a short fat roll. Set aside to cool for 40–60 minutes.

To make the filling, place the chocolate, sugar, vanilla and 2 tablespoons of the cream in a bowl and set over a pan with about 2cm of simmering water in it, stirring until smooth. Set aside to cool. Whip the remaining cream until soft peaks form and fold in the cooled melted chocolate.

To assemble the Swiss roll, carefully unroll the sponge and peel off the paper. Spread with the chocolate cream, roll it up again and tip onto a long serving plate, seam downwards. Dust over some icing sugar and decorate with chocolate curls if you wish. Chill, uncovered, for a couple of hours.

TIP
If you are making the Swiss roll in advance, bring it back up to room temperature for 30 minutes before eating. Dust it with icing sugar and decorate it at the last minute.

FOR THE CAKE

225g unsalted butter, diced

225g golden caster sugar

175g self-raising flour, sifted

50g cocoa powder, sifted

2 teaspoons baking powder, sifted

¼ teaspoon fine sea salt

1 teaspoon vanilla extract

4 medium eggs

100ml whole milk

FOR THE BUTTERCREAM

100g unsalted butter, softened

100g icing sugar, sifted

2 teaspoons cocoa powder, sifted

1 medium organic egg yolk

FOR THE ICING

100g milk chocolate, broken into pieces

15g unsalted butter

30g cocoa powder, sifted

50ml coffee (or water)

1 tablespoon golden syrup

KIT

20cm non-stick cake tin with a removable base, 9cm deep

Food processor

Electric whisk

Bread knife

LITTLE EXTRAS

Unsalted butter for greasing

classic tearoom chocolate victoria

This has to be one of my all-time favourite chocolate cakes, the one that greets you on the counter as you open the door of a West Country tearoom and the bell tinkles. It's very much cup-of-tea over dinner, which is its great appeal in an age when our chocolate cakes seem to get ever gooier.

Preheat the oven to 170°C fan oven/190°C electric oven and butter a 20cm non-stick cake tin with a removable base, 9cm deep. Place all the cake ingredients in the bowl of a food processor and cream together, for the whisked method see page 156. Transfer the mixture to the cake tin, smoothing the surface and bake for 45–55 minutes or until a skewer inserted into the centre comes out clean. Run a knife around the collar of the cake and leave it to cool completely.

To make the buttercream, blend the butter, icing sugar and cocoa together in a medium-sized bowl, then whisk with an electric whisk on high speed for a couple of minutes until really pale and fluffy. Add the egg yolk and whisk for a minute longer.

You can leave the cake on the base or remove it as you prefer. You may like to place it on a cake stand at this point. Slit with a bread knife, spread the buttercream over the lower half of the sponge and sandwich with the top half.

To make the icing, gently melt the chocolate and butter in a bowl set over a pan with a little simmering water in it, stirring until smooth. At the same time, combine the cocoa, coffee (or water) and golden syrup in a small saucepan and heat almost to boiling point, if necessary giving it a whisk until smooth. Add this to the melted chocolate and blend to a thick glossy icing. Smooth this over the top of the cake, taking it up to the sides, and leave it to drip down in whatever fashion it wants. The glaze needs to be prepared and used straightaway, if for any reason it starts to appear oily, simply whisk in a teaspoon of water until it returns to being glossy. Set aside to set for a couple of hours. The cake will keep well in a covered container for several days.

TIP

The art of a really fluffy buttercream is to whisk it for a good couple of minutes using an electric whisk until it is almost mousse-like. The addition of an egg yolk enriches it further but it isn't essential.

french and flourless

MAKES 1 X 20CM CAKE

FOR THE CAKE

250g unsalted butter, diced

250g dark chocolate (approx. 50 per cent cocoa solids), broken into pieces

6 medium eggs, separated

120g golden caster sugar

FOR THE GLAZE

100g dark chocolate (approx. 50 per cent cocoa solids), broken into pieces

3 tablespoons strong black coffee

KIT

20cm non-stick cake tin with a removable base, 7–9cm deep

Electric whisk

LITTLE EXTRAS

Unsalted butter for greasing

I included a recipe for this in *Gorgeous Cakes* and numerous friends have told me they have cooked it over the years. This updated recipe contains less sugar, but it is still rich – although that little bit less so.

It's pleasingly messy and rustic, a gooey crater surrounded by craggy mountainous sides, with a fine crispy top.

Preheat the oven to 160°C fan oven/180°C electric oven and butter a 20cm non-stick cake tin with a removable base, 7–9cm deep. Gently melt the butter and chocolate in a bowl set over a pan with a little simmering water in it, stirring occasionally. Meanwhile, whisk the egg yolks with half the sugar in a large bowl for several minutes until pale, thick and creamy. You can do this in a food processor and then transfer the mixture to a large bowl.

In a separate clean bowl, whisk the egg whites until stiff using an electric whisk. Gradually whisk in the remaining sugar in three goes, whisking for about 20 seconds with each addition so that you end up with a stiff glossy meringue.

Fold the melted chocolate mixture into the egg yolk and sugar mixture, and then carefully fold in the meringue in two goes. Pour the mixture into the prepared tin and give it a couple of taps on the worksurface to bring up any large bubbles. Bake for 1 hour until a skewer inserted into the centre comes out clean, or with just a few moist crumbs clinging. Run a knife around the edge and leave the cake to cool in the tin. It will sink in the centre, so you end up with a crater surrounded by chocolatey peaks – in an ideal world, the peaks should all be more less the same height, but should some happen to be much higher than others you can simply break or cut a little off to level them.

To make the glaze, melt the chocolate in a bowl set over a pan with a little simmering water in it. Whisk in the coffee until you have a smooth amalgamated glaze. Remove the cake collar, but leave it on the base of the tin. Transfer the cake to a plate or cake board and drizzle the icing over the crater and the surrounding peaked edges, allowing it to trickle down the sides. Set aside in a cool place overnight. The cake will keep well lightly covered or in a covered container for several days. It is also lovely eaten chilled.

FOR THE SPONGE

100g plain flour

pinch of fine sea salt

6 medium eggs

150g white caster sugar

FOR THE BUTTERCREAM

50g dark chocolate (70 per cent cocoa solids), broken into pieces

50g milk chocolate, broken into pieces

2 medium organic egg yolks

100g icing sugar

100g unsalted butter, softened and diced

FOR THE GLAZE

100g dark chocolate (approx. 70 per cent cocoa solids), broken into pieces

100g milk chocolate, broken into pieces

50g unsalted butter, diced

1–2 tablespoons strong black coffee

KIT

2 x 20cm non-stick cake tins with removable bases, 4cm deep

Electric whisk

Food processor

Palette knife

LITTLE EXTRAS

Unsalted butter for greasing

Chocolate scrolls (ideally milk) for decorating

blonde sponge cake with chocolate frills

A topsy-turvy chocolate cake, not quite the way round that we are accustomed to – a delicate pale yellow whisked sponge with chocolate buttercream and glaze. It's a good halfway house for those who want something chocolatey, but not too dense and fudgy.

Preheat the oven to 180°C fan oven/200°C electric oven. Butter two 20cm non-stick cake tins with removable bases, 4cm deep. Sift the flour into a bowl and add the salt. Place the eggs and sugar in a large bowl and whisk for about 6 minutes using an electric whisk, until the mixture is almost white and mousse-like. You can also do this in a food processor using the whisking attachment, in which case reduce the time to 3–4 minutes. Lightly fold in the flour in two goes. Divide the mixture between the prepared tins and give them a couple of sharp taps on the worksurface to eliminate any large bubbles. Bake for 12–14 minutes until the sponge is lightly golden, springy to the touch and shrinking from the sides. Remove from the oven, run a knife around the collars to loosen them and leave to cool in the tins, when they will contract and sink a little.

To make the buttercream, gently melt the two chocolates in a bowl set over a pan with a little simmering water in it. Spoon into a clean bowl and set aside to cool to room temperature. Meanwhile, place the egg yolks and icing sugar in a food processor and whizz for 3 minutes until pale and mousse-like. Now add the butter, a piece at a time, processing until it resembles a thick custard. Spoon the egg yolk mixture into the cooled melted chocolate and blend to a glossy butter icing.

Given the delicacy of the sponge, it is best to assemble it on the plate you want to serve it from. Remove the collars from the tins, loosen the two sponges using a palette knife and place one on a plate. Spread with the buttercream and sandwich with the second cake.

To make the chocolate glaze, place the two chocolates and butter in a bowl set over a pan with a little simmering water in it and whisk until smooth. Whisk in the coffee to give a thick, glossy icing and spread over the top and sides of the cake. Leave to cool to room temperature before decorating with chocolate scrolls. Set aside in a cool place for several hours for the icing to set properly. The cake should keep well in an airtight container for several days.

milk choc log
cabin log

MAKES 1 X 20CM LOG

FOR THE SPONGE

3 medium eggs

75g golden caster sugar

50g plain flour, sifted

pinch of fine sea salt

FOR THE FILLING

100g milk chocolate, broken into pieces

250g mascarpone

7–9 chocolate Flakes

KIT

32 x 23cm non-stick Swiss roll tin

Baking paper

Electric whisk

Palette knife

Food processor

Bread knife

LITTLE EXTRAS

Unsalted butter for greasing

Icing sugar for dusting

More timberyard than roulade, the top here is ranged with Flakes, with a creamy milk chocolate filling set between thin layers of sponge. Basically you make a thin sponge in a Swiss roll tin, which you then cut into strips and sandwich back together with a chocolate mascarpone cream. The whole thing is then decorated with chocolate Flakes.

Preheat the oven to 180°C fan oven/200°C electric oven. Butter a 32 x 23cm non-stick Swiss roll tin, line it with baking paper and butter this also. Place the eggs and sugar in a bowl and whisk for approximately 8 minutes using an electric whisk until the mixture is almost white and mousse-like. You can also do this in a food processor using the whisking attachment, in which case reduce the time to about 5 minutes. Lightly fold in the flour in two goes, and then the salt. Pour the mixture into the prepared tin, smooth the surface using a palette knife and give the tin a couple of sharp taps on the worksurface to bring up any large bubbles. Bake for 8–10 minutes until lightly golden and springy to the touch. Run a knife around the edge of the cake and leave it to cool.

To make the filling, gently melt the chocolate in a bowl set over a pan with a little simmering water in it. Remove from the heat and leave to cool to room temperature.

Place the mascarpone in the bowl of a food processor, add the cooled melted chocolate and whizz until smooth.

Turn the sponge out onto a board, peel off the paper and trim the edges using a bread knife. Cut it into three equal pieces across. Using a palette knife, spread one-third of the chocolate cream over each of the sponges and stack them up in three layers.

To decorate the cake, trim each Flake to the right length to lie across the cake – a serrated knife is best for this – and arrange over the surface of the cake, spacing them a little way apart. Dust the whole thing with icing sugar, cover loosely with clingfilm and chill the cake for an hour.

It will keep well overnight, in which case remove it from the fridge 15–30 minutes before serving.

FOR THE CAKE

225g ready-to-eat dried apricots

7cm cinnamon stick

finely grated zest and juice of
1 lemon

6 medium eggs

200g ground almonds

25g cocoa powder, sifted

200g golden caster sugar

1 teaspoon baking
powder, sifted

FOR THE CHOCOLATE CREAM

200g dark chocolate (approx.
50 per cent cocoa solids),
broken into pieces

200g soured cream

KIT

Food processor

20cm non-stick cake tin with a
removable base, 9cm deep

Palette knife

LITTLE EXTRAS

Unsalted butter for greasing

chocolate and apricot cake

If I had to pluck a favourite from the somewhat hearty school puds that used to get dished up, then a dried apricot crumble would come close to the top. Apricots acquire even greater depth when they're dried than when they're fresh, as well as a rich succulence. This cake reflects that, with its light soured cream and chocolate frosting.

Place the apricots, cinnamon stick, lemon zest and juice and 200ml water in a small saucepan. Bring to the boil and then simmer over a low heat for about 20 minutes or until the apricots are tender and have almost absorbed all the liquid. Watch carefully towards the end to make sure they don't catch. Remove the cinnamon stick and purée the apricots in a food processor. Transfer the purée to a bowl and leave to cool.

Preheat the oven to 170°C fan oven/190°C electric oven and butter a 20cm non-stick cake tin with a removable base, 9cm deep. Whisk the eggs in a large bowl, and then fold in the ground almonds, cocoa, sugar, baking powder and apricot purée.

Transfer the mixture to the prepared tin and smooth the surface. Bake for 50–55 minutes until a deep gold on top. A skewer inserted into the centre should come out with just a few moist crumbs clinging. Run a knife around the edge and leave it to cool in the tin.

To make the chocolate cream, gently melt the chocolate in a bowl set over a pan with a little simmering water in it. Remove from the heat and whisk in the soured cream.

Remove the cake collar and base and transfer the cake to a stand or serving plate. Smooth the chocolate cream over the cake using a palette knife and set aside in a cool place to set for a few hours. The cake should keep well in an airtight container in a cool place for several days.

CHAPTER EIGHT
cheesecakes

FOR THE PASTRY

85g plain flour, sifted

40g ground almonds

50g caster sugar

85g unsalted butter, melted

FOR THE FILLING

850g full-fat cream cheese

270g golden caster sugar

2 medium eggs, and 1 egg yolk

420ml whipping cream

50g plain flour, sifted

1½ teaspoons vanilla extract

freshly grated nutmeg

KIT

23cm non-stick cake tin with a removable base, 7cm deep

Food processor

Foil

LITTLE EXTRAS

Mixture of fresh berries, e.g. halved or small strawberries, raspberries, blueberries (optional)

Icing sugar for dusting (optional)

new york cheesecake

Many years ago, my husband's love of cheesecake rallied me into trying to produce something as delectable as the one he recalled from his childhood. I lost count of how many we went through before hitting on a formula that lived up to the hallowed memory – somehow either the crust was out of kilter, the curd not quite as he remembered it or the distribution of raisins just not right. But eventually we settled on this as 'the one'.

The filling is one for hot debate, and depends on how you like it. My preference is for a really creamy, loosely set curd over a drier one, and there is little to this other than a full-fat cream cheese cut with whipping cream and just a couple of eggs to hold it all together. But the final touch, and one that transports me back to the village bakery of my own childhood – to warm loaves of lardy cake and custard tarts – is a liberal grating of fresh nutmeg.

Preheat the oven to 150°C fan oven/170°C electric oven. Mix the ingredients for the pastry together in a bowl. Using your fingers, press the mixture onto the bottom of a 23cm non-stick cake tin with a removable base, 7cm deep. Bake for 20–25 minutes until pale gold, then set aside to cool.

Preheat the oven to 180°C fan oven/200°C electric oven. To make the filling, blend the cream cheese and sugar in a food processor. Add the eggs, extra yolk and cream and process briefly. Fold in the flour with the vanilla extract. Carefully pour the mixture into the tin and liberally dust the surface with freshly grated nutmeg. Bake in the oven for 1 hour until puffy around the edges and just set. It should wobble slightly if you move it from side to side. Leave the cheesecake to cool, and then run a knife around the collar and loosely cover the whole thing with foil (but not clingfilm). Chill overnight.

If wished, to serve, pile a mixture of berries in the centre of the cheesecake and dust with icing sugar. Accompany with extra berries.

TIP
Cheesecakes are one of the best keepers among cakes. A cheesecake needs to mature before you can eat it; there is no digging in straight away. Be sure to cover it with foil when chilling overnight to allow it to breathe; clingfilm will create a wet environment. Probably the best time to make it is during the afternoon so it will be ready for mid-morning coffee the next day.

As an alternative to fresh fruit you could include 100g raisins with the filling.

TIP
I like to flavour this with orange rather than lemon, which
I find too tart with the cheese, and the rosewater could just as
easily be an additional spoonful of orange juice should you wish.
As an alternative to rose petals, you could scatter over some
pomegranate seeds for decoration if you prefer.

german käsekuchen

This German-style cheesecake is made using quark rather than cream cheese, and with no additional cream it is much lighter than the norm, which is reflected in its crumbly texture.

To make the pastry, whizz the flour, sugar and butter together in a food processor to a fine crumb-like consistency, then add the egg and process briefly to bring the dough together in a ball. Pat into a flattened patty, wrap in clingfilm and chill for at least 1 hour.

Preheat the oven to 160°C fan oven/180°C electric oven. Knead the pastry on a lightly floured worksurface until it is pliable, then roll it out a few millimetres thick to fit the base and sides of a 20cm non-stick cake tin with a removable base, 8cm deep. Lay it in place, and then run a rolling pin across the top to tidy the sides. It's quite delicate pastry, so you may find you have to patch it; if it tears badly when you lift it into the tin, simply re-roll it and try again – it's generally easier second time around. Line the pastry case with foil, taking it over the top of the sides to secure them to the tin, and weight with baking beans or dried pulses. Bake for 15 minutes and then remove the foil and beans, using the back of a metal spoon to smooth the pastry sides. Return the pastry case to the oven for a further 15 minutes until very lightly coloured.

To make the filling, whizz all the ingredients, except the egg whites, in a food processor until smooth and creamy. Transfer the mixture to a large bowl. In a separate bowl, whisk the egg whites until stiff using an electric whisk, and then fold into the filling in two goes. Spoon the mixture into the pastry case, smoothing the surface – it should come to the top of the tin. Bake for 50 minutes until risen and puffy; the centre may seem slightly wobbly, which should leave it on the creamy side once it is chilled.

Set aside to cool completely in the tin, when it will level, and then loosely cover with foil and chill overnight. Like most baked cheesecakes this will keep well for a week, actually improving after several days.

To make the sauce, gently heat the redcurrant jelly, pomegranate juice and rosewater together in a small saucepan, whisking until smooth. Pour into a small bowl, cover and set aside to cool. To serve, cut the cheesecake into slices, drizzle over the sauce and scatter over a few rose petals if you wish.

MAKES 1 X 20CM CHEESECAKE

FOR THE PASTRY

250g plain flour

125g golden caster sugar

125g unsalted butter, chilled and diced

1 large egg

FOR THE FILLING

750g quark or curd cheese

125g golden caster sugar

100g unsalted butter, melted

3 large eggs, separated

1 heaped teaspoon cornflour

finely grated zest of 1 orange, plus 1 tablespoon juice

1 tablespoon rosewater

1 teaspoon vanilla extract

FOR THE SAUCE

200g redcurrant jelly

3 tablespoons pomegranate juice

1 tablespoon rosewater

KIT

Food processor

Clingfilm

20cm non-stick cake tin with a removable base, 8cm deep

Foil

Baking beans or dried pulses

Electric whisk

LITTLE EXTRAS

Plain flour for rolling

A handful of small edible red rose petals for decorating (optional)

magic lemon cheesecake

MAKES 1 X 20CM CHEESECAKE

200g digestive biscuits

100g unsalted butter, melted

300ml double cream

2 x 400g tins of condensed milk

finely grated zest and juice of
2 lemons

30g dulce de leche, e.g.
Nestlé Caramel

KIT

Food processor

2 plastic bags and a rolling pin
for the biscuit crumbs

23cm non-stick cake tin with a
removable base, 4cm deep

Skewer

A friend, Jo Higgo, told me about her 'magic' cheesecake that sounded too good to be true. No gelatine, no eggs and no baking – when the lemon juice combines with the cream and condensed milk it magically sets. So this one's a great standby.

Break the digestives into pieces, and whizz to crumbs in a food processor. Alternatively, you can place them in two plastic bags, one inside the other, and crush them using a rolling pin. Combine with the melted butter and press onto the base and sides of a 23cm non-stick cake tin with a removable base, 4cm deep. Pop into the freezer while you make the filling.

Combine the cream and condensed milk in a large bowl, fold in the lemon zest and gradually beat in the lemon juice using a large spoon, when the mixture will thicken. Spoon this over the base, smoothing the surface. The dulce de leche needs to be a thick trickling consistency, so if necessary blend it with a drop of water – about a teaspoon should do it. Spoon this in a spiral over the surface of the cheesecake and, using the tip of a metal skewer, marble it by tracing a figure-of-eight along the line.

Cover with clingfilm and chill for several hours, when it will set further. It keeps well for several days in the fridge.

retro lemon cheesecake

MAKES 1 X 20CM CHEESECAKE

FOR THE CRUST

50g unsalted butter

150g plain digestives

FOR THE FILLING

350g full-fat cream cheese

150g golden caster sugar

4 medium eggs

finely grated zest and juice of
2 lemons

1 teaspoon vanilla extract

300ml soured cream

KIT

2 plastic bags and a rolling pin
for the biscuit crumbs

20cm non-stick cake tin with a
removable base, 5cm deep

Food processor

This was one of my mother's party pieces, something I grew up with and have very fond memories of. An oldie but a goodie, digestives remain one of our best and easiest routes to a cheesecake base.

Preheat the oven to 180°C fan oven/200°C electric oven. Gently melt the butter in a small saucepan over a low heat. Place the digestives inside two plastic bags, one inside the other, and crush them to fine crumbs using a rolling pin. Tip them into the saucepan with the melted butter and stir to coat them. Transfer the mixture to a 20cm non-stick cake tin with a removable base, 5cm deep, and press down firmly using your fingers or the bottom of a tumbler.

Place all the ingredients for the filling, except the soured cream, in the bowl of a food processor and whizz until smooth. Carefully pour the mixture on top of the biscuit-crumb base – I like to use the back of the spoon as a chute to avoid disturbing the crumbs. Bake the cheesecake for 30 minutes until it is just set and slightly risen; it may also be starting to colour. Remove from the oven and allow it to settle for 5–10 minutes before smoothing the soured cream over the surface. Return to the oven for a further 10 minutes – it may still appear slightly shiny and liquid when you take it out of the oven, but it should firm up on cooling and chilling.

Leave the cheesecake to cool, then cover it with clingfilm and chill overnight. Serve chilled.

FOR THE CRUST

85g plain flour, sifted

40g fine polenta or cornmeal

50g golden caster sugar

85g unsalted butter, melted

FOR THE FILLING

550g low-fat cream cheese

150ml soured cream

180g golden caster sugar

3 medium eggs

a few drops of vanilla extract

½ teaspoon ground ginger

½ teaspoon ground cinnamon

1 heaped teaspoon black treacle

KIT

20cm non-stick cake tin with a removable base, 7cm deep

Food processor

Foil

LITTLE EXTRAS

Cocoa powder for dusting

indian cheesecake

This has a polenta biscuit base that gives it a lovely texture in contrast to the creamy curd and it couldn't be simpler, you just combine the ingredients and press them into the tin, as you might a digestive crust. The secret of the filling lies with the treacle, just a teaspoon of this powerful ingredient is enough to flavour the cream a gentle shade of butterscotch, which is highlighted with ginger and cinnamon too.

Preheat the oven to 150°C fan oven/170°C electric oven. Mix the ingredients for the crust together in a bowl. Using your fingers, press the mixture onto the bottom of a 20cm non-stick cake tin with a removable base, 7cm deep. Bake for 35 minutes until pale gold and allow to cool.

To prepare the filling, blend all the ingredients in a food processor until really smooth, scraping down the sides to make sure all the treacle is incorporated. Strain the mixture through a sieve on top of the crust and bake for 50 minutes. The very centre of the filling should quiver when gently shaken – it will set more firmly as it cools. Run a knife around the edge of the tin to prevent the filling cracking and leave to cool completely. Loosely cover with foil and chill overnight. Serve the cheesecake chilled, dusted with cocoa.

strawberry and clotted cream cheesecake

The alternative route to baked cheesecakes is to set them using gelatine. The results are altogether different – whereas a baked cheesecake has a grainy curd, here the filling is silkier, like a set mousse. Although the gelatine needs time to set, these cheesecakes don't need to mature in the same way as baked ones do.

These are great with summer fruits, strawberries especially. Some fresh ripe berries licked with runny jam spooned over the cheesecake is so very appealing. This one sings with that great summertime marriage of strawberries and clotted cream, with that little extra something of a few gingernuts thrown in.

Break up and whizz the gingernuts to crumbs in the bowl of a food processor. Gently melt the butter in a small saucepan over a low heat, tip in the crumbs and stir to coat them. Press into the base of a 20cm non-stick cake tin with a removable base, 7cm deep, to form the crust.

Place the gelatine strips in a small bowl, cover with cold water and soak for 5 minutes, then drain. Pour over a couple of tablespoons boiling water and stir to dissolve; if necessary, you can stand the bowl in a second bowl of boiling water.

Place the cream cheese and sugar in a small saucepan and heat gently, stirring constantly with a wooden spoon, until the mixture liquefies, and the sugar dissolves. Give the mixture a quick whisk to get rid of the lumps. Cool slightly, if necessary, to the same temperature as the gelatine solution. Beat the gelatine into the cream cheese mixture and stir in the vanilla extract. Transfer the mixture to a large bowl and if necessary cool slightly so it is lukewarm.

Add the clotted cream to the cooled cream cheese mixture and whisk together. Don't worry about the last few tiny little dots of cream. Pour the mixture over the crust, smoothing the surface with a spoon. Cover with clingfilm and chill for several hours, or overnight, until set.

To make the strawberry sauce, gently heat the jam in a small saucepan until it liquefies, then pass it through a sieve into a bowl. Stir in the lemon juice and leave to cool completely. Cover and set aside until ready to use.

Remove the cheesecake from the fridge about 15 minutes before serving to let the crust soften just a little. Stir the strawberries into the jam. Run a knife around the collar of the tin and remove it. Serve the cheesecake in slices with the strawberries and sauce spooned over.

SERVES 6–8

FOR THE CRUST

150g gingernuts

60g unsalted butter

FOR THE FILLING

4 gelatine leaves, e.g. Supercook, cut into broad strips

400g low-fat cream cheese

200g golden caster sugar

½ teaspoon vanilla extract

400g clotted cream

FOR THE SAUCE

200g strawberry jam

2 tablespoons lemon juice

400g strawberries, hulled and quartered, or sliced if large

KIT

Food processor

20cm non-stick cake tin, with a removable base, 7cm deep

SERVES 6

FOR THE CRUST

30g dark chocolate (50 per cent cocoa solids), broken
into pieces

75g unsalted butter, diced

80g plain flour, sifted

40g fine polenta or cornmeal

40g golden caster sugar

FOR THE FILLING

350g full-fat cream cheese

150g golden caster sugar

4 medium eggs

finely grated zest and juice of
2 limes

1 teaspoon vanilla extract

300g soured cream

KIT

20cm non-stick cake tin with a
removable base, 3cm deep

Food processor

Foil

LITTLE EXTRAS

Unsalted butter for greasing

Chocolate curls for decorating

Cocoa for dusting

chocolate lime cheesecake

The creative chocolatiers of this world have proved that chocolate goes pretty much with anything you care to marry it with, but we all have our favourites. I've always loved chocolate with lemon, and lime is just as successful. Here it's layered, chocolate top and bottom, with a bank of lime-sharp curd in between.

Preheat the oven to 180°C fan oven/200°C electric oven and butter a 20cm non-stick cake tin with a removable base, 3cm deep. Gently melt the chocolate and butter together in a bowl set over a small saucepan with a little simmering water in it. Stir in the remaining ingredients for the crust. Using your fingers, press the mixture onto the base of the prepared cake tin, taking care to seal the edge where the collar meets the base to prevent the cheesecake mixture leaking out. Bake for 15–20 minutes until starting to darken at the edges and then allow to cool.

Place all the ingredients for the filling, except the soured cream, in the bowl of a food processor and whizz until smooth. Pour the mixture through a sieve onto the base and level the surface. Bake the cheesecake for 25–30 minutes until just set and slightly risen; it may also be starting to colour. Remove from the oven and allow to settle for 4–5 minutes before smoothing the soured cream over the surface and returning to the oven for a further 10 minutes. Remove from the oven – it may still appear slightly shiny and liquid, but should firm up on cooling and chilling.

Set the cheesecake aside to cool and then cover it with foil and chill overnight. To serve, smother the surface with chocolate shavings and dust with cocoa.

TIP
If you can only find coarse polenta, simply give it a whizz in a coffee grinder.

TIP
For a little coulis to serve with
the cheesecake, place 200g
fresh or frozen redcurrants
(strung) and 100g caster sugar
in a small saucepan. Cover and
cook over a gentle heat for
10 minutes, then press
through a sieve into a bowl.
Cover the surface of the
purée with clingfilm and
leave to cool, then chill for
several hours or overnight.

MAKES 1 X 20CM TART

FOR THE PASTRY

200g plain flour

30g white caster sugar

100g unsalted butter, diced

1 medium egg yolk

FOR THE FILLING

9 medium eggs

200g white caster sugar

250g full-fat cream cheese

200ml sweet white wine

1 teaspoon vanilla extract

KIT

Food processor

Clingfilm

20cm non-stick cake tin with a removable base, 6cm deep

Foil

Baking beans or dried pulses

Baking tray

LITTLE EXTRAS

Plain flour for rolling

. summer
wine custard tart

This is halfway between a custard tart and a cheesecake, which is all very English, so you could dust the surface with nutmeg too should you desire.

To prepare the pastry, place the flour, sugar and butter in the bowl of a food processor, and reduce to a crumb-like consistency. Add the egg yolk and enough water to bring the dough together into a ball. Wrap in clingfilm and chill for at least 1 hour.

Preheat the oven to 180°C fan oven/200°C electric oven. Thinly roll out the pastry on a lightly floured worksurface and line the base and sides of a 20cm non-stick cake tin with a removable base, 6cm deep. Trim the edges, reserving the trimmings to patch any cracks once it is baked.

Line the pastry case with foil and baking beans (any dried pulses will do), securing the pastry sides firmly to the tin. Bake for 10 minutes until the pastry has set and then remove the foil and beans and bake for a further 10–15 minutes until lightly golden and fully baked. Allow it to cool for 10 minutes, and then patch any cracks that have appeared with the reserved pastry.

Turn the oven down to 130°C fan oven/150°C electric oven. Whizz the eggs and sugar in a food processor, then incorporate the cream cheese, wine and vanilla and continue processing until the mixture is completely smooth. Pour this mixture into the pastry shell, place it on a baking tray and bake for 1½–2 hours until it has set. It is important that the tart is removed from the oven as soon as it is set. Leave it to cool to room temperature and then trim the top of the pastry sides, leaving the collar of the tin in place. Cover loosely with foil and chill the cheesecake for several hours or overnight. Remove the cheesecake from the fridge 30 minutes before eating.

TIP

Sometimes when pre-baking a pastry case, small cracks can appear as the dough contracts. If you hang on to the pastry trimmings having rolled it out, these can be used to fill any offending crevices, which should prevent a custard filling from leaking below the pastry.

FOR THE PASTRY

40g unsalted butter, softened

40g white caster sugar

1 large egg yolk

100g plain flour, sifted

FOR THE ALMOND CREAM

100g amaretti biscuits

40g unsalted butter, diced

1 large egg

FOR THE FILLING

3 x 250g tubs of ricotta

175g white caster sugar

40g cornflour, sifted

4 medium organic eggs

2 teaspoons vanilla extract

150g fromage frais

KIT

Food processor

Clingfilm

20cm non-stick cake tin with a removable base, 7cm deep

Foil

LITTLE EXTRAS

Unsalted butter for greasing

Plain flour for rolling

ricotta cheesecake

This lovely light (or rather low-fat) cheesecake has a thin layer of almond sponge separating the pastry from the curd, which performs the double service of scenting it with almonds as well as shielding the pastry from any moisture in the filling, and thereby keeping it dry. It's fab eaten with a summery fruitcage style compote of raspberries, red and blackcurrants but, as ever, any summer berries will be good.

To make the pastry, cream the butter and sugar together until light and fluffy in a food processor. Beat in the egg yolk, and then add the flour. If necessary, add a couple of drops of water to bring the dough together. Wrap the pastry in clingfilm and chill for at least an hour.

Preheat the oven to 180°C fan oven/200°C electric oven. To make the almond cream, place the amaretti in a food processor and reduce to fine crumbs, almost a powder. Add the butter and blend with the amaretti to create a paste, then beat in the egg.

Butter the base of a 20cm non-stick cake tin with a removable base, 7cm deep. Roll out the pastry on a lightly floured surface to a round about 23cm in diameter and cut a circle to fit the base of the tin. Spread the almond cream over the pastry in the tin and bake in the oven for 20 minutes until golden and firm. Set aside to cool.

Reduce the oven temperature to 170°C fan oven/190°C electric oven. To make the filling, blend the ricotta, sugar and cornflour in a food processor for a couple of minutes until very creamy. Now add the eggs, one at a time, followed by the vanilla extract and fromage frais.

You are going to bake the cheesecake in a bain-marie, so to keep the base watertight you will need to wrap the outside of the tin tightly in foil so there are no gaps. Pour the filling over the base and smooth the surface. Place the tin in a roasting tray and fill it around the outside with 2cm hot, but not boiling, water. Bake the cheesecake for 1½ hours until the centre has set and the top is golden – it may still wobble slightly if moved from side to side, but it shouldn't have the appearance of being sloppy beneath the surface.

Once cooked, run a knife around the collar and remove it, keeping the cheesecake on the base. Set aside to cool completely. Cover with foil and chill for several hours or overnight, during which time it will set to the perfect consistency. Remove the cheesecake from the fridge about 20 minutes before eating.

salt caramel cheesecake

MAKES 1 X 20CM CHEESECAKE

FOR THE CRUST

150g HobNobs

50g unsalted butter

FOR THE FILLING

4 gelatine leaves, e.g. Supercook, cut into broad strips (or 1 sachet powdered gelatine, (see TIP)

1/3 teaspoon fine sea salt

400g low-fat cream cheese

250g dulce de leche, e.g. Nestlé Caramel

1 teaspoon black treacle

300ml double cream

KIT

Food processor

20cm non-stick cake tin with a removable base, 7cm deep

Electric whisk

LITTLE EXTRAS

Raspberries for decorating

Icing sugar for dusting (optional)

It's hard to get enough of this flavour, and this seems a logical extension of those French caramels – achieved with a little fine sea salt, dulce de leche and treacle. This is the cool, creamy kind of cheesecake, delicious served with some fresh raspberries.

Break up and whizz the HobNobs to crumbs in the bowl of a food processor. Gently melt the butter in a small saucepan over a low heat, tip in the crumbs and stir to coat them. Press into the base of a 20cm non-stick cake tin with a removable base, 7cm deep, to form the crust.

Place the gelatine in a medium-sized bowl, cover with cold water and leave to soak for 5 minutes. Drain off the water, pour over another couple of tablespoons of water, submerging them, add the salt and stand the bowl in a second bowl of boiling water. Stir for a few minutes until the gelatine dissolves.

Blend the cream cheese, the dulce de leche and the treacle in a large bowl using a wooden spoon until smooth, giving it a quick whisk if necessary. Blend 3 tablespoons of this with the gelatine solution, one spoonful at a time, and then add this back to the rest of the cream cheese mixture and blend until smooth.

In a separate bowl, whip the cream until it forms soft, fluffy peaks using an electric whisk. Fold into the cream cheese mixture in two goes, and then carefully pour the mixture over the crust, smoothing the surface with a spoon. Cover with clingfilm and chill for several hours or overnight until set.

Run a knife around the collar of the tin and remove it. Keeping the cheesecake on the base, transfer it to a serving plate and cut into slices. Decorate with the raspberries, dusting them with icing sugar if you wish.

TIP

Here HobNobs take up the role of digestives. They're butch and oaty and make excellent material for a biscuit crust.

If using powdered gelatine, sprinkle it onto about 3 tablespoons boiling water in a small bowl. Leave for 3–4 minutes and then stir to dissolve. If the gelatine has not completely dissolved, stand the bowl in another bowl of just-boiled water for a few minutes and stir again. Alternatively, set the bowl over a pan with a little simmering water in it.

FOR THE CRUST

180g shortbread biscuits

30g unsalted butter, melted

FOR THE FILLING

6 gelatine leaves, e.g.
Supercook, cut into broad strips
(or 1 sachet powdered gelatine),
see TIP page 219

600g low-fat cream cheese

200ml whipping cream

200g white caster sugar

2 tablespoons lemon juice

FOR THE TOPPING

1 gelatine leaf, cut into broad
strips (or ¼ sachet
powdered gelatine)

15g white caster sugar

4 passionfruit, halved

KIT

Food processor

20cm non-stick cake tin with
a removable base, at least
5cm deep

LITTLE EXTRAS

200g small strawberries, hulled
(optional)

Icing sugar for dusting (optional)

passionfruit cheesecake

This pretty-as-a-picture chilled cheesecake has a glassy, shimmering, jellied top, set with passionfruit seeds. I like to accompany it with some fresh strawberries, but you can serve it with any selection of berries – wild strawberries for a real treat.

Whizz the shortbread biscuits in a food processor to crumbs, add the melted butter and process again to blend. Press into the bottom of a 20cm non-stick cake tin with a removable base, at least 5cm deep, using the back of a spoon.

To make the filling, place the gelatine strips in a bowl, cover with cold water and soak for 5 minutes, then drain. Pour over 3 tablespoons boiling water and stir to dissolve.

Gently heat the cream cheese, cream, sugar and lemon juice in a medium-sized saucepan, stirring until the cheese liquefies, and then whisk until smooth – it should be warm but not boiling hot. Stir in the gelatine solution and combine thoroughly. Carefully pour the mixture over the cheesecake base. Cover and chill for several hours until set.

To make the topping, soak, drain and dissolve the gelatine as before. Add the sugar and stir to dissolve. Stir the passionfruit pulp, a tablespoon at a time, into the gelatine solution and make up if necessary to about 150ml with water. Pour the passionfruit topping over the surface of the cheesecake and chill for another few hours or overnight.

To serve, run a knife around the collar to remove it. If wished scatter some strawberries in the centre, with a few around the edge, and dust with icing sugar.

FOR THE CRUST

50g unsalted butter

150g digestive biscuits

FOR THE FILLING

6 gelatine leaves, e.g. Superccook, cut into wide strips (or 1 sachet powdered gelatine, see TIP page 219)

400g crème fraîche

100g white caster sugar

1 teaspoon vanilla extract

75g white chocolate, broken into pieces

400g ricotta

KIT

2 plastic bags and a rolling pin for the biscuit crumbs

20cm non-stick cake tin with a removable base, 9cm deep

Food processor

LITTLE EXTRAS

White chocolate shavings for decorating

white christmas cheesecake

An unctuously creamy white chocolate cheesecake that caters to our aspirations for a White Christmas, so pile it high with chocolate shavings to max the snowscape. This is very much a pud, and would be delicious served with a little fruit compote – a cranberry one for dramatics.

Gently melt the butter in a small saucepan over a low heat. Place the digestives inside two plastic bags, one inside the other, and crush them to fine crumbs using a rolling pin. Tip them into the saucepan with the melted butter and stir to coat them. Transfer to a 20cm non-stick cake tin with a removable base, 9cm deep, and press into the base using your fingers or the bottom of a tumbler, making sure there are no gaps around the edges. Set aside in the fridge while you do the next stage.

To make the filling, place the gelatine in a bowl, cover with cold water and soak for 5 minutes, then drain. Pour 3 tablespoons boiling water over the soaked gelatine and stir to dissolve. Place the crème fraîche in a small saucepan with the sugar and heat gently over a low heat, stirring constantly with a wooden spoon until the mixture liquefies and the sugar dissolves. Give the mixture a quick whisk to get rid of any lumps. It should be warm, roughly the same temperature as the gelatine solution. Stir the gelatine into the crème fraîche mixture, along with the vanilla extract. Transfer it to a bowl and leave to cool.

Gently melt the chocolate in a bowl set over a pan with a little simmering water in it. Place the ricotta in the bowl of a food processor and whizz until smooth. Add the melted chocolate and whizz again, then add the chilled cream mixture and process briefly until smooth. Pour this on top of the cheesecake base. Cover with clingfilm and chill overnight.

To serve, smother the surface with chocolate shavings and then run a knife around the collar to remove it. Leaving the cheesecake on the base, transfer it to a serving plate. Cover and chill until required.

CHAPTER NINE

fruitcakes and ginger cakes

napket's banana bread

MAKES 1 X 22CM LOAF

2 medium eggs

170g light brown sugar

80ml sunflower oil

80ml whole milk

3 small ripe bananas, peeled

170g plain flour

1 teaspoon bicarbonate of soda

60g walnuts, coarsely chopped

KIT

22cm/1.3 litre non-stick loaf tin

Baking paper

Electric whisk

Wire rack

LITTLE EXTRAS

Unsalted butter for greasing

Icing sugar for dusting (optional)

A really simple un-iced no-nonsense banana bread is one of the home baker's great staples, something to throw together for after-school teas or at the weekend. It is one of the most homely and unpretentious of cakes.

But a good one is an elusive thing, and I searched for years before I encountered my perfect banana bread. Sometimes finding myself in the environs of Regent Street I take refuge in a small café just off it called Napket, where they sell a banana bread to die for. They were kind enough to let me have this recipe, it is wonderfully moist but equally light, and the bananas are broken rather than mashed to a pulp, which leaves lovely big chunks of them in the cake.

Preheat the oven to 160°C fan oven/180°C electric oven. Butter a 22cm/1.3 litre non-stick loaf tin and line the base with baking paper. Whisk the eggs and sugar in a large bowl until pale and thick – you can use an electric whisk for this. Blend in the oil and the milk, then add the whole bananas and coarsely mash and break them up.

Sift and fold in the flour and bicarbonate of soda in two goes, and then fold in the walnuts.

Transfer the mixture to the prepared tin and bake for 60–70 minutes until golden and risen and a skewer inserted into the centre comes out clean. Run a knife around the edge of the cake and leave to stand for 10 minutes, then turn out onto a wire rack to cool, placing it the right way up. This keeps well for several days in an airtight container. You can give it a dusting of icing sugar before serving if you wish.

TIP

For a crunchy crystalline finish, scatter some demerara sugar over the top of the cake before baking.

MAKES 1 X 22CM LOAF

225g unsalted butter, diced

225g golden caster sugar

4 medium eggs, plus 1 egg yolk

90ml dark rum, Madeira or
vin Santo

1 teaspoon vanilla extract

200g currants

225g plain flour, sifted

1 teaspoon baking powder, sifted

35g flaked almonds

KIT

22cm/1.3 litre non-stick loaf tin

Food processor

Wire rack

LITTLE EXTRAS

Unsalted butter for greasing

Plain flour for dusting

Icing sugar for dusting

italian
currant cake

This fruitcake relies on currants, delicious little piquant bursts of flavour, set within a sponge scented with rum and vanilla. I would love to claim this as my own, having baked it on many occasions over the years, but the author is Carol Field, a San Franciscan, who specialises in artisan Italian breads and pastries.

Preheat the oven to 170°C fan oven/190°C electric oven and butter and flour a 22cm/1.3 litre non-stick loaf tin. Place the butter and sugar in the bowl of a food processor and cream for several minutes until very pale and fluffy. Add the eggs and the extra yolk, one at a time, scraping down the bowl if necessary. Incorporate the rum or whatever alcohol you are using and the vanilla, and continue to process for a couple of minutes. Transfer the mixture to a large bowl. Toss the currants with a little of the flour to coat them. Sift the remaining flour and baking powder over the cake mixture and gently fold in, then incorporate the currants. Transfer to the prepared tin, mounding it a little in the centre, and sprinkle the flaked almonds over the top.

Bake the cake for 60–65 minutes or until it is golden and risen and a skewer inserted into the centre comes out clean. Leave it to cool in the tin for several minutes, then run a knife around the edge and turn out onto a wire rack. Place it the right way up and leave to cool. Dust with icing sugar before serving.

TIP

Tossing the dried fruit with a little flour stops it from sinking to the bottom of the tin. If you like you can also soak the dried fruit in the rum overnight.

It may seem like a lot of almonds scattered over the top, but once the cake has risen they will spread out.

free-from pretty much everything cake

MAKES 1 X 20CM CAKE

200ml almond or groundnut oil

500ml apple juice

300g dates, pitted and chopped

350g raisins

200g sultanas

1 teaspoon bicarbonate of soda

300g ground almonds

1 teaspoon freshly grated
nutmeg

finely grated zest of 1 orange

100g chopped walnuts

KIT

20cm non-stick cake tin with a
removable base, 9cm deep

Baking paper

String

LITTLE EXTRAS

Unsalted butter or oil for
greasing

Icing sugar for dusting (optional)

For anyone suffering from multiple intolerances, this is the answer to pretty much every prayer – no wheat, no gluten, no dairy, no added sugar, and no eggs. It's every bit as luxurious as a traditional Christmas cake and can be wrapped in baking paper and fed small quantities of brandy or rum in the run-up. From there you can either marzipan and ice it, or my own preference would be a shower of icing sugar and to dish it up with a sliver of mature Cheddar or some creamy Stilton.

Pour the oil and apple juice into a medium-sized saucepan and stir in the dates, raisins and sultanas. Bring to the boil and simmer over a low heat for 5 minutes. Transfer the mixture to a large mixing bowl and stir in the bicarbonate of soda – the mixture will sizzle furiously. Set aside to cool for 10 minutes.

Meanwhile, preheat the oven to 140°C fan oven/160°C electric oven and butter or oil a 20cm non-stick cake tin with a removable base, 9cm deep. Line the bottom with baking paper and butter this also.

Fold the ground almonds, nutmeg and orange zest into the dried fruit mixture and then add the walnuts. Transfer the mixture to the cake tin, smoothing the surface.

Tear off a sheet of baking paper large enough to cover the surface of the cake and go about halfway down the sides of the tin. Cut out a small circle from the centre, about 2cm in diameter. Lay the paper over the top of the tin and tie it in place with string. Bake the cake for 3 hours, testing it with a skewer after about 2½ hours to be on the safe side – you can do this through the hole in the paper without removing it. Run a knife around the collar, remove it and leave the cake to cool on the base. It will be good to eat from the following day onwards. If you like you can give it a dusting of icing sugar before serving. It will keep well in a tin or covered container for several weeks.

TIP

For a classic Sticky Fruitcake, my favourite variation on this, replace the ingredients above as follows, adding the flour along with the ground almonds, and cooking for 2 ½ hours. There are no walnuts in this version: 300g unsalted butter, 500ml apple juice, 300g pitted and chopped dates, 350g raisins, 325g sultanas, 1 teaspoon bicarbonate of soda, 150g plain flour, sifted, 150g ground almonds, ½ teaspoon freshly grated nutmeg and the finely grated zest of 1 orange and 1 lemon.

200g unsalted butter, diced

200g demerara sugar

1 tablespoon treacle

4 medium eggs

300g chestnut flour

½ teaspoon ground cinnamon

1 teaspoon mixed spice

1½ teaspoons baking powder

4 tablespoons dark rum

300g raisins

200g sultanas

200g currants

100g glace cherries (undyed)

100g mixed peel

70–80g whole blanched almonds

KIT

20cm non-stick cake tin with a removable base, 9cm deep

Baking paper

Food processor

Foil

Pastry brush

LITTLE EXTRAS

Unsalted butter for greasing

150g apricot jam for glazing (optional)

chestnut dundee

Chestnut flour is rich and aromatic, and sticky by comparison to standard cake flour, which makes it perfect for fruitcakes that are that way inclined already. This dense fruited cake is based on a traditional Dundee, it's gorgeously squidgy and as ever a long-keeper.

Preheat the oven to 140°C fan oven/160°C electric oven. Butter a 20cm non-stick cake tin with a removable base, 9cm deep, and line the base and sides with baking paper. Also cut out a circle of baking paper for the top of the cake.

Cream the butter and sugar together in a food processor, then add the treacle, and the eggs one by one. Chestnut flour tends to be too sticky to sift, so just add this as it is to the cake mixture, but sift over the spices and the baking powder. Whizz briefly to blend, and then add the rum a tablespoon at a time.

Transfer the mixture to a large mixing bowl and fold in the dried fruit, cherries and mixed peel. Spoon the mixture into the prepared tin and smooth the surface using a spoon. Arrange the nuts in lines going out from the centre, spaced about 2cm apart at the outer edge, gently pressing the flat side into the cake mixture. This arrangement will make the cake easier to cut than simply scattering them over.

Cover the surface of the cake with the circle of baking paper and bake for 1 hour, then turn down the oven to 130°C fan oven/150°C electric oven and bake for a further 3 hours until a skewer comes out clean of cake mixture, or just with a few sticky crumbs clinging. Leave it to cool in the tin and then wrap it in foil or in a double thickness of baking paper and leave for 24 hours – although it can also be matured in the traditional fashion.

If you wish, you can also finish the cake with a glaze. Warm the jam in a small saucepan, press it through a sieve and lightly brush the top and sides of the cake. Leave to set for an hour.

TIP

You can also make this using plain flour, for a traditional Dundee, but in this case it benefits from maturing for 1–2 weeks, wrapped in a double thickness of baking paper. I would glaze it close to the time of cutting into it.

FOR THE CAKE

200ml groundnut or vegetable oil

250g golden caster sugar

3 medium eggs, separated

3 tablespoons whole milk

100g fresh pineapple

2 ripe bananas, peeled

300g plain flour

1 tablespoon baking powder

1 teaspoon ground cinnamon

75g sliced pecans

FOR THE FROSTING

180g unsalted butter, softened

150g icing sugar, sifted

450g full-fat cream cheese

1 teaspoon vanilla extract

KIT

2 x 20cm non-stick cake tins with removable bases, 5cm deep

Baking paper

Food processor

Electric whisk

LITTLE EXTRAS

Unsalted butter for greasing

Pecan halves for decorating

Icing sugar for dusting

hummingbird cake

This gorgeous cake belongs to the carrot cake family. This one is a marriage of pineapple, bananas and pecans – with the same thick bank of cream cheese frosting.

Preheat the oven to 170°C fan oven/190°C electric oven. Butter two 20cm non-stick cake tins with removable bases, at least 5cm deep. Line the base of each with baking paper and butter this too. Whisk the oil and caster sugar in a large bowl, then whisk in the egg yolks and milk. Whizz the pineapple flesh in a food processor to a coarse purée, then add the bananas and whizz again. Fold this into the sugar and oil mixture. Sift the flour and baking powder together and stir this into the mixture, then the cinnamon and pecans.

In a separate bowl, whisk the egg whites until stiff using an electric whisk. Fold them into the cake mixture in two goes, and then divide the mixture between the tins, weighing them for accuracy so you end up with two evenly deep cakes. Give the tins a couple of taps on the worksurface to bring up any large air bubbles and bake for 30–40 minutes until shrinking from the sides and a skewer inserted into the centre comes out clean. Run a knife around the edge of the cakes and leave them to cool.

To make the frosting, place the butter and icing sugar in the bowl of a food processor and cream together. Remove the butter icing to a large bowl, add the cream cheese a spoon at a time and blend until smooth with a wooden spoon. Finally, work in the vanilla extract. If you find the texture is still grainy, give it a quick whirl with an electric whisk – but not a food processor, which will liquefy the frosting.

Turn the cakes onto a board and remove the baking paper. Spread about a quarter of the frosting over the top of one of the cakes, sandwich with the other and use the remaining frosting to coat the top and sides. Decorate the top with pecans and dust these with icing sugar. Place in the fridge to set for about an hour.

If not serving straight away, cover with clingfilm and store in the fridge. Remove from the fridge about 30 minutes before eating.

FOR THE CAKE

110g light muscovado sugar

110g unsalted butter

150g golden syrup

70g runny honey

225g plain flour

½ teaspoon bicarbonate of soda

1 heaped teaspoon
ground ginger

2 medium eggs, beaten

2 tablespoons lager

FOR THE ICING

100g unsalted butter, softened

90g icing sugar, sifted

1 rounded teaspoon treacle

a squeeze of lemon juice

KIT

22cm/1.3 litre non-stick loaf tin

Skewer

Wire rack

Clingfilm (optional)

Electric whisk

LITTLE EXTRAS

Unsalted butter for greasing

.blonde
ginger cake

Not everyone goes for really dark ginger cakes, and this pale version has all the spicy charm we expect but remains light at heart.

Try to mature the cake for a couple of days before eating, which encourages the crust to soften and turn slightly sticky.

Preheat the oven to 160°C fan oven/180°C electric oven and butter a non-stick 22cm/1.3 litre loaf tin. Place the sugar, butter, syrup and honey in a small saucepan and gently heat until liquid and smooth, whisking if necessary. Sift the flour, bicarbonate of soda and ginger into a large bowl, add the melted ingredients and blend. Beat in the eggs and lager. Pour the mixture into the prepared tin and bake for 50–55 minutes until risen and a skewer inserted into the centre comes out clean.

Leave the cake to cool for 5–10 minutes, then run a knife around the edge, turn it out onto a wire rack and leave to cool the right way up. If maturing it, wrap it in clingfilm and store in an airtight container for a couple of days or up to a week before icing.

Place the upturned cake on a plate. To make the icing, whisk the butter in a bowl using an electric whisk for a couple of minutes until very pale and fluffy. Blend in the icing sugar and continue to whisk for another couple of minutes until really mousse-like and light, then whisk in the treacle and lemon juice. Spread the icing over the top of the cake, taking it up to the edge, and set aside in a cool place for a couple of hours to set. The cake will keep well in an airtight container in a cool place for several days.

TIP

Many ginger cakes benefit from maturing for a couple of days or more; it is as though they begin to sweat the treacle and honey, becoming stickier with time. Wrapping them in clingfilm encourages this further.

cherry crumble cake

A base of cake, a layer of juicy black cherries and a crumble above – three gorgeous textures that tumble around each other. This is a good recipe to dress up for pud with a dollop of crème fraîche.

Preheat the oven to 180°C fan oven/200°C electric oven and butter a 20cm non-stick cake tin with a removable base, 7cm deep. To make the cake, place the butter and sugar in the bowl of a food processor and cream until light and fluffy. Add the egg and then incorporate the milk, flour, baking powder and lemon zest. Spoon the mixture into the prepared tin.

To make the crumble, combine the flour, sugar, cinnamon and butter in the bowl of a food processor and whizz until the mixture just starts to form larger crumbs. Transfer it to a bowl and stir in the oats.

Scatter the cherries over the surface of the cake and pile the crumble mixture on top. Bake for 55–60 minutes or until a skewer inserted into the centre comes out clean. Run a knife around the edge of the cake and set aside to cool. Serve warm, about 30 minutes out of the oven, or at room temperature.

MAKES 1 X 20CM CAKE

FOR THE CAKE

100g unsalted butter, diced

100g golden caster sugar

1 medium egg

90ml whole milk

125g self-raising flour, sifted

½ teaspoon baking powder, sifted

finely grated zest of 1 lemon

250g black cherries, pitted

FOR THE CRUMBLE

90g plain flour

50g golden caster sugar

½ teaspoon ground cinnamon

90g unsalted butter, chilled and diced

25g porridge oats

KIT

20cm non-stick cake tin with a removable base, 7cm deep

Food processor

LITTLE EXTRAS

Unsalted butter for greasing

FOR THE CAKE

300g chopped dates

180ml smooth orange juice

1 heaped teaspoon bicarbonate of soda

3 medium eggs

180ml groundnut or sunflower oil

200g light muscovado sugar

225g plain flour

½ teaspoon ground cinnamon

75g walnuts, coarsely chopped

FOR THE BUTTERCREAM

200g unsalted butter, softened

250g icing sugar, sifted

1 teaspoon vanilla extract

1 tablespoon whole milk

KIT

2 x 20cm non-stick cake tins with removable bases, 4cm deep

Baking paper

Electric whisk

Clingfilm

LITTLE EXTRAS

Unsalted butter for greasing

Walnut halves for decorating

date and walnut cake

I think a date and walnut cake ranks as one of my favourites. This version is heart-stoppingly sticky, a little like a ginger cake, and it will get more so if you wrap it up for a day or two in clingfilm. But don't let that deter you from icing and eating it straight away. Like a banana or carrot cake, this will also stand on its own with a dusting of icing sugar, if you want something plain.

Place the dates in a small saucepan with the orange juice and bring to the boil, mashing them up. Stir in the bicarbonate of soda, which will fizz, and set aside for 20 minutes.

Preheat the oven to 170°C fan oven/190°C electric oven. Butter two 20cm non-stick cake tins with removable bases, at least 4cm deep, line with baking paper and butter this also. Whisk the eggs, oil and sugar together in a large bowl – you can use an electric whisk for this – and then stir in the date mixture. Sift and fold in the flour and cinnamon, and finally add the walnuts. Divide the mixture between the tins – you can weigh them for accuracy. Bake for 25–30 minutes until risen and a skewer inserted into the centre comes out clean. Run a knife around the edge of the cakes and leave them to cool for 10 minutes in the tins. Remove the hot cakes from their tins, lay top down on a sheet of clingfilm and wrap up, and set aside to cool completely – the clingfilm will encourage their stickiness.

Unwrap the sponges and remove the base paper. To make the buttercream, whisk the butter in a large bowl for a minute or two until very pale and creamy using an electric whisk. Gradually whisk in the icing sugar and continue to whisk for a couple of minutes until light and mousse-like. Finally whisk in the vanilla and the milk.

Spread just under half the buttercream over one of the sponges and sandwich with the second sponge. Spread the remaining buttercream over the top and sides and decorate with walnut halves around the rim. Chill for an hour until set and then cover with clingfilm. If chilling for longer, bring back to room temperature for 30–60 minutes before serving.

TIP

This sponge relies on bicarbonate of soda as a raising agent, and oil rather than butter – in type it is more like a carrot cake than a Victoria Sponge. I tend to choose Medjool dates over other varieties, as they are particularly luscious and aromatic.

good old-fashioned sticky ginger loaf

A home-baked version of our favourite shop-bought Jamaican ginger cake, no frills necessary, unless you fancy a lick of butter and a spoon of raspberry jam, which are ever delicious with ginger cakes.

Preheat the oven to 150°C fan oven/170°C electric oven and butter a 22cm/1.3 litre non-stick loaf tin. Gently heat the butter, treacle, syrup, milk and sugar together in a small saucepan until just melted, but without heating more than necessary, stirring frequently. Sift together the flour, ginger and bicarbonate of soda into a large bowl.

Add the treacle mixture and whisk until smooth, then whisk in the eggs. Pour the mixture into the tin and give it a couple of sharp taps on the worksurface to bring up any air bubbles. Bake for 50–60 minutes until risen and a skewer comes out clean.

Run a knife around the edge of the cake and leave to stand for 10 minutes. Turn out the warm cake onto a sheet of clingfilm, wrap it up and leave overnight when it will acquire that essential dense stickiness. Serve it on its own, or spread with unsalted butter or clotted cream and raspberry jam.

TIP

This cake needs maturing, but only overnight, so you won't have too long to wait before you can slice into it. The combination of treacle and golden syrup is responsible for that lovely, dark sticky finish that we prize so highly.

MAKES 1 X 22CM LOAF

125g unsalted butter, diced

115g treacle

115g golden syrup

150ml whole milk

50g light brown sugar

225g plain flour

1 teaspoon ground ginger

½ teaspoon bicarbonate of soda

2 medium eggs

KIT

22cm/1.3 litre non-stick loaf tin

Clingfilm

LITTLE EXTRAS

Unsalted butter for greasing

Unsalted butter or clotted cream, and raspberry jam, to serve (optional)

1.5kg Bramley apples, peeled, cored and sliced

finely grated zest of 1 lemon, and the juice of ½ lemon

75g demerara sugar

75g sultanas

3 cloves

1 teaspoon vanilla extract

120g unsalted butter

270g dry white breadcrumbs

75g ground almonds

120g golden granulated sugar

a few drops of almond extract

50g toasted flaked almonds

KIT

20cm non-stick cake tin with a removable base, at least 4cm deep

LITTLE EXTRAS

Icing sugar for dusting (optional)

danish apple cake

A gorgeous concoction of apple compote layered with crispy breadcrumbs, this cries out for a large spoonful of clotted cream or vanilla ice cream if you are prepared to sacrifice its healthy profile.

I first had it at the hands of a friend, the artist Val Archer, whose exquisitely detailed still-life oils so often illustrate cookery books, and she in turn gleaned it from the writer Karen Perry.

Place the apples in a large saucepan with the lemon zest and juice. Pour in just enough water to prevent the fruit from catching on the bottom, to a depth of a few millimetres. Add the demerara sugar, sultanas, cloves and vanilla and bring to the boil. Cover and cook over a low heat for 10–20 minutes until the apples are soft, stirring halfway through. If the apples are sitting in a lot of juice, simmer for a further few minutes to reduce it so you end up with a chunky purée. Discard the cloves.

You will need to fry the crumbs in two batches. Melt half the butter in a large frying pan over a medium heat, add half the breadcrumbs and half the ground almonds and fry until lightly golden, stirring almost constantly. Add half the sugar and continue frying until crisp. Transfer to a bowl and fry the remaining butter, breadcrumbs and almonds in the same way. Stir in a few drops of almond extract.

To assemble the cake, scatter a quarter of the breadcrumb mixture over the base of a 20cm non-stick cake tin with a removable base, at least 4cm deep. Spread a third of the apple purée on top and cover with two more layers of crumbs and apples, finishing with a topping of crumbs. Chill uncovered for 6–8 hours or overnight.

To serve the cake, run a knife around the collar and remove it. Scatter with the toasted almonds and dust with icing sugar if you wish. It is at its best chilled, eaten within a day while the crumbs on top are still crisp – although it will be tasty for several days afterwards.

TIP
You can ring the changes with this cake – pistachio or hazelnuts instead of walnuts, and dried cherries instead of raisins.

You can also replace the grated carrot with beetroot, which works a treat. To dye the icing a pale pink, simply add a few drops of the beetroot juice, squeezed through a garlic press.

As this cake relies on oil, rather than butter, it emerges from the fridge in exactly the same state as it goes in – unlike many butter-based sponges that never quite recover even if left at room temperature. This makes it a surprisingly good choice for the summer, even though its ingredients might suggest winter.

carrot cake

A truly fab cake with its zany blend of grated carrot, walnuts and spices. This makes a real statement with its deep layers, a large 23cm cake it serves eight at the very least.

Preheat the oven to 170°C fan oven/190°C electric oven. Butter two 23cm non-stick cake tins with removable bases, 7cm deep. Line the bases with baking paper and butter this too. Whisk the oil and caster sugar in a large bowl, then whisk in the egg yolks and milk. Fold in the carrot, nuts and raisins. Sift the flour and baking powder together and stir this into the mixture along with the spices.

In a separate bowl, whisk the egg whites until stiff peaks form using an electric whisk, and then fold them in two goes into the cake mixture. Divide the mixture between the tins, weighing them for accuracy, and smooth the surface of each. Bake for 30–35 minutes until shrinking from the sides and a skewer inserted into the centre comes out clean. Run a knife around the edge of the cakes and leave them to cool.

To make the frosting, whisk the butter in a large bowl using an electric whisk until very pale and fluffy. Add the icing sugar and vanilla and continue to whisk for a couple of minutes. Add the cream cheese and blend by hand using a wooden spoon until completely smooth.

Turn the cakes onto a board and remove the baking paper. Spread about a quarter of the frosting over the top of one of the cakes using a palette knife, sandwich with the other cake and use the remaining frosting to coat the top and sides. Swirl the top using a knife. Decorate with a spiral of chopped walnuts, taking them around the rim of the cake. Scatter a few slices of brazil nuts along the spiral and dust with icing sugar, finishing with a few 'pools' of ground cinnamon.

Place in the fridge to set for about an hour. If not serving straight away then cover with clingfilm. Remove from the fridge about 30 minutes before eating.

MAKES 1 X 23CM CAKE

FOR THE CAKE

240ml groundnut or vegetable oil

300g golden caster sugar

4 medium eggs, separated

4 tablespoons whole milk

180g finely grated raw carrot

120g walnuts, chopped quite finely

100g raisins

240g plain flour

2½ teaspoons baking powder

1 teaspoon ground ginger

1 teaspoon cinnamon

FOR THE FROSTING

200g unsalted butter, softened

175g icing sugar, sifted

1 teaspoon vanilla extract

525g full-fat cream cheese

KIT

2 x 23cm non-stick cake tins with removable bases, 7cm deep

Baking paper

Electric whisk

Palette knife

LITTLE EXTRAS

Unsalted butter for greasing

Finely chopped walnuts for decorating

Sliced brazils for decorating

Icing sugar for dusting

Ground cinnamon for dusting

FOR THE CAKE

200ml groundnut or vegetable oil

250g golden caster sugar

3 medium eggs, separated

3 tablespoons whole milk

100g finely grated raw carrot

2 ripe mashed bananas

300g plain flour

1 tablespoon baking powder

½ teaspoon ground ginger

½ teaspoon ground cinnamon

50g finely chopped walnuts

FOR THE FROSTING

180g unsalted butter, softened

150g icing sugar, sifted

450g low-fat cream cheese

1 teaspoon vanilla extract

KIT

2 x 20cm non-stick cake tins with removable bases, 5cm deep

Baking paper

Electric whisk

Food processor

LITTLE EXTRAS

Unsalted butter for greasing

passion cake

A passion cake is a gorgeous splash of an affair, a meeting between a carrot and a banana cake, with walnuts and spices.

Preheat the oven to 170°C fan oven/190°C electric oven. Butter two 20cm non-stick cake tins with removable bases, at least 5cm deep. Line the bases with baking paper and butter this too. Whisk the oil and caster sugar in a large bowl, then whisk in the egg yolks and milk. Fold in the carrot and banana. Sift the flour and baking powder together and stir this into the mixture along with the spices and walnuts.

In a separate bowl, whisk the egg whites until stiff using an electric whisk. Fold them in two goes into the cake mixture and divide between the tins, weighing them for accuracy so you end up with two evenly deep sponges. Bake for 30–40 minutes until shrinking from the sides and a skewer inserted into the centre comes out clean. Run a knife around the edge of the cakes and leave them to cool.

To make the frosting, place the butter and icing sugar in the bowl of a food processor and cream together. Remove the butter icing to a large bowl, add the cream cheese and blend until smooth with a wooden spoon. Finally, work in the vanilla extract.

Turn the cakes onto a board and remove the baking paper. Spread about a quarter of the frosting over the top of one of the cakes, sandwich with the other and use the remaining frosting to coat the top and sides. Place in the fridge to set for about an hour. If not serving straight away, cover with clingfilm and store in the fridge. Remove from the fridge about 30 minutes before eating.

TIP

I first cooked this as part of a celebratory organic lunch. It's a recipe you can really go to town with – using salty organic butter, unbleached white flour, golden caster sugar, or perhaps a thick and perfumed lime blossom honey. Dish it up with yellow untreated double cream.

upside-down apricot cake

Upside-down cakes come loaded with retro charm, like Tarte Tatin – perhaps the most famous topsy-turvy creation of this kind. The idea is that you lay the fruit in the bottom of the tin, so that when you turn it out you have a beautiful ready-decorated cake at hand.

To prepare the sauce, place the honey, 100ml water and lemon juice in a small saucepan and bring to the boil. Blend the potato flour or cornflour with 2 tablespoons of the liquid in a small dish and stir into the sauce. Simmer for a minute, stirring continuously, until the mixture thickens slightly, and then pour into a bowl and set aside to cool.

Preheat the oven to 180°C fan oven/200°C electric oven. To prepare the apricot base layer, cream together the light muscovado sugar and butter in a bowl.

Using your fingers, smear the mixture over the bottom of a 20cm non-stick cake tin with a removable base, 7cm deep. Place the apricots cut-side down on top of the butter and sugar mixture.

To make the cake, place the butter and sugar in the bowl of a food processor and cream together until light and fluffy. Add the eggs, one at a time, and then the lemon zest. Incorporate the milk, flour and baking powder. Spoon the mixture on top of the apricots, smoothing the surface. Bake for 45–50 minutes until the top is golden and a skewer inserted into the centre comes out clean.

Run a knife around the collar and leave the cake to cool for about 15 minutes. Place a plate on top of the cake tin and invert it, pressing the base down until the cake touches the plate. Now carefully run a knife between the base of the tin and the cake so the tin lifts off. The cake can be served hot or at room temperature, though it's best eaten the same day. Just before serving pour the honey sauce over, allowing it to trickle over the sides. Accompany with cream for those who want it.

MAKES 1 X 20CM CAKE

FOR THE SAUCE

100g set honey

juice of ½ lemon

1 teaspoon potato flour or cornflour

FOR THE APRICOTS

30g light muscovado sugar

30g lightly salted butter, softened

5 apricots, halved and stoned

FOR THE CAKE

150g lightly salted butter

150g golden caster sugar

2 medium eggs

finely grated zest of 1 lemon

125ml whole milk

200g plain flour, sifted

1½ teaspoons baking powder, sifted

KIT

20cm non-stick cake tin with a removable base, 7cm deep

Food processor

LITTLE EXTRAS

Double cream, to serve (optional)

molasses ginger squares

MAKES 9 SQUARES

150ml light beer (pale ale/lager)

175g molasses sugar

1 teaspoon bicarbonate of soda

200g self-raising flour

2 teaspoons ground ginger

3 large eggs

100g golden caster sugar

125ml groundnut or sunflower oil

2–3 knobs of stem ginger, finely sliced, and 3 tablespoons ginger syrup

KIT

23cm non-stick square brownie tin, 4cm deep

Clingfilm

LITTLE EXTRAS

Unsalted butter for greasing

This deep fluffy ginger cake is rich with molasses sugar, which is darker than the darkest muscovado – the ultimate brown sugar. The cake is rendered even stickier by a lick of stem ginger syrup after it is baked.

Place the beer and molasses sugar in a small saucepan and slowly bring to the boil, working out any lumps in the sugar with the back of a spoon. Remove from the heat, stir in the bicarbonate of soda and set aside to cool for about 30 minutes.

Preheat the oven to 160°C fan oven/180°C electric oven and butter a 23cm non-stick square brownie tin, 4cm deep. Sift the flour and ginger into a large bowl. Whisk together the eggs, caster sugar and oil in a medium-sized bowl, and then slowly add to the flour, stirring.

Add the beer mixture in two goes, gently mixing it in. Pour the cake mixture into the prepared tin and bake for 30–35 minutes until just firm to the touch – avoid opening the oven door during this time. Remove from the oven, run a knife around the edge of the cake and drizzle over the syrup using the back of a spoon to evenly coat the surface. Decorate with slivers of stem ginger. Cover with clingfilm and set aside to cool. Like other ginger cakes, this gets stickier overnight.

4 eating apples (approx. 500g), peeled, quartered and cored

90g unsalted butter

1 cinnamon stick

4 medium eggs

250g golden caster sugar

4 tablespoons sunflower oil

280g plain flour

2 heaped teaspoons baking powder

finely grated zest of 1 lemon

2 tablespoons Calvados or dark rum

200g apricot jam

KIT

23cm non-stick cake tin with a removable base, 7cm deep

Electric whisk

Pastry brush

LITTLE EXTRAS

Unsalted butter for greasing

french apple cake

This is comparatively light and low in fat. I would suggest serving it with a small bowl of rich yogurt or an apple compote.

Preheat the oven to 170°C fan oven/190°C electric oven. Butter a 23cm non-stick cake tin with a removable base, 7cm deep. Reserve four quarters of apple (i.e. one apple) for the top, and dice the remainder. Melt 30g of the butter in a large non-stick frying pan over a gentle heat, add the diced apple and cinnamon stick and fry for about 5 minutes until translucent but not coloured, stirring frequently. Transfer to a bowl or plate, discarding the cinnamon stick.

Whisk the eggs and sugar together in a large bowl using an electric whisk for 2 minutes until pale, thick and doubled in volume. Meanwhile, melt the remaining butter in a small saucepan. Fold the butter and oil into the egg mixture, and then sift and fold in the flour and baking powder. Finally add the lemon zest and Calvados or rum.

Carefully fold the cooked apple into the cake mixture and transfer to the buttered tin. Finely slice the reserved apple quarters lengthways and arrange in about three rows around the top, starting 2cm in from the edge. Bake for 50–60 minutes until risen and firm and a skewer inserted into the centre comes out clean. Run a knife around the edge and leave to cool.

Gently heat the jam until it liquefies, press it through a sieve and brush over the top and sides of the cake. Leave to set.

TIP

Apple cakes are rarely good keepers. Here the apple in the cake is fried in butter, which seals it, so the problem of the fruit juices leaking into the cake is reduced. You could also arrange the apple slices for the top in rows going out from the centre, to make it easier to cut into.

apple and olive oil cake

Beautifully moist, helped along by the olive oil which has a lovely affiliation with the apple. As with the cake before, one of the secrets is to fry the fruit first, which seals in the juices and stops them from seeping into the sponge. With its layer of vanilla mascarpone, this one is up for pud as well as tea.

Preheat the oven to 170°C fan oven/190°C electric oven. Brush two 23cm non-stick cake tins with removable bases, at least 4cm deep, with olive oil. Reserving four quarters of apple (i.e. one apple), dice the remainder. Heat 2 tablespoons oil in a large non-stick frying pan over a gentle heat, and fry the diced apple with the cinnamon stick for about 5 minutes until translucent but not coloured, stirring frequently. Transfer this to a bowl or plate, discarding the cinnamon stick.

Whisk the eggs and sugar together in a large bowl using an electric whisk for 2 minutes until pale, thick and doubled in volume. Fold in 120ml olive oil, and then sift and fold in the flour and baking powder. Finally add the lemon zest.

Fold the cooked apple into the cake mixture and divide between the tins, spreading it out evenly – you can weigh them for accuracy. Finely slice the reserved apple quarters lengthways, and arrange in two circles on the surface of one of the cakes. Place them at right angles to the tin, with the slices touching each other, starting about 1cm in from the edge. Bake the cakes for about 30 minutes or until risen and firm and a skewer inserted into the centre comes out clean. Leave the cakes to cool in their tins without running a knife around the edge.

Gently heat the jam until it loosens, press it through a sieve and brush it over the surface of the cake with the apple slices. You can assemble the cake on the other cake base or remove it to a serving plate as you prefer. Blend the mascarpone, syrup, icing sugar and vanilla together in a bowl and spread over the second sponge. Sandwich with the glazed sponge and leave to set in a cool place for about 30 minutes. The cake will keep well overnight, loosely covered and chilled. Remove it from the fridge an hour before serving.

MAKES 1 X 23CM CAKE

FOR THE CAKE

120ml extra virgin olive oil, plus 2 tablespoons for frying

3 eating apples, e.g. Granny Smith, peeled, quartered and cored

1 cinnamon stick

4 medium eggs

250g golden caster sugar

280g plain flour

2 heaped teaspoons baking powder

finely grated zest of 1 lemon

125g peach or apricot jam

FOR THE FILLING

250g mascarpone

25g golden syrup

10g icing sugar, sifted

1 teaspoon vanilla extract

KIT

2 x 23cm non-stick cake tins with removable bases, at least 4cm deep

Electric whisk

Pastry brush

LITTLE EXTRAS

Olive oil for greasing

MAKES 1 X 20CM CAKE

FOR THE TOPPING

50g unsalted butter

100g light brown sugar

1 x 400g tin of pear
halves, drained

a few walnut halves

FOR THE CAKE

125g plain flour

½ teaspoon bicarbonate of soda

1 teaspoon ground cinnamon

1 teaspoon ground ginger

¼ teaspoon grated nutmeg

pinch of ground cloves

¼ teaspoon fine sea salt

1 medium egg

125g light brown sugar

90g black treacle

125ml soured milk (see TIP)

50g unsalted butter, melted

KIT

20cm non-stick cake tin with a
removable base, 7cm deep

Baking tray

LITTLE EXTRAS

Crème fraîche, to serve
(optional)

grandpa beard's upside-down ginger cake

This recipe was given to me by some good friends, Kate and Alex Beard, who are great cooks. It is divinely sticky, quite the most wicked among the ginger cakes here. And surprisingly, perhaps, given how many recipes handed down over the generations within a family travel down the female line, this originates with Grandpa Beard rather than Grandma.

Preheat the oven to 160°C fan oven/180°C electric oven. To make the topping, gently melt the butter in a small saucepan, add the sugar and stir for 1–2 minutes. Smooth over the base of a 20cm non-stick cake tin with a removable base, 7cm deep. Arrange the pears on top, cut-side down, with a few walnuts around the outside flat-side down.

To make the cake, sift the flour, bicarb and spices into a bowl and add the salt. Blend the egg, sugar, treacle, soured milk and butter in a separate large bowl, and fold in the flour mixture. Beat with a wooden spoon for 1 minute and then pour the mixture over the fruit in the tin. Place on a baking tray and bake for 40–50 minutes until a skewer inserted into the centre comes out clean. Remove from the oven, run a knife around the edge and set aside to cool for about 10 minutes. To serve, remove the collar and invert the cake onto a plate or cake stand. Enjoy warm or at room temperature (but avoid chilling), with a dollop of crème fraîche on the side if wished.

TIP
To create soured milk, simply add a few drops of lemon juice to fresh milk.

CHAPTER TEN

celebration cakes

300g unsalted butter

300g runny honey, e.g. Acacia (see TIP)

300ml cranberry juice

350g dried sour cherries

325g raisins

1 teaspoon bicarbonate of soda

150g plain flour, sifted

150g ground almonds

½ teaspoon freshly grated nutmeg

100g finely diced candied orange peel (see TIP)

FOR THE MARZIPAN AND ICING

75g apricot jam

500g natural marzipan

500g icing sugar, sifted

1 medium organic egg white

1 heaped tablespoon liquid glucose

brandy for brushing

KIT

20cm non-stick cake tin with a removable base, 9cm deep

Baking paper

String

Pastry brush

Palette knife

Food processor

LITTLE EXTRAS

Unsalted butter for greasing

Icing sugar for rolling

Black writing icing

celebration fruitcake

Of all fruitcakes, it is the boiled variety (a description that scarcely does them justice, see also page 229) that I find are the most successful, and seductive. A term that we may not always apply to this genre of celebratory cake that is so often dry, with its desiccated marzipan and chalky icing. By comparison, this cake is decadently gooey, with dried sour cherries and cranberry juice that whisk it into the present, as does some spidery black icing traced over the blanket of white. But as ever with fruitcakes, you can use this as a blueprint and tweak the dried fruit and also the juice to taste. But if you are after a classic fruitcake, then the Traditional Christmas Cake on page 260 is a lovely time-honoured recipe, which can be marzipaned and iced in exactly the same fashion.

Heat the butter, honey and cranberry juice in a medium-sized saucepan until the butter melts. Stir in the cherries and raisins, bring to the boil and simmer over a low heat for 5 minutes. Stir in the bicarbonate of soda – the mixture will sizzle furiously – and leave to cool for 10 minutes.

Preheat the oven to 140°C fan oven/160°C electric oven and butter a 20cm non-stick cake tin with a removable base, 9cm deep. Line the bottom with baking paper and butter this also. Combine the flour, ground almonds and nutmeg in a large mixing bowl, pour over the butter and fruit mixture and beat to combine them. Fold in the peel and transfer the mixture to the cake tin, smoothing the surface. Tear off a sheet of baking paper large enough to cover the surface of the cake and go about halfway down the sides of the tin. Cut out a small circle from the centre about 2cm in diameter and butter the surface that will come in contact with the cake as it rises.

continued in the page 256

TIP
There are no eggs, and the cake relies on honey to sweeten it. Choose a light, mild honey rather than one that's dark and resinous.

celebration fruitcake

continued from page 254

Lay the paper over the top of the tin and tie it in place with string. Bake the cake for 2½ hours until a skewer inserted into the centre comes out clean. Run a knife around the collar to remove it and leave the cake to cool on the base.

Remove the cake from the base and peel off the paper on the bottom. Set the cake on a plate or board. Gently heat the jam in a small saucepan, press it through a sieve and lightly glaze the top and sides of the cake using a pastry brush. Measure the cake from the base of one side, over the top and to the base of the other. Thinly roll out the marzipan on a worksurface dusted with icing sugar into a circle a little bigger than this, about 30–35cm in diameter. Loosen it with a palette knife every now and again and if necessary sprinkle the surface with more icing sugar. Drape the marzipan over the rolling pin, lift it up and carefully lay it on top of the cake, letting it hang down the sides. Press it against the sides of the cake, cut out darts where folds appear and smooth these with your fingers. Trim it around the base so it is level. Set the cake aside overnight to allow the marzipan to semi-dry.

To make the fondant icing, place the icing sugar, egg white and liquid glucose in the bowl of a food processor and whizz to a crumb-like consistency. Tip the mixture onto a board and bring it together into a ball – it will look quite dry at first. Knead it with your hands for 5–10 minutes until very smooth and pliable and then roll it out in the same way as the marzipan. Brush the surface of the marzipan with brandy before laying the icing in place and trimming as before.

If wished you can roll out the trimmings and cut out some petals for a flower in the centre of the cake, securing them with a little brandy. You could also roll a few little balls for the centre of the flower. Using the black writing icing, decorate the cake with scrolls.

Embellish with any other little frills that take your fancy. Set the cake aside to dry for at least a couple of hours. Like most fruitcakes, this will keep well in a tin or covered container (see TIP).

TIP

If you want to make your own, see the Simnel Cake on page 272.

Like most fruitcakes, this can be matured for up to 6–8 weeks to allow its flavour and texture to develop. Wrap it in a double layer of baking paper and then foil, and feed with teaspoons of Calvados or brandy at weekly intervals (pierce the surface first with a skewer). Equally it can be eaten as soon as it is made – it'll be that little bit more crumbly when it's fresh, but that's no bad thing.

willy wonka marshmallow cake

This is one to have fun with – raid the sweet counter for jelly beans, Flumps or marshmallow twists, jelly loops and novelty marshmallows shaped like strawberries smothered in hundreds and thousands.

Preheat the oven to 170°C fan oven/190°C electric oven and butter a 20cm non-stick cake tin with a removable base, 9cm deep. Place all the cake ingredients in the bowl of a food processor and cream together. Transfer the mixture to the cake tin, smoothing the surface, and bake for 50–55 minutes or until a skewer inserted into the centre comes out clean. Run a knife around the collar of the cake and leave it to cool. You can leave the cake on the base or remove it as you prefer.

To make the frosting, blend the egg whites, sugar, orange juice, cream of tartar and salt in a large bowl using an electric whisk. Set the bowl over a pan with a little simmering water in it and whisk at a high speed for 5 minutes until you have a thick, mousse-like glaze that stands in peaks. Add the marshmallows and stir for several minutes until they begin to soften and melt, then whisk until the mixture is smooth and they have completely melted. Remove from the heat.

Spread the frosting thickly over the top and sides of the cake using a palette knife – you may not need quite all of it. Decorate with the sweeties and set aside for a couple of hours to set. The cake will keep well for several days in an airtight container.

TIP

The real treat here is the marshmallow frosting, which you can wheel out for all manner of sponges the same size, pale blush or plain white depending on the colour of the marshmallows.

MAKES 1 X 20CM CAKE

FOR THE CAKE

225g unsalted butter, diced

225g golden caster sugar

225g self-raising flour

2 teaspoons baking powder

finely grated zest of 1 orange

4 medium eggs

100ml smooth fresh orange juice

FOR THE MARSHMALLOW FROSTING

2 medium organic egg whites

150g white caster sugar

2 tablespoons smooth fresh orange juice

½ teaspoon cream of tartar

pinch of sea salt

11 pink or white marshmallows, halved

KIT

20cm non-stick cake tin with a removable base, 9cm deep

Food processor

Electric whisk

Palette knife

LITTLE EXTRAS

Unsalted butter for greasing

Selection of marshmallows, jelly beans and jelly hoops for decorating

FOR THE CAKE

120g unsalted butter, diced

300g golden caster sugar

2 large eggs

300g plain flour, sifted

230g buttermilk

1 teaspoon fine sea salt

1 teaspoon vanilla extract

20g cocoa powder, sifted

approx. ½ teaspoon red food colour paste

1 tablespoon white wine vinegar

1 teaspoon bicarbonate of soda

FOR THE FROSTING

180g unsalted butter, softened

150g icing sugar, sifted

450g full-fat cream cheese

1 teaspoon vanilla extract

KIT

2–3 x 20cm non-stick cake tins with removable bases, 5cm deep

Baking paper

Food processor

Wire rack

LITTLE EXTRAS

Unsalted butter for greasing

red velvet cake

A velvet cake is so stunning it makes a great celebratory offering – be it Christmas, Easter, a birthday or any other occasion. Legend has it the recipe was leaked from the kitchens of the Waldorf-Astoria some time in the 1920s, and it has held Southerners captive ever since.

Preheat the oven to 170°C fan oven/190°C electric oven. Butter two (or three if you have them) 20cm non-stick cake tins with removable bases, 5cm deep, and line the bases with baking paper.

To make the cake, cream the butter and sugar together for 3–4 minutes in a food processor until really light and fluffy. Add the eggs one at a time, scraping down the sides of the bowl between each addition. Add the flour in three batches, alternating it with the buttermilk so you start and end with the flour. Next mix in the salt, vanilla and cocoa. Start to add the red food colouring, a knife-tip at a time, until the mixture is a dramatic dusky red – I find it needs about ½ teaspoon in all. Mix the vinegar and bicarbonate of soda together in a small bowl, they will fizz, and add to the batter. If using three cake tins,* divide the mixture between them, weighing them for accuracy to ensure you get evenly thick sponges at the end. Bake for 20–25 minutes or until shrinking from the sides and firm when pressed in the centre. Leave to cool in the tins for 10 minutes, then turn the cakes out onto a wire rack, remove the paper and leave to cool top upwards.

To make the frosting, place the butter and icing sugar in the bowl of a food processor and cream together. Transfer to a bowl and blend in the cream cheese and vanilla extract, beating with a wooden spoon until smooth.

Use about one-third of the buttercream to sandwich the three layers and the rest to coat the top and sides. Place the finished cake on a plate or board, cover with clingfilm and chill for 1 hour until set. If chilling it any longer than this, remove from the fridge 30 minutes before serving. It keeps well in an airtight container for several days.

*If using two tins, add a third of the mixture to each one, bake these, and then bake the third sponge while the other two are cooling.

TIP

I find food colour paste much more effective than liquid for dyeing the sponge a rich vermillion red (see page 21).

traditional christmas cake

An old-fashioned rich fruitcake reads like a spell out of the *Sorcerer's Apprentice*; it is the most magical creation, you only have to read through this ingredients list to understand its subtle complexity. As a rule of thumb, I try to avoid this type of complication, but a Christmas cake is something special that we only bake once a year, and it is the most pleasurable of rituals to set to on a rainy November weekend. It takes a little while to assemble everything and half a day to bake, and then of course it needs to be lovingly fed at weekly intervals in the run-up. It's no quick fix, but it is something unique.

This recipe is completely authentic, and true to the longstanding tradition of fruited Christmas cakes that goes back so many years. It comes via a dear friend, the artist Val Archer, whose mother Gladys Archer made wedding and other celebration cakes on a small-scale basis. Val recalls vividly the painstaking process of making them, and how as a little girl her job was to carefully lay the blanched almonds for a Dundee in rows around the top of the cake. She was also given the task of cutting every sultana going into a wedding cake in half. This was so that when the cake was cut into small squares for placing in cardboard boxes, which were given to guests to take home, and to those who had been unable to attend, the cake didn't break in an unseemly fashion; the fruit was small enough to withstand the size of morsel.

Like me, Val inherited her mother's handwritten notebook with recipe after recipe for different fruitcakes. And this was her classic Christmas cake, heavily fruited and full of subtle mystery. On looking through the book she found that her mother changed the cooking time constantly over the years. The timings below are actually based on an entry in 1972 that reads: 'the perfect cooking time'. I love the fact that she had been baking this cake for decades by then, but still felt it could be improved year on year. That for me captures the spirit of the passionate lifetime baker.

225g dark muscovado sugar

180g plain flour

125g self-raising flour

¼ teaspoon each of ground cinnamon, ginger, nutmeg and allspice

225g unsalted butter, softened

finely grated zest of 1 lemon

finely grated zest of 1 orange

5 medium eggs

1 tablespoon treacle

1 teaspoon vanilla extract

1 teaspoon almond extract

1 generous tablespoon brandy

1 level teaspoon fine sea salt

50g ground almonds

225g sultanas

225g raisins

350g currants

125g mixed chopped peel

50g blanched almonds, chopped

100g glace cherries

KIT

23cm cake tin with a removable base, 8cm deep

Baking paper

Electric whisk

Newspaper

String

LITTLE EXTRAS

Unsalted butter for greasing

Preheat the oven to 130°C fan oven/150°C electric oven and butter a 23cm cake tin with a removable base, 7cm deep. Line the base and sides with baking paper.

If the sugar seems claggy, give it a whizz in a food processor; sift together the two flours and the spices into a bowl.

Whisk the butter with the lemon and orange zest in a large mixing bowl using an electric whisk for about 1 minute until light and fluffy. Add the sugar and continue to whisk for another 2 minutes until really mousse-like. Now whisk in the eggs, one at a time, whisking well with each addition, then the treacle, vanilla, almond extract, brandy and salt. As lightly as possible, fold in the flour in two goes, and the ground almonds. Finally, fold in the dried fruit, mixed peel, almonds and cherries. Transfer the mixture to the prepared tin, smoothing the surface with a wooden spoon. Loosely cover the surface with a circle of baking paper and tie a wad of newspaper, 7–10 sheets thick, around the outside with string. Bake the cake for 1 hour, then turn the oven down to 120°C fan/140°C electric and bake for a further 3¼ hours until a skewer inserted into the centre comes out very slightly tacky, but comes out clean if inserted in the outside. Turn the oven off and leave the cake inside for 10 minutes, then remove and set aside to cool in the tin overnight.

The cake should ideally be matured for at least two weeks, up to six weeks, before icing (see page 256). I would leave the top and side paper in place, and tape the sides to the top, then place it in a tin in a cool place.

TIP

You can marzipan and ice the cake as for Celebration Fruitcake, see page 256, but if all you want is a lovely, plain fruitcake for serving with cheese for instance, then it can be simply glazed. Warm 150g apricot jam in a small saucepan, press it through a sieve and lightly brush the top and sides, then leave for an hour to set. In this case, when maturing it I would pierce the base of the cake rather than the top.

FOR THE FILLING

150g dark chocolate (approx. 50 per cent cocoa solids), broken into pieces

300ml soured cream

FOR THE CAKE

5 medium eggs, separated

200g golden caster sugar

1½ teaspoons baking powder, sifted

1 teaspoon almond extract (optional)

100g ground pistachios

200g ground almonds

FOR THE ICING

150g milk chocolate, broken into pieces

25g unsalted butter

50g cocoa powder, sifted

1 generous tablespoon golden syrup

KIT

2 x 20cm non-stick cake tins with removable bases, at least 4cm deep

Baking paper

Electric whisk

Bread knife

LITTLE EXTRAS

Unsalted butter for greasing

Birthday candles

chocolate pistachio birthday cake

One of the problems of acquiring a taste for any ersatz food stuff is that you spend the rest of your life trying to recreate its artificiality, and I have long been addicted to lurid green pistachio ices. A kind of Venetian fairground attraction, I will ever associate them with Canalettos and gondolas. If however you have tried to make pistachio ice cream at home then you will know how fake it really is. But it is amazing what you can do with the addition of a little almond extract in support of the nut, which is how this particular cake arose. And while the pistachio layer does give it an added dimension, you can also add ground almonds for all three layers.

To make the filling, gently melt the dark chocolate in a bowl set over a pan with a little simmering water in it. Spoon the soured cream into a medium-sized bowl and beat in the melted chocolate with a wooden spoon. Cover the bowl with clingfilm and chill for a couple of hours.

Preheat the oven to 180°C fan oven/200°C electric oven and butter two 20cm non-stick cake tins with removable bases, at least 4cm deep, and line with baking paper. Whisk the egg whites in a large bowl until stiff peaks form using an electric whisk. In a separate large bowl, whisk the egg yolks with the sugar, without letting the mixture become too pale and thick. Gently fold the egg whites into the yolk and sugar mixture in two goes, and then fold in the baking powder and almond extract (if using). Transfer one-third of the mixture to another bowl (or weigh out one-third and two-thirds respectively into two clean bowls). Fold the pistachios into the one-third, and the ground almonds into the other.

Pour the mixtures into the tins and bake the smaller cake for 20 minutes and the larger cake for 25 minutes – or until the tops feel springy to the touch and a skewer inserted into the centre comes out clean. Without running a knife around the collars, invert the cake tins and leave to cool, this will minimise any shrinking.

Run a knife around the collar of each sponge and remove it, then peel off the base paper. Slit the larger cake in half using a bread knife and place the base on a serving plate. Slice off and discard the brown surface from the pistachio sponge. Sandwich the three cake layers together with the chocolate filling, placing the pistachio layer in the middle.

To make the icing, gently melt the chocolate and butter in a bowl set over a pan with a little simmering water in it, stirring until smooth. At the same time, combine the cocoa, golden syrup and 75ml water in a small saucepan and heat almost to boiling point – if necessary, whisking until smooth. Pour the hot syrup mixture over the melted chocolate and blend with a wooden spoon to a thick glaze. Smooth two-thirds of the chocolate glaze over the top of the cake and one-third around the sides. Set aside in a cool place for a couple of hours for the glaze to set fully. The cake can be chilled for up to a couple of hours, but is best stored out of the fridge in a cool place. Decorate with candles to serve.

MAKES 1 X 20CM CAKE

FOR THE FILLING

75g dried sour cherries

3 tablespoons brandy

300g cherry jam, ideally morello

350ml double cream

FOR THE CAKE

225g unsalted butter, diced

200g light muscovado sugar

1 tablespoon golden syrup

200g self-raising flour, sifted

2 teaspoons baking
powder, sifted

50g cocoa powder, sifted

4 medium eggs

150g fromage frais

¼ teaspoon bicarbonate of soda

FOR THE DECORATION

4–5 tablespoons coarsely grated
dark or white chocolate

KIT

20cm non-stick cake tin with a
removable base, 9cm deep

Food processor

Electric whisk

Bread knife

Pastry brush

LITTLE EXTRAS

Unsalted butter for greasing

Icing sugar for dusting (optional)

A handful of undyed
glace cherries

black forest gateau

This celebratory classic also lends itself to a Christmas take, the Black Forest in the snow if you shower it with white rather than dark chocolate and liberally dust the surface with icing sugar.

Soak the dried cherries for the filling in the brandy for 2–3 hours. Preheat the oven to 170°C fan oven/190°C electric oven and butter a 20cm non-stick cake tin with a removable base, 9cm deep.

To make the cake, place all the ingredients in the bowl of a food processor and cream together. Transfer the mixture to the prepared tin, smoothing the surface, and bake for 45–55 minutes or until a skewer inserted into the centre comes out clean. Run a knife around the collar of the cake and leave it to cool in the tin.

Work the jam in a bowl to loosen it, drain the cherries, reserving the brandy, and fold them into the jam. In a separate bowl, whisk the cream using an electric whisk until it forms soft peaks – be careful not to overbeat or it will stiffen to a buttery consistency making it difficult to spread. You can leave the cake on the base or remove it as you prefer.

If the cake has risen unevely, you can slice a small sliver off the top to even it using a bread knife, and then slit the cake into three layers. Drizzle half the reserved brandy over the bottom layer. Place on a plate and spread with half of the jam, and then half of the cream. Repeat with the next layer, using up the remaining jam and cream, and then place the top layer on top. Use the jam coating the sides of the bowl to lightly glaze the top of the cake with a pastry brush, and then scatter over the grated chocolate. Dust with icing sugar if you wish and scatter over a few glace cherries. Chill the cake for 1 hour before serving. It is best eaten within a couple of days. Bring it back up to room temperature for 30–60 minutes before serving it.

FOR THE CAKE

350g chopped roasted hazelnuts

6 medium eggs, separated

250g golden caster sugar

1½ teaspoons baking powder

FOR THE FILLING

100g unsalted butter, softened

50g icing sugar

½ teaspoon ground cinnamon

100g thick ready-prepared custard

FOR THE ICING AND DECORATION

450g ready-to-roll white icing

100g apricot jam

130g ready-to-roll red icing

KIT

2 x 20cm non-stick cake tins with removable bases, at least 4cm deep

Coffee grinder

Electric whisk

Bread knife

Pastry brush

LITTLE EXTRAS

Unsalted butter for greasing

Icing sugar for rolling

Edible red and green sprinkles (optional)

Thick red or green ribbon for the outside

poinsettia cake

Having grown up with poinsettias, the sight of their cheery red leaves outside a flower shop in the run up to Christmas brings back the same nostalgic memories as Christmas trees, when they first start to arrive in the shops. So this is an ode to this plant – in essence, a hazelnut sponge with a French buttercream filling scented with cinnamon, and a white icing surround.

Preheat the oven to 180°C fan oven/200°C electric oven and butter two 20cm non-stick cake tins with removable bases, at least 4cm deep. Grind the nuts in batches in a coffee grinder, taking care to stop the motor before they turn to a paste at the bottom. Whisk the egg yolks and sugar together in a large bowl using an electric whisk – the mixture should not be too pale and thick. In a separate bowl, whisk the egg whites until stiff using an electric whisk, and then gently fold them into the cake mixture in three batches. Fold in the ground nuts and baking powder.

Divide the cake mixture between the tins and give them a couple of taps on the worksurface to bring up any air bubbles. Bake for about 25 minutes until the top feels springy to the touch and the sides are shrinking away from the tin. A skewer inserted into the centre should come out clean. Remove the collar from the cakes and leave them to cool.

To make the filling, beat the softened butter in a medium-sized bowl with an electric whisk until creamy and almost white. (If it's on the hard side you can cream it in a food processor first and then transfer it to a bowl.) Sift over the sugar and cinnamon and beat together. Gradually beat in the custard, whisking for several minutes – first on a low speed and then on a higher speed – until fluffy and mousse-like.

Remove the sponges from their tins and place them upside down, if necessary trim the edges to level them. Spread one of the cakes with the buttercream and sandwich with the second one. Transfer the cake to a stand or serving plate. Measure the cake from the base of one side, over the top, and to the base of the other side – it should be about 35cm. Thinly roll out the white icing on a worksurface lightly dusted with icing sugar to a circle the same diameter. Rotate the icing now and again, rather than turning it over as you would pastry.

Gently heat the jam in a small saucepan until it liquefies, press it through a sieve and use it to brush over the top and sides of the cake. Carefully drape the icing over the cake, pressing it against the sides. Cut out darts where there is excess icing and smooth the edges together, then trim the base.

Cut out a poinsettia leaf about 7cm long from a piece of paper (if in doubt about their shape, search for an image on the internet or refer to a Christmas card). Roll out the red icing as thinly as possible in the same way as the white icing, and cut out some leaves. Use these to make a flower on top of the cake – you should have enough for two rows of leaves, securing them with a little jam. Tie a thick green or red ribbon around the outside. The cake will keep well for several days in a cool place, loosely covered with clingfilm, or in an airtight container.

FOR THE CAKE

12 medium egg whites

1/3 teaspoon fine sea salt

1½ teaspoons cream of tartar

375g icing sugar, sifted

200g white plain flour, sifted

FOR THE RASPBERRY CREAM FILLING

250g mascarpone

100g raspberry jam, e.g. St Dalfour 'no added sugar'

FOR THE FROSTING

120g unsalted butter, softened

100g icing sugar, sifted

1 teaspoon vanilla extract

300g full-fat cream cheese

KIT

Electric whisk

2 x 23cm non-stick cake tin with removable bases, 7cm deep

Bread knife

Small palette knife

LITTLE EXTRAS

Several tubes of Smarties

Candles or sparklers for decorating

angel smartie cake

I get to make this one every year on demand, for my son's birthday. He's a great traditionalist, I first made it when he was six as he grew out of the Bob the Builder/Batman phase. The time had come to get back in the kitchen, rather than relying on shop-bought birthday cakes, and I have been making it ever since on demand.

But this is the new improved version, with slightly thicker layers of sponge. Decorate it as befits with a spiral, the child's age, a dinosaur or a rose traced with pink and mauve Smarties.

Preheat the oven to 150°C fan oven/170°C electric oven. This is a large quantity of meringue to whisk, so you may prefer to do it in two batches in two separate bowls; otherwise use your biggest mixing bowl. Whisk the egg whites with the salt and cream of tartar until stiff peaks form using an electric whisk.

Now whisk in the sugar, a couple of tablespoons at a time, sprinkling it over the egg whites and whisking for about 20 seconds with each addition. Fold the sifted flour into the meringue in three goes. Divide the mixture between two unbuttered 23cm non-stick cake tins with removable bases, 7cm deep – I like to weigh the mixture for accuracy.

Bake the sponges for 35–40 minutes until lightly golden on the surface and springy to the touch. Invert the tins and set the sponges aside to cool, without running a knife around the edge.

To make the filling, blend the mascarpone with the jam in a bowl.

To make the frosting, whisk the butter in a large bowl for about 1 minute using an electric whisk, then add the icing sugar and continue whisking for a further minute or two until really fluffy. Whisk in the vanilla, and then blend in the cream cheese using a large spoon.

Run a knife around the collars of the tins to remove them. Using a bread knife, split one of the sponges in half. Slice the top off the other one, then cut the sponge off its base to make up the middle layer of cake. Spread half the raspberry mascarpone filling over the base of the sponge, lay the middle section in place, spread with the remaining raspberry filling, and then lay the top over. Smooth the cream cheese frosting over the top and sides of the cake using a small palette knife. Transfer the cake to a 25cm cake board, keeping it on the base of the tin. Store in the refrigerator for up to two days, removing it from the fridge 30–60 minutes before serving. Decorate with Smarties and candles, or sparklers, close to the time of eating.

chocolate chestnut log

SERVES 6–8

100g dark chocolate, e.g. Lindt 70 per cent cocoa solids, broken up

50g unsalted butter, diced

1 x 435g tin of unsweetened chestnut purée

75g golden caster sugar

100g extra-thick double cream

1 teaspoon vanilla extract

KIT

Food processor

20 x 8cm stand or plate for the log

Foil

Palette knife

LITTLE EXTRAS

Christmas figurines or chocolate leaves for decorating

Icing sugar for dusting

My mother used to make this every Christmas without fail, as I do now for my own children. Somewhere between a fudgy cake and a mousse, its main drawback, as with anything that belongs in the fridge, is that all your usual hiding places are obsolete. Once cut into, I find this one has disappeared next time I check if there's enough leftover for supper.

Essentially it is a 'buche de Noel', the French equivalent of our Christmas pudding. They go to town with coloured icing, Santa and reindeers, and it is indeed readily dressed up if you have any decorations. More austerely, you can throw some chocolate leaves at it and dust them with icing sugar.

Place the chocolate and butter in a bowl set over a pan of simmering water and gently melt them, stirring now and again until smooth and amalgamated. Remove the bowl from the heat and set aside to cool to room temperature. Place the chestnut purée, sugar, cream and vanilla extract in the bowl of a food processor and whizz until creamy, then add the chocolate and butter mixture and whizz again until you have a silky purée. This should be the consistency of whipped butter icing – that is, firm enough to pile into a log. If the mixture seems too loose, simply transfer it to a bowl, cover with clingfilm and chill until it firms up sufficiently to shape.

You will need a stand for the log, a minimum of 20 x 8cm. You could use a small chopping board, otherwise the card that comes inside the chocolate bar wrapper.

Wrap the stand or plate in foil and pile the chocolate chestnut mixture along its length. Run the tines of a fork along the length of the log to resemble wood, and smooth the ends with a palette knife. Decorate the forked surface with chocolate leaves, and place in the fridge for several hours, or overnight until set. I like the log best about 30 minutes out of the fridge. Dust it with icing sugar just before serving.

TIP

Delicious with whipped cream or a spoonful of sweetened crème fraîche with a drop of liqueur in it.

FOR THE MARZIPAN

200g ground almonds

200g icing sugar

1 teaspoon lemon juice

1 teaspoon brandy or dark rum

1 medium organic egg, separated

FOR THE CAKE

225g plain flour

½ teaspoon each ground cinnamon, nutmeg and allspice or ginger

180g unsalted butter, diced

50g demerara sugar

3 medium eggs

1 rounded tablespoon treacle

½ teaspoon fine sea salt

100ml whole milk

400g currants

225g sultanas

finely grated zest of 1 lemon and 1 orange

200g coarse-cut marmalade

KIT

Food processor

Clingfilm

20cm non-stick cake tin with a removable base, 9cm deep

Baking paper

Pastry brush

LITTLE EXTRAS

Unsalted butter for greasing

Icing sugar for dusting

Yellow or white organza or other thick ribbon

simnel cake

A Simnel cake is decorated with twelve marzipan balls that represent the twelve apostles. The marzipan is toasted under the grill, which gives it a delicate fine crust.

To make the marzipan, place the almonds, icing sugar, lemon juice, brandy or rum and egg yolk in the bowl of a food processor and whizz together. Add just enough of the egg white to form a pliable paste. Wrap the marzipan in clingfilm and chill. If necessary, the marzipan can be made a day in advance.

Preheat the oven to 130°C fan oven/150°C electric oven and butter a 20cm non-stick cake tin with a removable base, 9cm deep. Line the base with baking paper, and then the sides, and butter again. Also cut out another circle of paper the diameter of the tin for the top of the cake and cut a hole in the centre about 2.5–3cm in diameter.

To make the cake, sift the flour and spices together in a large mixing bowl. Place the butter and sugar in the bowl of a food processor and cream together, then add the eggs one at a time, with a little flour in between, and then the treacle. Now add the rest of the flour with the salt and finally the milk. Transfer the mixture to the large mixing bowl. Stir in the dried fruit and zest. Gently warm 150g of the marmalade and press it through a sieve. (Reserve the sieved jam for later.) Finely chop and stir the marmalade peel into the cake mixture.

Spoon half of the cake mixture into the prepared tin, smoothing the surface. Roll out a little under half of the marzipan on a worksurface lightly dusted with icing sugar into a circle the diameter of the cake tin, trimming to fit. Lay the marzipan on top of the cake mixture in the tin. Reserve the trimmings with the remainder of the marzipan.

Spread the sieved marmalade in a thin layer on top of the marzipan and then spoon over the remaining cake mixture. Loosely cover the surface with the paper circle and bake for 2¾–3¼ hours. The cake should be firm to touch and if you insert a skewer down as far as the marzipan it should come out clean. Leave it to cool completely. You can now mature the cake for up to a couple of weeks if you wish, wrapping it in a double thickness of baking paper and storing it somewhere cool, which allows the crumb to settle.

To decorate the cake, preheat the grill to medium-high and peel the lining paper off the cake. Thinly roll out the remaining marzipan on a worksurface lightly dusted with icing sugar into a circle about 2cm bigger than the cake, using the tin as a guide. Gently warm and sieve the remaining 50g marmalade as before, and use to paint the top of the cake and the top 1cm of the sides. Lay the marzipan over the cake, gently pressing it against the top and sides and use your finger to mark the edge. Roll the trimmings into 12 balls, slightly smaller than a cherry, dab a little jam onto the base of each and arrange around the outside of the cake. Place the cake under the grill to toast the surface – this happens quite quickly – turning the cake to colour the balls evenly. Set aside to cool completely. To serve tie a pretty yellow and white organza or other thick ribbon around the outside.

TIP
If maturing the cake, make up half the
marzipan at a time as required.

FOR THE FILLING

1 small butternut squash
(approx. 600g)

125ml double or whipping cream

100g golden syrup

1 teaspoon lemon juice

1 teaspoon vanilla extract

¼ teaspoon ground cinnamon

½ teaspoon ground ginger

pinch of fine sea salt

2 medium eggs

freshly grated nutmeg

FOR THE PASTRY

100g plain flour

30g ground almonds

30g golden caster sugar

75g unsalted butter, chilled
and diced

1 medium egg yolk

KIT

Skewer

Food processor

20cm tart tin with a removable
base, 3cm deep

Clingfilm

Baking tray

Foil

pumpkin pie

A pumpkin pie was something of a curiosity I heard constantly about from people I knew living in the States – it became one of those friend of friends that I was dying to meet. My first encounter was when I actually set about making my own, and I was instantly smitten.

Pumpkin pie is, in fact, an egg custard tart by another name. Like our own custard tarts it is flavoured with nutmeg, but it also has that alluring slightly soggy pastry that comes of baking the filling inside an unbaked pastry case – which is the main reason custard tarts make us go weak at the knees in the first place. So I can completely see its appeal and understand why it gets the applause that it does at those times of the year when it is a centrepiece of the Thanksgiving table or at Halloween.

Preheat the oven to 160°C fan oven/180°C electric oven. Prick the squash all over using a fine skewer, place it in a roasting or baking dish and bake for 1 hour. Turn the oven up to 170°C fan oven/190°C electric oven. To make the pastry, whizz the flour, ground almonds, sugar and butter to a fine crumb-like consistency in a food processor. Add the egg yolk and 1 teaspoon of water and process briefly to bring the dough together in a soft, squidgy ball. Press the pastry onto the base and sides of a 20cm tart tin with a removable base, 3cm deep. Level the surface by laying a sheet of clingfilm over the top and smoothing it out with your fingers, taking it very slightly higher than the rim of the tin. Either trim the rim using a knife to neaten it or smooth it using a teaspoon. Place the case on a baking tray.

Cut the squash open, discard any seeds and scoop out and weigh 200g of the flesh. Place the flesh in a food processor with all the ingredients for the filling, except the nutmeg, and whizz to a smooth cream. Pour into the pastry case and grate over a liberal dusting of nutmeg. Bake for 35–40 minutes until lightly golden and set; it may wobble slightly but will firm as it cools and chills. Set aside to cool and then loosely cover with foil and chill for at least a couple of hours. It will keep well in the fridge for several days.

TIP
The chances are that you will end up with more squash than you need, so purée and freeze the remainder for the next time.

tarts and. pies

FOR THE PASTRY

60g unsalted butter, softened

60g golden caster sugar

½ medium egg

125g plain flour, sifted

15g ground almonds

FOR THE FILLING

100g unsalted butter, softened

100g golden caster sugar

100g ground almonds

1 tablespoon plain flour

2 medium eggs

1 large eating apple (approx. 200g), e.g. Granny Smith's, peeled, quartered, cored and thinly sliced lengthways

KIT

Food processor

Clingfilm

23cm tart tin with a removable base, 3cm deep

Baking paper

Baking beans or dried pulses

LITTLE EXTRAS

Plain flour for rolling

Icing sugar for dusting (optional)

apple and almond tart

This is a classic French apple tart that we see more of across the Channel than we do here, a pastry case filled with almond sponge set with apples.

To make the pastry, cream the butter and sugar together in a food processor. Mix in the egg, then add the flour and ground almonds. As soon as the dough comes together in a ball, wrap it in clingfilm and chill for at least 2 hours; it can be kept in the fridge for several days.

Preheat the oven to 170°C fan oven/190°C electric oven. Thinly roll out the pastry to a thickness of about 2–3mm on a lightly floured worksurface and use to line the bottom and sides of a 23cm tart tin with a removable base, 3cm deep. Don't worry if the pastry tears and you end up partly pressing it into the tin. Trim the edges, line the case with baking paper and weight it with baking beans or dried pulses. Bake in the oven for 20 minutes until starting to colour at the sides, then remove the paper and beans and leave to cool.

Preheat the oven to 170°C fan oven/190°C electric oven if you have turned if off. To make the filling, place the butter, sugar, ground almonds and flour in a food processor and blend together, then add the eggs and mix to a smooth cream. Smooth over the base of the pastry case and arrange the apple slices on top in a tight row around the outside edge, with any leftover slices in the centre. Bake for 30–35 minutes until golden, risen and firm. Leave to cool and dust with icing sugar if you wish.

TIP

This quantity of pastry makes for quite a tight fit, which is fine if you are an old hand, but if you are unsure or new to working with pastry, then it might be worth doubling the quantity, which will make it that much easier to handle. The addition of just a small amount of ground almonds gives it a delicate crispness.

FOR THE FRANGIPANE

200g unsalted butter, softened

150g golden caster sugar

125g ground almonds

125g ground hazelnuts

100g plain flour

3 medium eggs

FOR THE TART

225g puff pastry

9 slightly under-ripe Victoria plums, quartered and stone removed

3 tablespoons apricot jam, warmed and sieved

KIT

Food processor

23cm tart tin, 4cm deep

Pastry brush

LITTLE EXTRAS

Plain flour for rolling

plum and frangipane tart

This recipe derives from one of my favourite patisseries in London, Baker and Spice, and it is typical of their generous rustic style. Plums do make a particularly lovely tart; cooking brings out the best in this fruit.

Preheat the oven to 180°C fan oven/200°C electric oven. To make the frangipane, cream the butter and sugar together in a food processor for a few minutes. Add the ground nuts and flour and process briefly, then add the eggs one at a time. Set aside while you get on with the pastry.

Roll out the pastry into a thin circle on a lightly floured worksurface and cut out a circle to fit a 23cm tart tin, 4cm deep. Draping the pastry over the rolling pin, gently lift it into the tin and press it to line the bottom and sides. Run a rolling pin across the top to trim the sides.

Spread the frangipane over the pastry base, and arrange the plum quarters cut-side up on top, laying them in circles starting at the outside. Bake for 15 minutes, then turn down the oven to 140°C fan oven/160°C electric oven and bake for a further 35–45 minutes – by which time the frangipane will have risen up around the plums and set. Brush the surface of the tart with the warmed jam and leave to cool.

TIP

Ground hazelnuts are an ingredient that I readily find in France, but less so elsewhere. They can be used in exactly the same fashion as ground almonds, but are more aromatic as might be expected. If you can't find them ready-ground, simply grind blanched nuts in a coffee grinder. Alternatively, substitute ground almonds instead.

bakewell tart

MAKES 1 X 23CM TART

FOR THE PASTRY

60g unsalted butter, softened

60g golden caster sugar

½ medium egg

125g plain flour, sifted

15g ground almonds

FOR THE FILLING

125g marzipan

50g unsalted butter, diced

75g golden caster sugar

2 medium eggs

120g ground almonds

½ teaspoon baking powder, sifted

50g raisins

100g raspberry jam

30g flaked almonds

KIT

Food processor

Clingfilm

23cm tart tin with a removable base, 3cm deep

Baking paper

Baking beans or dried pulses

LITTLE EXTRAS

Plain flour for rolling

Icing sugar for dusting (optional)

The essential character of a bakewell tart is the scent of almonds married with raspberry jam, and here it's given a boost with a layer of marzipan. Further to its appeal is the combination of the two differing textures of pastry and sponge.

To make the pastry, cream the butter and sugar together in a food processor. Mix in the egg, then add the flour and ground almonds. As soon as the dough starts to come together in a ball, wrap it in clingfilm and chill for at least 2 hours; it can be kept in the fridge for several days.

Preheat the oven to 170°C fan oven/190°C electric oven. Thinly roll out the pastry on a lightly floured surface and use it to line the bottom and sides of a 23cm tart tin with a removable base, 3cm deep. Don't worry if the pastry tears and you end up partly pressing it into the tin. Line the case with baking paper and weight it with baking beans or dried pulses. Bake for 15–20 minutes until lightly coloured and then remove the paper and beans.

While the pastry is baking, thinly roll out the marzipan on a lightly floured worksurface and cut out a 23cm circle. To make the filling, cream the butter and sugar together in a food processor. Add the eggs one at a time, and then the ground almonds and baking powder. With the motor off, stir in the raisins.

Lay the circle of marzipan over the pastry base and spread with the raspberry jam. Spoon the almond sponge mixture on top, smoothing the surface. Scatter over the flaked almonds and bake in the oven for 25–30 minutes until golden and risen.

The tart is delicious eaten 20–30 minutes out of the oven, otherwise leave it to cool and dust with icing sugar. The tart should keep well for several days in an airtight container.

FOR THE PASTRY

75g unsalted butter, softened

75g golden caster sugar

1 medium egg

200g plain flour

20g ground almonds

FOR THE FILLING

70g unsalted butter, softened

100g golden caster sugar

100g ground almonds

1 medium egg, and 1 egg white

125g fresh or frozen blackcurrants (strung weight)

KIT

Food processor

Clingfilm

23cm tart tin, 3cm deep

Foil

Baking beans or dried pulses

LITTLE EXTRAS

Plain flour for rolling

Icing sugar for dusting (optional)

Crème fraîche, to serve (optional)

blackcurrant frangipane tart

An elegant thin French tart consisting of blackcurrants set into a creamy almond sponge.

To make the pastry, cream the butter and sugar in a food processor. Beat in the egg, and then add the flour and ground almonds. Bring the dough together into a ball, wrap in clingfilm and chill for at least an hour; it will keep well for several days.

Preheat the oven to 170°C fan oven/190°C electric oven. Allow the dough to come to room temperature for a few minutes and then knead it until pliable. Thinly roll it out on a lightly floured worksurface and use it to line the base and sides of a 23cm tart tin, 3cm deep. Trim the excess around the sides, reserving the trimmings. Line the case with foil and baking beans or dried pulses and bake for 15–20 minutes. Remove the foil and beans and bake for a further 5–10 minutes until starting to colour. Patch any cracks that have appeared with the reserved trimmings.

To make the filling, cream the butter and sugar in a food processor until light and fluffy. Add the ground almonds, along with the egg and egg white and mix to a smooth cream. Smooth the cream over the base of the tart case. Scatter the blackcurrants evenly over the surface and bake for 45 minutes until spongy, golden and firm. Leave to cool and dust with icing sugar if you wish. Delicious served with crème fraîche.

FOR THE PASTRY

100g spelt or plain flour

30g ground almonds

30g icing sugar

75g unsalted butter, chilled and diced

1 medium egg, separated

FOR THE FILLING

150g marzipan

50g unsalted butter, diced

75g golden caster sugar

2 medium eggs

1 teaspoon almond extract

120g ground almonds

½ teaspoon baking powder, sifted

50g strung redcurrants or raspberries, or half and half (see TIP)

KIT

Food processor

20cm tart tin with a removable base, 2–3cm deep

Clingfilm

LITTLE EXTRAS

Plain flour for rolling

swedish mazarin

This lovely fudgy almond tart is very similar to a Bakewell Tart. The redcurrants provide welcome sharp relief, but it could also be raspberries or a mixture of the two, or no fruit at all. Quite often this tart is iced with a simple glace icing. Some recipes include the marzipan in the sponge, but as commercial brands vary considerably I find it safest to include it as a layer below the almond sponge.

Preheat the oven to 170°C fan oven/190°C electric oven. To make the pastry, whizz the flour, ground almonds, icing sugar and butter together to fine crumbs in a food processor, then add the egg yolk. (Reserve the egg white for the filling.) Process briefly to bring the dough together in a soft, squidgy ball. Press the pastry onto the base and sides of a 20cm tart tin with a removable base, 2–3cm deep. Level the surface by laying a sheet of clingfilm over the top and smoothing it with your fingers. Now smooth the top rim using a teaspoon to neaten it.

Thinly roll out the marzipan on a lightly floured worksurface, cut out a circle about 20cm in diameter and fit it inside the pastry base. Cream the butter and sugar for the filling in a food processor. Add the eggs, one at a time, the egg white, almond extract, ground almonds and baking powder. Whizz to a smooth cream.

Smooth the almond cream over the marzipan and scatter over the redcurrants or raspberries. Bake for 35 minutes until golden, risen and firm. Set aside to cool. The tart should keep well for several days in an airtight container.

TIP
The easiest route to redcurrants is to run a fork down each sprig to remove them, working over a bowl.

plum pie

This is especially good with a rich custard or with whipped cream for a teatime treat.

First make the pastry. Cream the butter and sugar until soft and fluffy in a food processor. Beat in the eggs until well combined and then gradually add the flour and ground almonds. Bring the dough together in a ball, wrap it in clingfilm and chill for at least 2 hours; it will keep for several days.

To make the filling, toss the plums with a couple of tablespoons of the brown sugar in a bowl and set aside for 30 minutes to draw out the juices. Drain, discarding the juice.

Preheat the oven to 180°C fan oven/200°C electric oven. Allow the dough to come to room temperature for a few minutes and then knead it until pliable. On a lightly floured surface, thinly roll out two-thirds of the dough and use it to line the base of a 1.7 litre pie dish (I use an oval gratin dish), letting the extra hang over the sides. Don't worry if the dough tears and you end up partly pressing it into the dish.

Toss the plums with the remaining brown sugar, the flour and lemon zest, and tip them into the pie dish. Roll out the remaining pastry, incorporating any spare trimmings, to fit the top of the dish. Paint the pastry rim of the dish with milk and lay the lid on top. Press the edges together to seal them and trim off the excess. Crimp the edges using the tip of your finger or else the tip of a knife. Brush the surface of the pastry with milk, cut several diagonal slits in the centre to release the steam and dust with caster sugar. Bake the pie for about 35 minutes until the pastry is golden and the plums are tender. If the fruit needs a little longer, you can cover the pastry with foil to stop it colouring any further. Serve hot, about 10 minutes out of the oven, or at room temperature.

SERVES 6

FOR THE SWEET SHORTCRUST PASTRY

150g unsalted butter, softened

150g golden caster sugar

2 medium eggs

400g plain flour, sifted

50g ground almonds

FOR THE FILLING

900g plums, stoned and quartered

125g light muscovado sugar

2 tablespoons plain flour

finely grated zest of 1 lemon

KIT

Food processor

Clingfilm

Shallow 1.7 litre pie dish, e.g. oval gratin dish

Pastry brush

LITTLE EXTRAS

Plain flour for dusting

Milk for brushing

Golden caster sugar for dusting

FOR THE PASTRY

200g plain flour

30g golden caster sugar

100g unsalted butter, chilled and diced

1 medium egg yolk

FOR THE CUSTARD FILLING

9 medium eggs

300g golden caster sugar

finely grated zest and juice of 2 lemons

finely grated zest and juice of 2 oranges

250ml double cream

KIT

Food processor

20cm non-stick cake tin, at least 7cm deep

Foil

Baking beans or dried pulses

Electric whisk

Baking tray

LITTLE EXTRAS

Icing sugar for dusting

lemon custard tart

I like to 'cut' the lemon juice with some orange, which gives a gentler but perfectly balanced tart.

To make the pastry, place the flour, sugar and butter in the bowl of a food processor and reduce to a crumb-like consistency. Add the egg yolk and enough water to bring the dough together into a ball. Reserve a small amount of the pastry to patch any cracks once the case is cooked and press the remainder into a 20cm non-stick cake tin, at least 7cm deep, so the pastry comes about 6cm up the sides. Chill for 1 hour.

Preheat the oven to 180°C fan oven/200°C electric oven. Line the pastry case with foil and baking beans (any dried pulses will do), securing the pastry sides firmly to the tin. Bake for 10 minutes until the pastry has set, then remove the foil and beans and bake for a further 10–15 minutes until lightly golden and fully baked. Allow it to cool and then patch any cracks that have appeared with the reserved pastry.

Preheat the oven to 130°C fan oven/150°C electric oven or turn it down. To make the custard filling, whisk together the eggs and sugar in a large bowl using an electric whisk until blended. Whisk in the lemon and orange zest and juice and the cream, again until blended. Pour this mixture into the pastry shell and place it on a baking tray. Bake for 1½ hours until it has set. Check it after 45 minutes to make sure it is starting to set, turn the oven up if it is still a barely warm liquid; turn the oven down if it appears to be cooking too quickly. It is important that the tart is removed from the oven as soon as it has set.

Remove from the oven and leave it to cool to room temperature before trimming the top of the pastry level with the custard, leaving the collar of the tin in place. Cover and chill the tart for several hours, removing it 30 minutes before eating. Liberally dust the surface of the tart with icing sugar just before serving it.

FOR THE PASTRY

230g plain flour (see TIP)

70g golden caster sugar

130g unsalted butter, chilled and diced

1 medium egg, separated

1–2 teaspoons whole milk

FOR THE FILLING

200g pecan nuts

finely grated zest of 1 lemon, and the juice of ½ lemon

300g golden syrup

3 medium eggs, and 2 egg yolks

300ml double cream

pinch of fine sea salt

KIT

Food processor

Clingfilm

23cm tart tin with a removable base, 4–6cm deep

Foil

Baking beans or dried pulses

Baking tray

Pastry brush

Small whisk

LITTLE EXTRAS

Plain flour for rolling

pecan pie

This pie is luxuriously deep and creamy, which offsets the texture of the nuts and the pastry.

To make the pastry, place the flour, sugar and butter in the bowl of a food processor and give it a quick burst at high speed to reduce it to a crumb-like consistency. Add the egg yolk (reserving the white for later) and then, with the motor running, trickle in just enough milk for the dough to cling together in lumps. Bring the pastry together into a ball using your hands and then pat into a flattened patty. Wrap in clingfilm and chill for at least 1 hour or overnight.

Preheat the oven to 180°C fan oven/200°C electric oven. Lightly dust a worksurface with plain flour and knead the pastry until it is pliable. Thinly roll out the pastry and use it to line the base and sides of a 23cm tart tin with a removable base, 4–6cm deep – I usually slide the base of the tin under the rolled out pastry and then lift the whole thing into the tin. Don't worry if you end up partly pressing it into the tart tin.

Trim the edges by running a rolling pin across the top and reserve the trimmings. Line the case with foil and baking beans (any dried pulses will do), securing the sides to the tin. Place on a baking tray and bake for 15 minutes. Remove the foil and beans, paint the case with the egg white and patch any cracks with the trimmings. Return to the oven for a further 10 minutes until the case is evenly golden. Patch again if any cracks appear.

Turn the oven down to 150°C fan oven/170°C electric oven. Thinly slice two-thirds of the pecan nuts, reserving the rest for the top. In a large bowl, whisk the lemon zest and juice with the syrup using a small whisk. Beat in the eggs and egg yolks, and finally the cream. Fold in the sliced nuts and salt and then pour the mixture into the precooked tart case. Arrange the reserved pecan halves, flat-side down, over the surface, discarding any broken ones. Bake for 60 minutes until lightly golden and puffy at the edges – if you move the tart around the filling should wobble slightly without showing any signs of being liquid. Remove the tart from the oven and set aside to cool for a couple of hours, then chill it for another couple of hours. If chilling for more than a few hours, cover with clingfilm and remove from the fridge 30 minutes before serving.

TIP
I have also made this pastry successfully using spelt flour; its character works well with the pecan filling.

FOR THE PASTRY

230g plain flour

70g golden caster sugar

130g unsalted butter, chilled
and diced

1 medium egg, separated

a little whole milk

FOR THE FILLING

3 medium eggs, and 2 egg yolks

juice and finely grated zest of
1 lemon

300ml golden syrup

300ml double cream

100g fresh breadcrumbs

1 eating apple, peeled and
grated

KIT

Food processor

Clingfilm

23cm tart tin, 4–6cm deep

Foil

Baking beans or dried pulses

Pastry brush

Small whisk

Baking tray

LITTLE EXTRAS

Plain flour for rolling

Clotted cream, to serve
(optional)

treacle tart

This treacle tart is deep and creamy; and the lemon and the apple
cut through the sweetness of the syrup.

To make the pastry, place the flour, sugar and butter in the bowl of a food processor
and give it a quick burst at high speed to reduce it to a crumb-like consistency. Add
the egg yolk (reserving the white for later) and then, with the motor running, trickle
in just enough milk for the dough to cling together in lumps. Transfer the pastry to a
large bowl and bring it together into a ball using your hands. Wrap it in clingfilm and
chill for at least 1 hour or overnight.

Preheat the oven to 180°C fan oven/200°C electric oven. Lightly flour a worksurface.
Thinly roll out the pastry and use it to line the base and sides of a 23cm tart tin,
4–6cm deep – I usually slide the base of the tin under the rolled out pastry and then
lift the whole lot into the tin. Don't worry if you end up partly pressing it into the tart
tin. Trim the edges by running a rolling pin across the top and reserve the trimmings.

Line the case with foil and baking beans (any dried pulses will do), securing the sides
to the tin. Bake for 15 minutes. Remove the foil and beans, paint the case with the
reserved egg white and patch any cracks with the trimmings. Bake for a further 10
minutes until the case is evenly gold. Patch again if any cracks appear.

Turn the oven down to 150°C fan oven/170°C electric oven. To make the filling, whisk
the eggs and yolks in a large bowl with the lemon juice and zest, using a small whisk.
Add the golden syrup and cream and continue whisking until the mixture emulsifies.
Stir in the breadcrumbs along with the grated apple and pour straight away into the
precooked tart case. Place on a baking tray and bake in the oven for 60 minutes
until lightly golden and puffy at the edges, and if you move the tart around the filling
wobbles slightly without showing any signs of being liquid. Remove from the oven
and leave the tart to cool for a couple of hours. Accompany with some clotted cream
if wished.

TIP

This tart is also good chilled, in which case cover with clingfilm
and place in the fridge for several hours or overnight. Just before
serving, dust with icing sugar if wished.

FOR THE SWEET SHORTCRUST PASTRY

150g unsalted butter, softened

150g golden caster sugar

2 medium eggs

400g plain flour, sifted

50g ground almonds

FOR THE FILLING

600g fresh cherries, pitted

a generous squeeze of lemon juice

75g light muscovado sugar

1 tablespoon plain flour

KIT

Food processor

Clingfilm

23cm tart tin, 3cm deep

Pastry brush

LITTLE EXTRAS

Plain flour for rolling

Milk for brushing

Golden caster sugar for dusting

all-american cherry pie

The pastry settles over the cherries as the pie bakes in an alluring cartoon-esque fashion – you can just imagine the mama in *Tom and Jerry* padding in her slippers from kitchen to dining room, the triumph of a cherry pie held high in her hand. It goes without saying, a big jug of custard on the table would further its homely appeal.

To make the pastry, cream the butter and sugar in a food processor. Beat in the eggs until well combined, then gradually add the flour and ground almonds. Bring the dough together in a ball, wrap it in clingfilm and chill for at least 2 hours; it will keep for several days.

Preheat the oven to 180°C fan oven/200°C electric oven. Allow the dough to come to room temperature for a few minutes and then knead it until pliable. On a lightly floured surface, thinly roll out two-thirds of the dough and use it to line the base of a 23cm tart tin, 3cm deep. Don't worry if the dough tears and you end up partly pressing it into the tin. Trim the sides, reserving the trimmings.

To make the filling, toss the cherries with the lemon juice, brown sugar and flour. Tip them into the tart tin, spreading them out evenly. Roll out the remaining pastry, including any trimmings, to form a circle the same diameter as the tin. Paint the edge of the pastry in the tin with milk and lay the pastry over the top.

Press the pastry together around the sides and trim to neaten, then crimp the edge using the tip of your finger. Cut a couple of small slits in the centre to release the steam. Brush the surface of the pastry with milk and dust with caster sugar. Bake for about 35 minutes until the pastry is golden and the cherries are tender. Serve hot, about 20 minutes out of the oven, or at room temperature.

TIP

You can also decorate the pie. Roll out the pastry trimmings and cut out an apple or two with a stalk. Brush the shapes with milk and lay them in place, and then brush with milk all over.

If necessary the pie can be reheated for 20 minutes at 160°C fan oven/180°C fan oven.

good old-fashioned apple pie

Good and old-fashioned, this is that little bit more sophisticated than your average apple pie. Baked in a shallow dish, it takes advantage of eaters and cookers – the first hold their shape, while the latter collapse to a purée and offer the richest flavour.

Soak the raisins in the rum in a small bowl for several hours or overnight. To make the pastry, place the flour and butter in a food processor, give it a quick burst at high speed to reduce it to a crumb-like consistency, then add the icing sugar and give it another quick burst. Add the egg yolk and enough water to bring the dough together, wrap it in clingfilm and chill for several hours.

Preheat the oven to 160°C fan oven/180°C electric oven. Allow the dough to come to room temperature for a few minutes and then knead it until pliable. On a lightly floured surface, thinly roll out two-thirds of the dough and use it to line the base of a 30cm oval gratin dish, letting the extra hang over the sides; trim the excess. Don't worry if the dough tears and you end up partly pressing it into the dish.

Toss the apples with the sugar and flour in a bowl, and then mix in the soaked raisins along with any rum left in the bottom of the bowl. Tip the fruit mixture into the pie dish. Roll out the remaining pastry, incorporating any trimmings, to fit the top of the dish. Paint the pastry rim of the dish with milk, lay the lid on top and press around the sides to seal. Trim the edges and push them down slightly below the fruit, which will sink as it bakes, and crimp them with the tines of a fork. Brush all over with milk and dust with caster sugar.

Bake the pie for 35–45 minutes until the pastry is lightly golden and the apples are tender. Leave to stand for 10 minutes and serve hot or warm with cream.

SERVES 6

FOR THE FILLING

50g raisins

2 tablespoons dark rum

600g Bramley cooking apples, peeled, cored and thickly sliced

300g eating apples, peeled cored and thickly sliced

100g golden caster sugar

1 tablespoon plain flour

FOR THE PASTRY

450g plain flour

250g unsalted butter, chilled and diced

100g icing sugar

1 medium egg yolk

KIT

Food processor

Clingfilm

30cm/2 litre oval gratin dish

LITTLE EXTRAS

Plain flour for rolling

Milk for brushing

Golden caster sugar for dusting

Whipped or clotted cream, to serve

banoffee pie

MAKES 1 X 23CM PIE

FOR THE CRUST

250g digestive biscuits

125g unsalted butter, melted

FOR THE TOFFEE FILLING

125g unsalted butter, diced

100g light muscovado sugar

1 x 400g jar dulce de leche, e.g.
Nestlé Caramel

1 teaspoon vanilla extract

FOR THE TOPPING

1–2 small bananas, peeled and
finely sliced

a squeeze of lemon juice

1 gelatine leaf, e.g. Supercook,
cut into broad strips

2 tablespoons strong black
coffee, hot

275ml double cream

KIT

Food processor

23cm tart tin, 3cm deep

Clingfilm

Electric whisk

LITTLE EXTRAS

Dark chocolate shavings
for decorating

It's easy to see why this absurdly indulgent creation is the hit that it is. Calories? Off the scale, don't even try counting. Nestlé now makes tins of 'caramel' that do away with the need for boiling up tins of condensed milk for hours to create the gooey layer of toffee beneath the cream and bananas.

Break the digestives into pieces and whizz to crumbs in a food processor. Alternatively, you can place them in two plastic bags, one placed inside another, and gently crush them using a rolling pin. Combine with the melted butter and press onto the base and sides of a 23cm tart tin, 3cm deep.

To make the filling, melt the butter with the sugar in a small non-stick saucepan. Add the dulce de leche and vanilla extract and bring to the boil, stirring constantly; if necessary, whisk until smooth. Pour the mixture over the biscuit base, cover the surface with clingfilm and set aside to cool for about 1 hour.

Toss the banana slices with the lemon juice to coat them and arrange in a single layer on top of the toffee, starting at the outside just inside the tart rim.

Place the gelatine in a medium-size bowl, cover with cold water and leave to soak for 5 minutes, then drain. Pour over the hot coffee and stir to dissolve. Stir the cream into the gelatine solution, a tablespoon at a time to begin with. Whip the cream with an electric whisk until soft peaks form. Spread on top of the bananas, taking it up to the sides but not covering them. Scatter the surface with chocolate shavings and chill for a couple of hours. Cover with clingfilm and store in the fridge for up to 48 hours.

250g plain flour

125g ground almonds

200g golden caster sugar

finely grated zest of 1 lemon

250g unsalted butter, chilled and diced

approx. 300g eating apples, peeled, cored and thinly sliced

approx. 200g Bramley cooking apples, peeled, cored and thickly sliced

300g blackberries

KIT

Food processor

20cm non-stick cake tin with a removable base, 9cm deep

LITTLE EXTRAS

Icing sugar for dusting (optional)

deep blackberry and apple streusel

A streusel is a winning German take on a crumble, and derives from the word scatter or sprinkle. The great thing is it comes in cake form, which opens the doors to serving it at tea and coffee time as well as for pud.

This is a blackberry and apple pie by any other name, a relaxed take that is deliciously deep but delicate. This version plays on the strengths of both cookers and eaters – Bramleys for that jammy intensity and eaters, which hold their shape.

Preheat the oven to 170°C fan oven/190°C electric oven. Place the flour, ground almonds, 125g of the caster sugar and the lemon zest in the bowl of a food processor. Add the butter and reduce the mixture to crumbs (it's very important that the butter is cold, otherwise it will cream into a dough). Using your fingers, press half the mixture into the base of a 20cm non-stick cake tin with a removable base, 9cm deep – as if you were making shortbread.

Toss the apples and blackberries with the remaining 75g sugar in a large bowl. Spoon the fruit over the shortcake base. Tip the crumble mixture on top and level – it will come to the top of the tin, but will sink as it cooks. Bake for 1 hour until the top is golden and crisp and the juices are bubbling at the sides. Allow the streusel to cool in the tin. Run a knife around the edge of the collar, then liberally dust with icing sugar if wished.

TIP

You can also make a rhubarb and apple version of this pie: omit the lemon zest from the crumble mixture, and use approx. 450g eating apples, peeled, cored and sliced, and 300g rhubarb, trimmed and cut into 3cm lengths.

mad hatter jam tarts

MAKES APPROX. 12

2 medium eggs

90g salted butter, diced

70g icing sugar

120g plain flour

approx. 200g seedless raspberry jam, worked until smooth

approx. 12 raspberries

KIT

Food processor

Clingfilm

8cm fluted cutter

Fairy cake tray

LITTLE EXTRAS

Plain flour for rolling

This slightly mad pastry, made with hard-boiled egg yolks, is typical of some French biscuits and makes for a really short and cakey finish. These soften after a day, but are still very good.

Bring a small pan of water to the boil, carefully lower in the eggs and cook for 10 minutes. Drain and refill the pan with cold water and leave to cool. Shell the eggs, discarding the whites, and mash the yolks with a fork.

Cream the butter and sugar together in a food processor, then add the hard-boiled yolks, and finally the flour. It will be very sticky and soft at this point. Wrap the dough in clingfilm and pat into a flattened block. Chill for several hours or overnight.

Preheat the oven to 170°C fan oven/190°C electric oven. Roll out the dough about 5mm thick on a lightly floured surface, and cut out circles using an 8cm fluted cutter, then roll out the trimmings. Press into a fairy cake tray, and fill with a heaped teaspoon of jam. Bake for about 15 minutes until the pastry rims are golden. Remove and leave to cool. Decorate each one with a raspberry. They are at their crispest fresh but still good the following day, in which case decorate shortly before serving.

fig streusel squares

MAKES APPROX. 12 SQUARES

200g plain flour

110g ground almonds

110g golden caster sugar

225g unsalted butter, chilled and diced

500g fresh figs, stalks trimmed, cut into quarters

2 tablespoons runny honey

40g flaked almonds

KIT

Food processor

30cm x 23cm non-stick traybake tin, 4cm deep

LITTLE EXTRAS

Icing sugar for dusting (optional)

This is a streusel in traybake form for cutting into squares. The marriage of figs, almonds and honey is the stuff that Greek islands are made of – somehow they seem to go hand in glove as a trio.

Preheat the oven to 170°C fan oven/190°C electric oven. Place the flour, ground almonds and caster sugar in the bowl of a food processor. Add the butter and reduce the mixture to crumbs (it's very important that the butter is cold, otherwise it will cream into a dough). Scatter half the crumble mixture over the bottom of a 30 x 23cm non-stick traybake tin, 4cm deep, and press it onto the base with your fingers as if you were making shortbread. Scatter the fig quarters over the top and drizzle over the honey. Stir the flaked almonds into the remaining crumble mixture and scatter this over the figs – there should be tips of fruit showing through.

Bake for 45 minutes until the top is golden and crisp. Remove and allow the traybake to cool, then dust the surface with icing sugar if you wish. To serve, run a knife around the edge of the tin and cut the streusel into squares.

150g currants

125g raisins

25g blanched almonds,
finely chopped

1 knob of stem ginger,
finely chopped

1 eating apple, peeled
and grated

50g shredded suet (beef
or vegetable)

¼ teaspoon ground cinnamon

¼ teaspoon ground nutmeg

knife tip of ground cloves

finely grated zest and juice
of 1 lemon

2 tablespoons brandy

1 tablespoon dark
muscovado sugar

homemade mincemeat

Mincemeat is one of those eccentric British confections that is a masterpiece in its own right, a blend of dried fruit and nuts, spices, brown sugar and brandy. It is good to know how to make your own, if time allows, although frequently I end up titivating a good jar of ready-made, given the enormity of preparing for the festive season. A splash of dark rum, Calvados or Armagnac, and some lemon zest and juice and a knife tip of ground cinnamon work wonders to enliven it.

Going back to the real thing, it is incredibly easy to make. My own blend employs stem ginger in lieu of crystallised fruit, lots of currants, grated apple and lemon. The mix is drier than the commercial stuff, which is almost jammy by comparison, but once baked the suet, grated apple and dark brown sugar meld to coat everything in a lovely spicy slick.

Combine all the ingredients for the mincemeat in a bowl, cover and set aside for at least 12 hours. Use within 24 hours.

TIP

The pleasure of mincemeat is creating it to suit your own taste, so use this as a guideline. You may be partial to glace cherries and candied peel, or prefer rum in lieu of brandy and orange instead of lemon.

TIP
These can be stored in an airtight container for up to a week, and reheated on demand for 5 minutes at 150°C fan oven/170°C electric oven. They can also be frozen.

good old-fashioned mince pies

MAKES APPROX. 18

FOR THE PASTRY

450g plain flour

125g unsalted butter, chilled and diced

125g lard, chilled and diced

100g icing sugar, sifted

1 medium egg yolk

a little milk or water

FOR THE FILLING

1–2 tablespoons brandy

a squeeze of lemon juice

approx. 300g mincemeat (see page 302)

golden caster sugar for dusting

KIT

Food processor

Clingfilm

8cm and 6cm fluted cutters

2 non-stick fairy cake trays

Pastry brush

LITTLE EXTRAS

Plain flour for rolling

These are a classic take on a mince pie. Even though I try endlessly to re-invent them, it's hard to beat a down-to-earth little pie. The lard is a British touch that allows for really short pastry, and it does give the pies their quintessential flavour and texture, but it could just as well be all-butter should you prefer.

To make the pastry, place the flour, butter and lard in a food processor. Give it a quick burst at high speed to reduce it to a crumb-like consistency, then add the icing sugar and give it another quick burst. Add the egg yolk and enough milk or water to bring the dough together, wrap it in clingfilm and chill for 1 hour or overnight.

Preheat the oven to 170°C fan oven/190°C electric oven. Stir the brandy and lemon juice into the mincemeat. Roll two-thirds of the pastry to the thickness of about 3–4mm on a lightly floured worksurface, and cut out circles using an 8cm fluted cutter to fit a couple of non-stick fairy cake trays. Place in the trays and fill with a heaped teaspoon of mincemeat.

Roll out the remaining pastry with the trimmings and cut out lids using a 6cm fluted cutter. Brush the rim of the pies with milk or water, lay the lids on top and gently press the edges together. Dust with sugar and bake for 15–20 minutes until the pastry is a pale gold. Serve warm, about 20 minutes out of the oven, or at room temperature.

rum butter

A little rum butter on top or slipped under the lid while they're warm keeps them in traditional mode.

Whisk the butter and icing sugar together using an electric whisk until light and fluffy, then gradually whisk in the rum, until you have a smooth creamy butter. Transfer to a bowl, cover and chill until required. Remove the butter from the fridge about 20 minutes before serving.

SERVES 6–8

175g unsalted butter, softened

175g icing sugar, sifted

6 tablespoons dark rum

KIT

Electric whisk

FOR THE FILLING

300g mincemeat

2 tablespoons brandy

a squeeze of lemon juice

FOR THE PASTRY

225g unsalted butter, chilled and diced

200g plain flour

110g golden caster sugar

110g ground almonds

KIT

Non-stick fairy cake tray

Food processor

8cm fluted cutter

LITTLE EXTRAS

Unsalted butter for greasing

Plain flour for rolling

Icing sugar for dusting

mince pie crumbles

Could these short, buttery mince pies be the speediest yet? With no resting of the pastry needed, you can whip them up as a last minute solution – and the crumble topping is so much easier than making pies with lids. If you want to make up a larger quantity, I would make up the dough in batches so as not to overcrowd the machine.

Preheat the oven to 170°C fan oven/190°C electric oven and butter the moulds of a non-stick fairy cake tray. Blend the mincemeat with the brandy and lemon juice in a medium-sized bowl. Place all the ingredients for the pastry in a food processor and whizz until the mixture forms crumbs that just start to cling together into nibs. Set aside 4 heaped tablespoons of this mixture for the topping and whizz the remainder until it comes together into a dough. Roll out the pastry on a well-floured worksurface to a thickness of about 5–7mm (slightly thicker than usual, allowing for its shortbread-like texture).

Cut out circles using an 8cm fluted cutter, rolling the dough twice, to give 12 bases in all. Lay them in the prepared tray and divide the mincemeat between them, filling each case with about 1½ teaspoons. Spoon a heaped teaspoon of the reserved crumble on top, carefully spreading it out within the pastry rim – some of the mincemeat may show through.

Bake for 25 minutes until the pies are golden around the edge. Set aside to cool in the tin for 30 minutes before loosening the bases with a knife. Dust with icing sugar to serve. Like most mince pies, these keep well for many days in an airtight container.

calvados cream

SERVES 6–8

225g crème fraîche

1–2 tablespoons Calvados

50g icing sugar, sifted

A thick, sweet pouring cream laced with Calvados, lovely with warm mince pies as well as apple pies and the like. You can use any fruit eau-de-vie, Armagnac or brandy here.

Whisk the ingredients together in a bowl, cover and chill until required.

sahara mincemeat

MAKES 9–16 SQUARES

225g self-raising flour, sifted

110g golden caster sugar

110g icing sugar, sifted

225g lightly salted butter, diced

3 medium eggs, separated, and 2 egg yolks

¾ teaspoon vanilla extract

1 x 400g jar of mincemeat

KIT

Food processor

Clingfilm

23cm non-stick square brownie tin, 4cm deep

Electric whisk

LITTLE EXTRAS

Unsalted butter for greasing

My brothers and I grew up with this one, as much of a tradition in our house as mince pies – in part, I am sure, because it is so easy to make by comparison. We prized its generous, gooey shortbread base and lick of souffléd mincemeat, great with custard.

But did my mother just hear it wrong from a friend before she entered it in her handwritten book of recipes, something I treasure now that she is gone? The name certainly seems plausibly 1970s, but I cannot find any mention of Sahara Mincemeat elsewhere, and have never encountered anything similar. A mystery.

Place the flour, two sugars and butter in the bowl of a food processor and whizz until the mixture forms a crumb-like consistency. In a separate bowl, blend the 5 egg yolks with the vanilla. Pour into the processor with the dry ingredients and whizz to a soft, sticky dough. Wrap in clingfilm and chill for at least a couple of hours.

Preheat the oven to 170°C fan oven/190°C electric oven and butter a 23cm non-stick square brownie tin, 4cm deep. Press the dough into the tin, laying a sheet of clingfilm over the top and smoothing it with your fingers. Bake for 25 minutes until lightly golden, crusty and risen.

Spoon the mincemeat into a large bowl. In a separate bowl, whisk the egg whites until stiff using an electric whisk and then fold into the mincemeat in two batches.

Smooth the mixture over the shortcake base and bake for 15–20 minutes until lightly coloured on the surface. Leave to cool completely in the tin before carefully running a sharp knife around the outside and cutting into 9–16 squares. It should keep well for several days loosely covered in clingfilm.

easy breads and pancakes

160g wholegrain spelt flour

130g refined spelt flour

25g sunflower seeds, plus a few extra for the top

25g pumpkin seeds, plus a few extra for the top

1 teaspoon sea salt

½ teaspoon bicarbonate of soda

1 medium egg

180ml buttermilk

KIT

Non-stick baking tray

Wire rack

LITTLE EXTRAS

Wholegrain spelt flour for kneading and dusting

seeded spelt soda bread

The simplest of breads, you can knock this one up in 10 minutes, as there's no rising involved. This is best eaten on the day it is made, though it does make fine toast the day after and will also freeze on the day. Delicious eaten newly cooled or slightly warm with some farmhouse Cheddar and chutney.

Preheat the oven to 170°C fan oven/190°C electric oven. Combine the flours, seeds, salt and bicarbonate of soda in a large bowl. Whisk the egg and buttermilk together in another bowl, tip onto the dry ingredients and mix with a wooden spoon until blended, then bring the dough together using your hands. It will be sticky at this point, so throw another handful of wholegrain flour over and knead it on a lightly floured worksurface to smooth out any large cracks.

Form it into a ball, place this on a non-stick baking tray lightly dusted with wholegrain flour and mark a cross on the top, cutting about 1cm down. Scatter over a few more seeds and bake for 45–50 minutes until risen and golden and the base sounds hollow when tapped. Leave it to cool on a wire rack. It is best eaten the day it is made.

TIP
Like American muffins, the art here lies with slapdash mixing.

pain d'épices

MAKES 1 X 22CM LOAF

120g unsalted butter, diced

150g dark resinous honey, e.g. pine or Greek mountain

110g rye flour (wholemeal or plain)

110g plain flour

100g light muscovado sugar

pinch of sea salt

¾ teaspoon bicarbonate of soda

½ teaspoon ground cinnamon

½ teaspoon ground ginger

½ teaspoon ground nutmeg

¼ teaspoon ground cloves

180ml whole milk

3 medium eggs

KIT

22cm/1.3 litre non-stick loaf tin

Clingfilm

LITTLE EXTRAS

Unsalted butter for greasing

Unsalted butter and marmalade, to serve (optional)

This lovely lightly spiced and moist honey cake is half bread and half cake, neither too rich or too sweet. It is one of the few cakes that I would choose to make using a wholemeal flour, which you can use on its own if wished, or as suggested here cut half and half with plain white. Try serving it with a rhubarb or apple compote, or poached pears and crème fraîche. And on a savoury note it is lovely with a sliver of creamy chicken liver pâté.

Preheat the oven to 140°C fan oven/160°C electric oven and butter a 22cm/1.3 litre non-stick loaf tin. Gently heat the honey and butter together in a small saucepan, whisking until melted and amalgamated.

Place the flours, sugar and salt in a large bowl and sift over the bicarbonate of soda and the ground spices. Add the honey mixture and whisk to a thick paste, gradually whisk in the milk and then the eggs one at a time. Pour this into the prepared tin, and bake for 1¼ hours until risen and firm and a skewer inserted into the centre comes out clean.

Run a knife around the edge of the cake and leave it to stand for about 15 minutes. Then turn it out onto a sheet of clingfilm while still hot, wrap up and set aside for at least 24 hours when it will develop its classic sticky crust. It will be good for some days in an airtight container. It's particularly good with unsalted butter and marmalade.

TIP

This is a great keeper courtesy of the honey, it matures over a number of days even though you can start cutting into it after 24 hours. Keep it somewhere cool, but not the fridge.

MAKES 1 X 22CM LOAF

15g unsalted butter

1 small onion, peeled and chopped

125g tinned sweetcorn kernels

sea salt and black pepper

125g cornmeal or polenta

140g self-raising flour, sifted

15g golden caster sugar

1 tablespoon baking powder, sifted

2 medium eggs

200ml whole milk

KIT

22cm/1.3 litre non-stick loaf tin

Wire rack

LITTLE EXTRAS

Unsalted butter for greasing

Cornmeal or polenta for dusting

cornbread loaf

This must be to the Deep South what soda bread is to Ireland, and it is easy to see how its scent would soon call up nostalgic memories were you raised on it. Unusually for cornbread this has real sweetcorn in it as well as the ground, which makes for a decadently moist bread. It will keep well for several days in an airtight container, and is especially good with roasted ham.

Preheat the oven to 170°C fan oven/190°C electric oven and butter a 22cm/1.3 litre non-stick loaf tin. Melt the butter in a large frying pan over a medium heat. Add the onion and fry for several minutes until softened, without colouring, then add the sweetcorn and fry for a little longer, seasoning the mixture.

Combine the cornmeal or polenta, flour, sugar, baking powder and a teaspoon of salt in a large bowl. In another bowl, whisk the eggs with the milk, then stir in the fried onions and sweetcorn. Tip the wet ingredients into the dry ones and loosely combine, leaving the mixture on the lumpy side.

Pour the mixture into the prepared tin and bake for 30–35 minutes until golden and crusty on the surface and a skewer inserted into the centre comes out clean. Run a knife around the outside and turn onto a wire rack to cool. You can dust it with a little more cornmeal or polenta if you wish.

TIP

Cornbread is mixed with the same abandon as muffins, where dry and wet ingredients are acquainted in a sloppy fashion – in fact, you could use the mixture for just these. I particularly like this bread for its lengthy shelf life, it stays nicely moist for days.

Cornbread is especially good eaten with crispy bacon and maple syrup. Bake for about 15 minutes on a rack set over a baking tray at 200°C fan oven/220°C electric oven, brushing the bacon either side with maple syrup 5 minutes before the end. You can serve with more syrup drizzled over.

fruited
yogurt loaf

MAKES 1 X 22CM LOAF

100g unsalted butter, softened

100g golden caster sugar

300g live set natural yogurt, stirred

3 tablespoons smooth orange juice

1 teaspoon vanilla extract

250g plain flour

1 teaspoon bicarbonate of soda

75g raisins

75g currants

KIT

Electric whisk

22cm/1.3 litre non-stick loaf tin

Wire rack

Such is the calm outlook of my lovely Krishna plumber, there are no problems, just solutions. He has long waxed lyrical about the cakes his wife bakes using yogurt – Krishnas are not allowed to eat eggs.

Eggs are one of the hardest ingredients of all to omit from a cake, given the role they play in making it rise and its structure generally.

You would never guess from this fruited teabread that they were not present and correct; it's much moister than a scone, in fact moister than a sponge generally, more in keeping with a yeasted loaf.

Preheat the oven to 150°C fan oven/170°C electric oven. Whisk the butter in a large bowl using an electric whisk for about 1 minute until fluffy, then add the sugar and continue to whisk for another minute until very light. Whisk in the yogurt, orange juice and vanilla; the mixture may appear slightly curdled at this point. Sift the dry ingredients together, and toss the raisins and currants with a little of the mixture.

Lightly fold the remaining flour into the cake mixture in two goes and then fold in the dried fruit.

Spoon the mixture into an unbuttered non-stick 22cm/1.3 litre non-stick loaf tin, leaving it mounded in the centre. Bake for 1 hour until risen and golden and a skewer inserted into the centre comes out clean. Lay the tin on its side and set aside to cool for 15 minutes, then turn it over and set aside for a further 15 minutes. Slip the loaf out of the tin, place it the right way up on a wire rack and leave to cool completely.

500g plain flour

75g icing sugar

25g baking power

½ teaspoon fine sea salt

125g unsalted butter, chilled and diced

2 medium eggs, beaten

a little whole milk

KIT

Food processor

7cm cutter, plain or fluted

2 non-stick baking trays

Pastry brush

LITTLE EXTRAS

Plain flour for rolling

Milk for brushing

Unsalted butter or clotted cream, to serve

Strawberry or other jam, to serve

a good plain scone

I am inclined to judge all scones from childhood memories of Devon cream teas. It was one of the great treats of any holiday, a rainy day solution, driving down some muddy lane to a hidden farmhouse, tramping through to a backroom where we would settle to the most enormous tea of warm scones, mounds of clotted cream and strawberry jam. Heaven.

For anyone who eschews yeast cookery, scones are the answer. They are so very easy to knock out and, as with pancakes, what is perhaps most useful is a really good recipe for the basic. These ones are big and blowsy, and promise to be thick and fluffy within. But you can also make them smaller as shown here.

Sift the flour, icing sugar and baking powder into the bowl of a food processor and add the salt. Add the butter and whizz to crumbs. Incorporate the eggs and add just enough milk to bring the dough together. You can also make the dough by hand.

Roll the dough out to a thickness of 2cm on a lightly floured worksurface and cut out about eight 7cm scones, only rolling the dough twice. Arrange on one or two non-stick baking trays, spacing them well apart, and leave to rest for 20 minutes.

Preheat the oven to 180°C fan oven/200°C electric oven. Brush the tops of the scones with milk and bake for 17–20 minutes. They are most delicious eaten warm, split and spread with butter and jam, or clotted cream for a treat, but are also good at room temperature.

TIP

To prevent scones from toughening, work the mixture as quickly as possible. Avoid kneading the dough and roll it just twice.

Add the milk a little at a time – you can always add more – but if the dough is wet the scones will spread. If doing this by hand, use a fork. Try squeezing a handful of crumbs together to see if they stick before adding more milk.

Scones, like muffins, are best eaten the day they are made. You can, however, bring them back to life the following day by reheating them at 180°C fan oven/200°C electric oven for 5–10 minutes, depending on their size.

400g plain flour

125g icing sugar

1 teaspoon mixed spice

25g baking powder

75g wholemeal flour

finely grated zest of 1 orange

½ teaspoon sea salt

125g unsalted butter, chilled
and diced

2 medium eggs, beaten

100g currants

a little whole milk

KIT

Food processor

7cm cutter, plain or fluted

2 non-stick baking trays

Pastry brush

LITTLE EXTRAS

Plain flour for rolling

Milk for brushing

Golden caster sugar for dusting

Unsalted butter and honeycomb
or honey, to serve

big and fruity scones

Sweet and spicy, scented with orange and studded with currants,
these also contain a small amount of wholemeal flour, which gives
them a slightly more robust texture.

Sift the flour, icing sugar, mixed spice and baking powder into the bowl of a food
processor and add the wholemeal flour, orange zest and salt. Add the butter and
whizz to crumbs, then incorporate the eggs. Transfer the mixture to a large mixing
bowl, stir in the currants and add just enough milk to bring the dough together.

Roll the dough out to a thickness of 2cm on a lightly floured worksurface and cut out
about eight 7cm scones, only rolling the dough twice. Tidy the edges, pressing any
loose currrants into the dough. Arrange the scones on a couple of non-stick baking
trays, spacing them well apart, and leave to rest for 20 minutes

Preheat the oven to 180°C fan oven/200°C electric oven. Brush the tops with milk,
scatter over some caster sugar and bake for 17–20 minutes. They are most delicious
eaten warm, split and spread with butter, and honeycomb or honey for the sweet of
tooth. But they're also good at room temperature.

MAKES 12

125g self-raising flour

50g golden caster sugar

pinch of sea salt

1 medium egg

150ml whole milk

30g unsalted butter, melted

KIT

Large non-stick frying pan

Palette knife or spatula

LITTLE EXTRAS

Salted or unsalted butter,
to serve

Strawberry or other jam, or
maple syrup, to serve

scotch pancakes

Scotch pancakes are pretty much the easiest of all. Small, soft and pudgy, they are more readily turned than thin pancakes with no tossing involved. Gorgeous eaten with lashings of salty butter and homemade jam or maple syrup. They have the added advantage of being good eaten cold too.

Place the flour, sugar and salt in a medium-sized bowl. Break in the egg and then whisk in the milk in two goes. Stir in the melted butter.

Heat a large non-stick frying pan over a medium-low heat for several minutes. Drop tablespoons of the mixture into the pan and fry for about 1 minute until the top-side starts to pit with bubbles. Flip over using a palette knife or spatula and cook the undersides for 30–45 seconds until they puff up. Dish up with butter and jam or maple syrup.

TIP

The trick here is to cook them at a relatively low temperature, so they don't darken overly before the insides cook. The inclusion of melted butter in the batter means the pancakes can be turned without sticking and without having to grease the pan further.

welsh cakes

MAKES APPROX. 14

350g plain flour

120g golden caster sugar

½ teaspoon sea salt

1 teaspoon baking powder

¼ teaspoon ground mace

180g unsalted butter, diced

1 medium egg, beaten

120g currants

a little whole milk

KIT

Food processor

Clingfilm

8cm cutter, plain or fluted

Cast-iron griddle or frying pan
(or large non-stick frying pan)

LITTLE EXTRAS

Plain flour for rolling

Lard or vegetable oil for cooking

Salted or unsalted butter,
to serve

This recipe for Welsh cakes was given to me by my mother-in-law, who in turn garnered it from her grandmother who came from the Welsh valleys. So it's very traditional and authentic. Welsh cakes are somewhere between a scone and a pancake, scented with mace and studded with currants. Traditionally cooked on a griddle or in a cast-iron frying pan, they are crisp on the outside and gorgeous split open and eaten hot with a sliver of butter.

Place the flour, sugar, salt, baking powder, mace and butter in the bowl of a food processor and whizz to fine crumbs, then incorporate the egg.

Transfer the mixture to a large bowl and stir in the currants. Using a fork, mix in just enough milk for the dough to start to cling together into lumps. Bring it together into a ball using your hands, wrap in clingfilm and chill for 30 minutes. (The dough can be made the night beforehand.)

Roll the dough out to a thickness of 1cm on a lightly floured worksurface. Cut out scones using an 8cm cutter, rolling the dough twice – you should get about 14.

To cook the Welsh cakes, heat a cast-iron griddle or frying pan over a low heat for several minutes, or failing that use a large non-stick frying pan. Grease with lard or brush with vegetable oil and griddle the scones for about 3 minutes on each side until mottled with brown. You will need to do this in batches, re-greasing the pan in between. Slice while hot and spread with butter. They are also good newly cooled.

TIP

If you can lay your hands on some lard, this will give the pancakes their inimitable flavour. I know it's not wildly good for you, but just a little won't harm. Otherwise, a brushing with vegetable oil will stand in.

pancake lore

The fact that most of us can rustle up the ingredients for pancakes – eggs, milk, flour and butter – makes them one of the great convenience foods. There are various lazy options for making the pancake mixture, such as whizzing the ingredients in a liquidiser, but whisking the batter by hand to a smooth, buff-coloured cream really is the easiest thing in the world – more foolproof than, say, making a béchamel when even with the best of intentions you can end up with lumps.

I would hesitate to strive for ultra-thin pancakes, achieved in part by cutting the milk with water, as the results are of negligible improvement in delicacy – and for the heartache of cooking anything that flimsy, I would say are not worth it. A perfectly delicate pancake can be achieved with milk alone.

What matters more is the final flourish of a little melted butter. I find the first pancake (or two) inevitably hit the bin, before you alight on the right temperature and knack of turning them, but from here on the butter ensures making them is plain sailing – there is no further need to oil the pan and it enriches the finished pancakes to boot.

The other key is a non-stick pan, the saviour of pancakes, they slide out with the merest loosening at the edges. Now whether or not you toss them will depend on your theatrical skills. They won't taste any better, and to tell a cautionary tale the last time I tried this the pancake ended up in the bowl of batter itself, which was a real hat-trick.

My advice is to play safe and slip a palette knife or non-stick spatula under the pancake and gently turn it.

The heat is another consideration – too low and the pancakes fail to cook to that golden lacy finish, and too hot and they dry out and singe. A lively heat somewhere in between medium and hot should ensure that the mixture sings as it hits and coats the pan and then colours in the way you want it to.

I find with two hungry recipients seated at the table, I can just about keep up with the demand for the next pancake – even if diplomacy runs thin when you get down to the bottom of the bowl. Little can beat the cosy experience of eating them hot as they come out of the pan, with a squeeze of lemon juice and the crystalline crunch of some sugar, or a drizzle of honey.

125g plain flour

1 heaped teaspoon golden caster sugar

pinch of sea salt

2 medium eggs

300ml whole milk

20g unsalted butter, melted

KIT

24cm non-stick frying pan

Palette knife or non-stick spatula

Foil

LITTLE EXTRAS

Lemon wedges and caster sugar

Nutella

Jam

Maple syrup or honey

simple pancakes

The call for pancakes in our house is pretty much any breakfast that involves a sleepover. And that spans many mornings throughout the year, so we have this one down to a fine art – someone whisking, someone frying, someone laying. This quantity does for about three children, or two children and a lurking parent, or simply two children with a passion for pancakes. One child? Probably best not to go there, but it has been known.

The fun is turning them into a pancake bar with lemon and sugar, Nutella, strawberry jam, maple syrup – the list is endless, and you can be sure everyone will want one of each. I usually throw in some strawberries too, in idle hope.

I see little point in getting clever with a pancake mix. Ultimately you want something that's going to work and can be whisked up in a jiffy. For double the quantity use 250g flour, 1 tablespoon sugar, 3 large eggs and 2 egg yolks, 600ml whole milk and 40g unsalted butter.

To prepare the pancakes by hand, place the flour, sugar and salt in a large bowl, add the eggs and mix to a lumpy wet paste using a wooden spoon. Now whisk in the milk, a little to begin with to smooth out the lumps, then in bolder streams once you have a creamy batter. Alternatively, place all the ingredients except for the butter in a blender and whizz until smooth. Give the sides and bottom of the blender a stir to make sure there's no flour clinging, and whizz again. Finally stir in the melted butter, transferring the batter to a bowl if you've made it in a blender.

Heat a non-stick frying pan with an 18cm base (i.e. a 24cm pan) over a medium-high heat for several minutes. Ladle in just enough batter to coat the base, tipping it to allow it to run evenly over the surface. Once the pan is hot enough, the pancake mixture will sizzle immediately as it hits the pan. Cook for 30 seconds, or until the top side appears dry and lacy at the edges and is golden and lacy underneath. Loosen the edges using a palette knife or non-stick spatula, slip this underneath and flip the pancake over. Give it another 30 seconds on the other side before sliding it onto a plate. I always discard the first one – for no explicable reason other than it never seems to work properly. Cook the remainder in the same way. You can either dish up the pancakes as they are cooked, or pile them up on a plate and cover with foil to keep warm. Serve with lemon and sugar, Nutella, jam, maple syrup, honey… the list is endless.

pancake bar

Scatter over fresh raspberries and blueberries with a dollop of Greek yogurt.

Warm 150g strawberry jam with 1 tablespoon lemon juice, press it through a sieve and serve hot or cold as a drizzly sauce.

Serve with a scoop of ice cream or buy a selection of mini-tubs – chocolate fudge, caramel, strawberry cheesecake – for an ice-cream bar.

Gently melt 2 sliced Mars Bars with 3 tablespoons whipping cream in a bowl set over a pan with a little simmering water in it, whisking until smooth. For praline pancakes, scatter with roasted chopped hazelnuts.

For banoffee pancakes, spread with dulce de leche, scatter over sliced banana and dollop with whipped cream.

Wrap a chocolate Flake up in a pancake and let the warmth gently melt it.

For a cut above the classic, serve with halved lemons wrapped in muslin and vanilla sugar.

pancake race

I cannot be alone in being fascinated by pancake races. There is something heartwarming about this tradition, which has been going on since 1445 when pancakes were a popular treat. The origins are something of a mystery. They are thought possibly to have started as an harassed housewife, hearing the shriving bell, dashed off to church frying pan in hand. Though I prefer the notion that it was a bribe for the ringer or sexton to ring the bell sooner than intended, to indicate the start of the holiday – Shrove Tuesday being a day of last fling celebrations before the start of Lent.

Either way, it is with some relief that I do not qualify to enter Olney's famed pancake race, where you have to have been resident for three months before the event. But I love the idea, and am there in spirit cheering on those women game enough to race in their pinnies as they toss to the finishing line, before receiving a kiss from the verger.

TIP

As the result of many mornings when I've needed to speed things up, I've come to the conclusion that resting the batter doesn't make any difference at all. You can start frying as soon as you've finished mixing.

I swear by a non-stick frying pan (see page 21) – and if you want to speed things up then have two on the go. Select a frying pan with an 18cm base (i.e. a 24cm pan), although for small children you could use a slightly smaller pan than this.

You can also make these in advance, cover and chill the pancakes once they are cool, and reheat them briefly on each side in a dry frying pan. In this case, they keep well for several days.

mock blinis

These mock blinis, which rely on a raising agent rather than yeast, are pudgy and slightly sour – as heavenly spread with salty butter and honeycomb as they are with the traditional line-up of smoked salmon or roe and soured cream.

Sift the dry ingredients into a large bowl. Whisk the egg yolk and milk in another bowl until blended. Pour this mixture onto the sifted dry ingredients and whisk until smooth. In a separate bowl, whisk the egg white until stiff using an electric whisk and fold into the pancake mixture.

Preheat a cast-iron frying pan or flat griddle on a lowish heat for 10 minutes until it reaches an even snug warmth. Grease the hot pan with oil, and then drop tablespoons of the mixture into the pan spaced slightly apart. Cook for 1–2 minutes until the surface pits with bubbles, and then carefully turn the pancakes over using a palette knife. Cook for a further minute until golden on the underside. You should find the first side is completely smooth, while the underside looks more like a crumpet.

Remove them to a plate. To serve, smear with a little salted butter and a dollop of honey, and eat while you put some more on to cook, re-oiling the pan now and again between batches as it needs it.

TIP

Buckwheat (*Fagopyrum esculentum*) is no relation to wheat, and is gluten free. It is actually a member of the rhubarb family, and looks like dock. It is quite widely available from specialist flour producers.

If you are making the pancakes in advance, keep them covered with foil on a plate for up to half an hour. If storing for longer than this, they can be reheated in an oven at 160°C fan oven/180°C electric oven. Stack them about six high, wrap in foil and heat for 20 minutes.

MAKES 25

80g plain flour

80g buckwheat flour

pinch of sea salt

pinch of golden caster sugar

2 teaspoons baking powder

1 medium egg, separated

300ml whole milk

KIT

Electric whisk

Cast-iron frying pan or flat griddle

Palette knife

LITTLE EXTRAS

Vegetable oil for greasing

Softened salted butter, to serve

Honeycomb, to serve

FOR THE BATTER

75g plain flour, sifted

50g caster or vanilla sugar

3 medium eggs

425ml whole milk

25g unsalted butter

FOR THE APPLES

150ml dark rum, plus
1 tablespoon

50g caster or vanilla sugar

2 eating apples, peeled, cored
and cut into 8 wedges

KIT

Liquidiser

35cm oval gratin dish

LITTLE EXTRAS

Unsalted butter for greasing

Caster or vanilla sugar for
dusting

Icing sugar for dusting (optional)

apple
clafoutis

This French batter pudding is at its most delicious eaten hot
or warm about 30 minutes out of the oven. There's no need for
additional cream, but there are no rules against it.

Blend the flour, sugar, eggs and milk in a liquidiser and set aside to rest for 30
minutes; you may need to re-whisk it at the end.

Preheat the oven to 220°C fan oven/240°C electric oven. Butter a 35cm oval gratin
dish and dust with caster or vanilla sugar, tipping out the excess. Place 150ml rum
and the sugar in a small saucepan, bring to the boil and simmer until thick, syrupy
and reduced by half. Toss the apple wedges into the syrup and stir to coat.

Pour the batter into the prepared dish and scatter the apples and syrup evenly over
the surface. Dot with the butter and bake for 25–30 minutes until impressively puffed
and golden – although it will sink after a few minutes out of the oven. Sprinkle over
the remaining tablespoon of rum. If you like you can give it a flourish of dusted icing
sugar just before serving.

SERVES 6

50g unsalted butter, melted

125g golden caster sugar

2 medium eggs

500ml whole milk

1 tablespoon dark rum

1 teaspoon vanilla extract

125g plain flour

125g ready-soaked prunes

KIT

23cm non-stick square brownie tin, 4cm deep

Liquidiser

LITTLE EXTRAS

Melted unsalted butter for greasing

Golden caster sugar for dusting

Icing sugar for dusting

breton prune far

This is often sold in slabs in patisseries in Brittany and Normandy, much as bread-and-butter pudding might be sold in village bakeries here. It is a thick, set flan studded with prunes – deliciously comforting.

Preheat the oven to 180°C fan oven/200°C electric oven. Brush a 23cm non-stick square brownie tin, 4cm deep, with butter and dust with caster sugar. Whizz all the ingredients, except the prunes, in a liquidiser. Scrape down the sides and whizz again.

Pour the batter into the prepared tin and scatter the prunes evenly over the surface – a few may peek out at the top. Bake for 35–40 minutes until puffy and golden. Set aside to cool, when it will sink. Liberally dust with icing sugar and cut into squares or rectangles to serve.

index

For my Mother

Acknowledgements

With enormous thanks to everyone who has helped in putting this beautiful book together.

Many of these recipes began life in *YOU Magazine* in the *Mail on Sunday*, and I am hugely indebted to Angela Mason, Associate Editor, for inspiring them in the first place, and to Sue Peart, Editor of the magazine.

With many thanks to my agent Lizzy Kremer at David Higham for all her wisdom and support, to Kyle Cathie for championing the project, and to Judith Hannam, Managing Editor. To Vicky Orchard for steering the book from start to finish, Catherine Ward for her painstaking copy-editing, to Rashna Mody Clark for her lovely design, Julia Barder, as Sales and Marketing Director, Victoria Scales for publicity.

In particular thanks to Con Poulos, for going out of his way and landing in London en route between New York and Australia, for his exceptional photography and his understanding of what was wanted from the word go, and to his assistant Matthew Embury. And to Susie Theodorou for her artistic flair in styling the shots, and to leading so many debates about cakes, also to her assistants Camilla Baynham, Sammie Bell and Maddie Rix. Thanks to Brickett Davda for their beautiful crocks that feature in so many of the photographs.

Lastly where would any cake be without Jonnie, Rothko and Louis? My key tasters and central to everything I cook. And to all those family members and friends who have been willingly led astray over a cup of coffee.

An Hachette UK Company
www.hachette.co.uk

Thio odition publiohod in Croat Britain in 2019 by Kyle Books, an imprint of Kyle Cathie Ltd
Carmelite House
50 Victoria Embankmont
London EC4Y 0DZ
www.kylebooks.co.uk

First published in Great Britain in 2012 by Kyle Books,
an imprint of Kyle Cathie Ltd

ISBN: 978 0 85783 746 2

A CIP catalogue record for this title is available from the British Library

Annie Bell is hereby identified as the author of this work in accordance with Section 77 of the Copyright, Designs and Patents Act 1988

Text © Annie Bell 2012
Photographs © Con Poulos 2012
Design © Kyle Books 2012

Editor: Vicky Orchard
Design: Rashna Mody Clark
Design Assistant: Paola Guardiani
Photography: Con Poulos
Styling: Susie Theodorou
Copy editor: Catherine Ward
Production: Nic Jones and Gemma John

Printed and bound in China